PLAYING NICE and losing

Sports and Entertainment
Steven A. Riess, *Series Editor*

PLAYING
NICE
and losing

The Struggle for Control of Women's
Intercollegiate Athletics, 1960–2000

Ying Wushanley

 Syracuse University Press

Library of Congress Cataloging-in-Publication Data

Wushanley, Ying.
Playing nice and losing : the struggle for control of women's
intercollegiate athletics, 1960–2000 / Ying Wushanley.— 1st ed.
p. cm.—(Sports and entertainment)
Based on the author's thesis (Ph. D.—Penn State University, 1997).
Includes bibliographical references and index.
ISBN 0–8156–3045-X (cl. : alk. paper)
1. Sports for women—United States—History. 2. College
sports—United States—History. 3. Sex discrimination in sports—United
States—History. I. Title. II. Series.
GV709.18.U6 W87 2004
796'.082—dc22
2003024656

Manufactured in the United States of America

To Geraldine, Sophia, and Lily

Ying Wushanley (formerly Ying Wu), born in Shanghai, China, received his Ph.D. at Penn State University, his M.S. at Washington State University, his B.S. at Shanghai Teachers' University, and a Diploma in German at Shanghai International Studies University. Dr. Wushanley is an associate professor at Millersville University in Pennsylvania and a former council member of the North American Society for Sport History. He has published in the *Journal of Sport History, Sport History Review, International Journal of the History of Sport, International Review for the Sociology of Sport, International Encyclopedia of Women and Sports,* and the *Scribner Encyclopedia of American Lives.*

Contents

    Table
    A Comparison of AIAW Expenses
    on Legal Services and Championships   118

Illustrations

ix

Preface

MY TRAINING in sport history began at Penn State University in the early 1990s, where I also started my research on women's intercollegiate athletics. Women's intercollegiate athletics, however, was not my original choice of dissertation topic. I wanted to write a history of the political issues of the "two Chinas" in the modern Olympic Movement. Subconsciously, I assumed that my knowledge about China and my command of the Chinese language would be advantageous for me on the strenuous journey toward my doctoral degree. This advantage was not the case, however, because neither my mother tongue nor my knowledge about China could compensate for the disadvantages I might encounter in my endeavor.

I was born into a counterrevolutionary family during the Great Leap Forward movement in China. My father was a high military officer in the nationalist government. Disillusioned with the widespread corruptions in the old regime, however, he refused to join the nationalists in Taiwan in 1949. Instead, he surrendered to the Communists and hoped that the new rulers of the Middle Kingdom would be better servants to its people. His dream was soon shattered. When the Korean War escalated and the U.S. military engagement in the Far East became a threat to China's national defense, my father, along with tens of thousands of former counterrevolutionaries, was rounded up by the government and sent to prison, where he spent more than thirty years of his life completely cut off from his family. Consequently, I grew up without a father, although the public knowledge that my father was a Guomindang (nationalist) military officer never ceased to be a stigma in my life in China.

I was raised by two women—my mother, Jia-an Wu, and her mother, Shu-yao Chen. Grandma Shu-yao was the third wife of my grandfather, a well-established doctor and wealthy heir of a high-ranking official in the Qing Dynasty. It is not difficult to imagine the inferior status of Grandma Shu-yao and her children in the family. Not surprisingly, when my mother graduated from college and became financially independent, she "rescued" her mother from the big family—a vestige of the archaic feudal system—and left it forever.

My mother was a rebel in her time, ideologically and physically. In a society where the thousand-year-old tradition of foot-binding still existed, my mother chose to become a career physical educator. She was an outstanding athlete in many sports, from basketball to track, volleyball, tennis, table tennis, badminton, swimming, diving, gymnastics, Chinese martial arts, and even flying. For a woman, flying a glider in China in the 1930s–40s was symbolically similar to Amelia Earhart's attempt to circle the world in a real aircraft. In my mother's case, the cost of such acts was also similar. Earhart lost her own life; my mother lost her best friend, who died in a crash while flying a glider. Both Earhart and my mother paid a big price for their unconventional endeavors. But Earhart never gave up her dreams, nor did my mother. Despite the political hardship she endured as the wife of a counterrevolutionary, my mother never ceased to pursue what she believed to be her rights. She certainly made me believe that women could do anything men could, if not more. The life of my mother has been the major inspiration in my personal life and professional endeavors. Indirectly, it has prepared me for the writing of this book with an open mind and a strong conviction that men and women are equal.

There were, nevertheless, disadvantages for me in writing a history of women's intercollegiate athletics in the United States. The first disadvantage was language. I grew up in China in an era when anything "foreign," including foreign languages, was taboo. Even when English became part of the university curriculum after the revival of higher education in China in 1977—when I joined that first class of university students—my college training in English did not go much further than memorizing the alphabet and shouting a few Communist Party slogans. Later, my employment at Shanghai Foreign Languages School (a subdivision of Shanghai International Studies University) gave me the opportunity to learn a foreign language. I chose German. German was great fun, but it did not help much with my postgraduate pursuit in the United States. I still remember vividly those very first days of my life as a graduate assistant at Washington State

University, in the small town of Pullman, Washington. Teaching six activity classes independently while being a full-time graduate student was by no means easy, let alone teaching them in a second foreign language. It was a great challenge, and I don't know how I survived. I suspect that my growing up in China made any other challenges in life relatively easier. Dictionaries and a tape recorder certainly helped. But nothing helped me more than the people around me. Washington State offered probably the best learning environment I could have dreamed of. While my teaching load seems heavy for a graduate scholarship, it provided me twelve formal contact hours weekly with my students, who possibly taught me more than what they learned from me. There is no better way to learn a language than to be placed in an environment where the language to be learned is the only means of verbal communication. Learning English became a lot easier for me because of the friendship I soon established with my students, my peers, and my professors. Within two years of my life in Pullman, I began to *think* in English, a giant step in conquering the language barrier.

Another major challenge for me was to understand the sporting culture of the United States. Like most people in the world, I had little idea about American college sports until I arrived in this country in 1988. Nor did I know much about the culture of men's and women's intercollegiate programs and the disparity between the two. College football epitomized my initial experience with the phenomenon of college sports. The game was confusing but the event exciting. For a foreigner, American football was difficult to comprehend. There were so many huddles, stoppages, and time-outs; there were so many coaches and players on the sidelines; but there was not much playing action. The most amazing of all were the tens of thousands of fans packed in the stadium, apparently content with the lack of action but enjoying themselves tremendously. It did not take long for me to begin enjoying the festivity of college football. When the unranked Washington State team, a nineteen-point underdog, beat the top-ranked UCLA Bruins on national TV in October 1988, my heart pumped as hard as any other fan of the Cougars. I knew at that moment that my initiation into intercollegiate athletics was complete. My understanding of the phenomenon was yet to come.

I did not really begin to understand big-time college athletics or to contemplate its cultural significance until I began my doctoral study at Penn

State University in 1991. The sport history program at Penn State was one of the most intellectually stimulating and challenging in the nation. Outside the classroom, there was no better place to experience the magnitude of college football than in State College, Pennsylvania. Every home game weekend in the fall, one could not fail to notice that the traffic leading to Happy Valley, central Pennsylvania, would begin to congest on Friday afternoon. By midday Saturday the avalanche of cars, camper-vans, and trucks and trailers had covered the rolling hills around Beaver Stadium, the Mecca of Nittany Lion football. I had the opportunity to serve as the supervisor for Penn State football program sales. For two seasons, with an "all facilities" pass, I had access to all venues imaginable inside and outside the stadium of nearly one hundred thousand seats. I did not have to try very hard to imagine the power of college football in American society or the influence of the male-dominated intercollegiate athletics upon American higher education, because even I, a near-insignificant figure in the complex operation of Penn State football, was given the escort of a police officer at every game to ensure the safe transfer to the bank of tens of thousands of dollars from proceeds of program sales, merely a fraction of total revenues generated from the game.

Historian Larry R. Gerlach once wrote: "Sport is like religion. Many follow, but few understand." The big-time college athletics, which contains mainly Division I football and men's basketball, is a powerful social and cultural institution in the United States of America. Its power comes directly from the following of millions of fans. The supposedly amateur but commercialized big-time intercollegiate athletics is indeed difficult to understand. Yet understanding the complexity of that institution is a prerequisite to comprehending another phenomenon in intercollegiate athletics: the less conspicuous development and existence of the women's program. A decade ago, my doctoral advisor, Ronald A. Smith, asked me a seemingly uncomplicated question: Why did women lose their control of women's intercollegiate athletics after Title IX became the law of the land? I did not know the answer then. But I agreed to find out. It took me years to construct my answer in the form of a nearly five-hundred-page dissertation.

Playing Nice and Losing is based on my doctoral dissertation from Penn State University in 1997. Yet the making of this book has been the result of a continuous journey that began a decade ago. I was fortunate to have excellent mentors at Washington State University—professors Karen

DePauw, Georgia Hulac, Jo Washburn, Sue Durrant, and Robert Peavy—who not only laid down a solid foundation for my graduate work but also provided invaluable support in my early adjustment to American life. My good fortune continued at Penn State University, where I embarked on my most challenging and rewarding training in historiography, history of sport, and various other historical studies under the tutelage of professors Ronald Smith, John Lucas, James Thompson, James Sweeney, William Duiker, Gary Cross, and Paul Harvey.

I wish to thank numerous individuals and institutions for their aid in researching and writing this book. The Department of Wellness and Sport Sciences, the School of Education, the Faculty Professional Development Grants Committee, and the Commission on the Status of Women at Millersville University have contributed immensely in funding my research and in giving me a teaching schedule that allowed time for both researching and writing. Lauren Brown, Beth Alvarez, Jennie Levine, and the rest of the staff at the University of Maryland Archives provided excellent services during my research of the AIAW Papers and the reproduction of AIAW photos included in the book. I am very grateful to Ursula Walsh, Todd Petr, and their staff at NCAA Library for their assistance during my research of Walter Byers Papers and other NCAA archival materials. In the past several years, I have continually received invaluable assistance from NCAA archivist Ellen Summers. My research at AAHPERD Archives was equally rewarding thanks to the assistance of archivist Michie Shaw. I also appreciate the gracious help I have received from archives and libraries at the following institutions: Millersville University, Texas Women's University, Ithaca College, Immaculata College, and Philadelphia Archdiocesan Historical Research Center.

Two sport historians and former leaders of women's sports, Joan Hult and Jody Davenport, were instrumental in formulating my research approaches. Despite their close personal association with the AIAW and our differing perceptions on certain issues, they not only recognized the need for this study but gave me generously their time, knowledge, encouragement, and valuable sources in personal collections. I owe my gratitude to many of my colleagues in the North American Society for Sport History, who throughout the years have provided me with invaluable insight and constructive criticism or inspiration through their own scholarship: Melvin Adelman, William Baker, Robert Barney, Nancy Bouchier, Joan

Chandler, James Coates Jr., John Dewar, Lynne Emery, Jerry Gems, Larry Gerlach, Allen Guttmann, Susan Hamburger, Stephen Hardy, Patrick Harrigan, Thomas Jable, Roberta Park, Susan Rayl, Barbara Schrodt, Peggy Stanaland, Mila Su, Patricia Vertinsky, and John Watterson.

Steven Riess was one of the few sport historians outside of my thesis committee who first recognized the significance of this study. He also provided the most valuable advice in converting my dissertation into a publishable book manuscript. Ellen Goodman of Syracuse University Press skillfully conducted the complex, and for a while seemingly never-ending, process of the manuscript acquisition. I was fortunate to have Jill Root as my copy editor, whose critical eye, expertise, and efficiency made the last stage of publishing this book a pleasure.

No one has been more influential in my academic career and more helpful in the making of this book than my long-time mentor and friend Ronald Smith, who critiqued the entire manuscript from its first form to the last one. His critique was meticulous, challenging, and mostly constructive. But nothing could match his generosity with his time and care, a trait well known to all his students and those who seek his help.

Finally, I want to thank my wife, Geraldine, always the first and most faithful critic of my work, for her unyielding love, patience, understanding, and support, which have made the completion of this book possible. I dedicate this book to Geraldine and to our daughters, Sophia and Lily, with the hope that someday in our lifetime our choice to participate in sports, or in any other activities, will not be restrained by who we are, be it gender, race, or whatever label the humankind is capable of producing.

Lancaster, Pennsylvania   Ying Wushanley
October 2003

Abbreviations

AAHPER	American Association for Health, Physical Education, and Recreation
AAHPERD	American Alliance for Health, Physical Education, Recreation, and Dance
AAU	Amateur Athletic Union
ACE	American Council on Education
AIAW	Association for Intercollegiate Athletics for Women
AOA	American Olympic Association
AOC	American Olympic Committee
APEA	American Physical Education Association
BFUSA	Basketball Federation of the United States
CCWAA	Council of Collegiate Women Athletic Administrators
CIAW	Commission on Intercollegiate Athletics for Women
CWA	Committee on Women's Athletics
DGWS	Division for Girls' and Women's Sports
HEW	U.S. Department of Health, Education, and Welfare
IOC	International Olympic Committee
NAAAA	National Association of Amateur Athletes of America
NAAF	National Amateur Athletic Federation
NAGWS	National Association for Girls and Women in Sport
NAIA	National Association of Intercollegiate Athletics
NAPECW	National Association for Physical Education of College Women
NCAA	National Collegiate Athletic Association

NEA	National Education Association
NFSHSAA	National Federation of State High School Athletic Associations
NJCAA	National Junior Collegiate Athletic Association
NJCESCW	National Joint Committee for Extramural Sports for College Women
NSGWS	National Section for Girls' and Women's Sports
NSWA	National Section on Women's Athletics
NWBC	National Women's Basketball Committee
USOC	United States Olympic Committee
USTFF	United States Track and Field Federation
WAC	Western Athletic Conference

PLAYING NICE and losing

Introduction

Women's Intercollegiate Athletics in a Male-Dominated Society

> When placed alongside the male, the female
> basketball player is a slow pygmy. . . . If judged
> on the same spectator interest criteria as men's
> athletics, women's athletics will always be
> considered an inferior product.
> —Donna A. Lopiano, former AIAW
> president (1982)

DONNA A. LOPIANO was testifying in court for the Association for Intercollegiate Athletics for Women (AIAW) in its antitrust lawsuit against the National Collegiate Athletic Association (NCAA).[1] Arguing that the physiological inferiority of the female body should justify sex separation in athletic contests, Lopiano maintained that men's and women's intercollegiate athletics should also remain under sex-separate control. She was trying to convince the court that combining men's and women's championships into a single event, as the NCAA allegedly did, would harm the development of women's athletics; thus, the newly-established NCAA women's program must be stopped. The AIAW eventually lost the litigation, partially because Lopiano failed to prove that the NCAA would certainly harm the development of women's athletics if it continued to provide programs for both sexes.

Since the demise of the AIAW in 1982, women's intercollegiate athletics has experienced considerable changes. In May 2001, water polo became the nineteenth NCAA national championship sport for women. The new

1

addition was historically significant in the movement toward gender equity in intercollegiate athletics. With water polo, the NCAA could claim that it provides an equal number of championship sports to both men and women, and is thus in compliance, at least symbolically, with Title IX of the Education Amendments of 1972, which prohibits sex discrimination in all federally assisted educational activities. Few would dispute that opportunities for women in intercollegiate athletics have increased dramatically since the enactment of Title IX. In the three decades since passage of the law in 1972, the number of women participating in intercollegiate athletics has grown more than 400 percent, from 30,000 to over 150,000. In contrast, the number of men participating fell from 248,000 to 234,000.[2] The growth of women's intercollegiate athletics continues in the twenty-first century.

One of the most remarkable changes in women's intercollegiate athletics is the practice of awarding athletic scholarships. In 1972, the AIAW banned women from competing in its national championships if they received any form of financial aid for their athletic talent. By 2000, the NCAA member institutions had spent on average more on athletic scholarships for women than for men, exceeding the mandate by the federal government under Title IX regulations.[3]

Participation rates and scholarships are not the only measures of success for women's intercollegiate athletics. Today's college sport, especially at the Division I level, is foremost a serious business despite its proclaimed amateur nature and educational experience. More often than not, its success is measured by how much revenue it generates. Generating revenue, however, has not been synonymous with women's intercollegiate athletics. Until the early 1970s, most women's programs operated on a shoestring budget compared to men's. For those programs, success most often meant being able to survive. At the national level, lack of financial strength also contributed to the demise of the AIAW—the major governing body of women's intercollegiate athletics between 1972 and 1982. In the past two decades, however, women's intercollegiate athletics has grown steadily under the impact of Title IX legislation. Individual institutions have either voluntarily or been forced by law to increase administrative and financial support to their women's programs. The NCAA, with its wealth and power, has guaranteed full and equal funding for both men and women individual and team competitors at its championships—that is, full reimbursement of transportation cost and per diem allowance throughout the competition.[4] The wealth of the NCAA comes mainly from its commercial success. The NCAA Division I men's basketball championship alone brings in hundreds of millions of dollars annually through television rights fees. That income has provided the major funding for most other NCAA men's and women's championships.

The financial dependence of women's programs at the national level, however, is about to change. In July 2001, the NCAA and the television cable network ESPN reached an eleven-year, $200 million contract for broadcasting rights to the women's basketball championship and twenty other NCAA men's and women's championships through 2013. This new television agreement involving women's programs is a promising step in the commercial growth of women's intercollegiate athletics. Yet it matches only a fraction of the $6 billion deal between the NCAA and the CBS network for television rights primarily to the NCAA Division I men's basketball championship for the same period.[5]

Critics of commercialized college sports may question the philosophical reorientation of women's college athletics growth. To them, the increasingly commercialized big-time college sports reflect little trace of the spirit of amateurism and educational values. In July 2001, the Knight Foundation's Commission on Intercollegiate Athletics, a group comprised of academic leaders, public officials, and corporate executives, issued a new call to reform college athletics. It proposed to create a coalition of college presidents to take charge of collegiate athletics independently of the NCAA. The main goals of the new coalition were to raise academic standards for student athletes, to reduce the "arms race" in athletics expenditure—especially in football and men's basketball programs—and to deemphasize commercialism in all college sports.[6] Ten years before, the commission made a similar attempt that had little result. It is unlikely that much more will be accomplished this time around because college presidents already have the power to control the NCAA.

The philosophical orientation of intercollegiate athletics, however, deserves a separate treatment and is beyond the scope of this book. Ideology aside, the status of women's intercollegiate athletics is not short of controversies. Despite the rising participation rate and the more-than-equal share of the scholarship dollars, women's programs on average are still underfunded in recruiting, coaches' salaries, and operations. Men continue to hold the vast majority of athletics director positions, and the percentage of women coaching women's teams is at its lowest ever.[7] This reality seems to reflect a trend that began twenty years ago when the NCAA launched its women's programs: The opportunities for women in intercollegiate athletics continue to increase while women are losing more and more power and control of women's programs to men. "How could this happen?" one may ask.

This book attempts to answer this question from a historical perspective. The narrative of the book centers around two seemingly inseparable but independent issues: the development of intercollegiate athletics for women, and the control of women's intercollegiate athletics. Five major themes emerge from the narrative: the movement from protectionism to sex-separation of women's college sports; the ascendance of women's sports as a result of the Cold War and power struggle within U.S. amateur sports; the challenge to the sex-separatist philosophy in the legal and social reality; the NCAA "takeover" and the financial bankruptcy of the AIAW; and the AIAW's defeat in court as a defender of the "separate but equal" doctrine.

This book is not intended to be praiseworthy of AIAW's attempt at creating an educational model for women's athletics or of whatever successes it achieved in a decade of operation.[8] Readers are reminded that the focus of this study is on what contributed to the demise of the AIAW rather than on a general history of the AIAW. The research is based on the primary sources found in the AIAW Papers located in the University of Maryland archives, in the Walter Byers Papers and other NCAA documents located in the NCAA headquarters, and in material from other archival and personal collections. In addition, I conducted interviews with persons directly involved in the AIAW-NCAA conflict in order to better understand and interpret the written documents. Knowledge of the NCAA's historical interest in amateur sports and involvement in women's sports and of the impact of Title IX is fundamental to the understanding of the development of women's intercollegiate athletics in the last quarter of the twentieth century. The conflict between the AIAW's philosophical commitment and the legal and social reality, and the internal conflict and legal and financial dilemma of the AIAW, show that the demise of the AIAW was more than just an "NCAA takeover."

It has often been charged that the male-dominated NCAA took over women's intercollegiate athletics after the AIAW's "educational model" had become financially successful.[9] The thesis of this book is that the NCAA became interested in women's athletics during the Cold War era because it had not been successful in its struggle with the Amateur Athletic Union over the control of amateur sports. The repeated U.S. defeats by the Soviet Union at the Olympics during the Cold War not only highlighted the importance of women's sports but also spurred their growth in the 1960s. For the NCAA, traditionally a men's organization, controlling women's programs could mean a great increase of its power in U.S. amateur sports. Yet it was not easy for men to take control of women's college sport programs, which for three-quarters of a century were sheltered within the sex-separate sphere of college campuses. The passage of Title IX in 1972, however, changed the landscape of intercollegiate athletics, especially for women. Title IX meant greater opportunity for women's participation in college athletics traditionally afforded men only. At the same time, the court of law as well as many feminists used the men's model to judge women's parity in sport. Such a perception of the law, although not its intention, "created" an "obligation" for the NCAA to provide equal opportunities and championship competitions for both men and women. It also brought legal and social challenges to the AIAW's sex-separatist policies of the women's programs. Under Title IX, intercollegiate athletics became a legal issue rather than a philosophical one. Consequently, the women's "educational model" was converted to the men's "commercial model"; sex-separation gave way to integration; the financially less successful AIAW lost its members to the financially more successful NCAA; and ultimately, women lost power and control of women's intercollegiate athletics. All this change seems to have begun with the passage of Title IX. As former AIAW president Donna Lopiano maintained, "Title IX was the first step toward the demise . . . the end of the AIAW."[10] Title IX did not kill the AIAW, but the AIAW's own sex-separatist philosophy did. With Title IX and formerly men's organizations entering the governance of women's intercollegiate athletics, the sustaining of the sex-separatist AIAW become untenable in American society.

The Background of Women's Intercollegiate Athletics

1890s–1960s

> Unless we guard our athletics carefully in the
> beginning many objectionable elements will
> quickly come in . . . [and] the great desire to win
> and the excitement of the game will make our
> women do sadly unwomanly things.
> —Senda Berenson (1900)

COLLEGE EDUCATION in America remained a male privilege for nearly two centuries in the colonial and early national periods. From the founding of Harvard University in 1636 to the opening of Oberlin College in 1833, only men attended college. Even after women were admitted to Oberlin, women's going to college remained a rare social and cultural phenomenon in the first half of nineteenth-century America. Opportunities for quality higher education were not afforded the female sex until the 1860s. Women's college education, however, was separated from men's for most of the nineteenth and early twentieth centuries. Consequently, a "separate sphere" of sport for women was formed, which lasted well into the twentieth century.[1]

College Education and Physical Activities for Women

College education for women was part of the nineteenth-century women's rights movement. For women, attending college was not only a direct challenge to the traditional place of women in American society but also a crusade to prove that women possessed equal mental ability and deserved an

6

education previously afforded only to men. Such a crusade would prove to be a difficult task in Victorian America.

A dominant belief of the nineteenth century was that each human body possessed a limited amount of energy and that the use of the energy in one place was necessarily removed from another. Thus, it would be dangerous should one try to exert both physically and mentally at the same time. Women, however, would risk much greater health danger than men. The popular assumption was that women, from puberty to menopause, would be periodically weakened by menstruation, and that they would break down both physically and mentally if they had to assume any other work beyond domestic duties.[2]

Many physicians of the nineteenth century believed that the physical condition of American women was deteriorating and that education was responsible for that deterioration. They argued that girls would suffer from education, especially during puberty and adolescence, because education would consume the energy that was vital for achieving the state of "true womanhood."[3]

The image of the physically and mentally "frailer" nineteenth-century American women was largely a product of male-biased Victorian values rather than of female anatomy and physiology. Such a male-created image of women justified men's resistance to women's rights to higher education as well as to other opportunities traditionally dominated by men, often in the name of protecting the "weaker" sex.[4]

There were certainly people, men and women, who challenged the traditional sex roles. Yet the development of female intellect and physical energy meant different things even among female reformers who promoted education for women. Catherine Beecher, one of the earliest and most influential reformers in furthering the cause of women's education, advocated physical vigor and health of women through exercise and hygienic living. Her crusade toward that end was manifested in her invention of a system of calisthenics and the founding of two female seminaries in the 1820s and 1830s, where calisthenics was a major form of daily exercise. Beecher's advocacy for women's health and education, however, was confined within the concept of domesticity, which determined that the proper place for women was in the private world of home. For Beecher and her peer believers, a woman's improved health and better cultivated mind were only useful when she stayed home to serve as a nurturer and moral guardian of her husband and children. Beecher's calisthenics continued to be a popular form of exercise for women in the decades to come; her philosophy of women's education, however, would soon be outdated by the women's rights movement that demanded broader equal opportunities for women.[5]

More liberal thinkers and educators believed not only that women should have equal right to higher education, but that they also possessed the same capacity to succeed as men. Those who established women's colleges or were associated with women in coeducational institutions in the late 1800s insisted that physical fitness was essential for women to be successful at intellectual endeavors. Physical education, thus, was incorporated as an essential part in women's experience of higher learning. Matthew Vassar, a nineteenth-century American philanthropist and founder of Vassar College, probably best represented such a belief and practice.

In the school's philosophical blueprint, *Prospectus for Vassar Female College*, Vassar made clear his belief regarding physical education's role in the success of education. "Good health," it stated, "is essential to the successful prosecution of study, and to the vigorous development of either the mental or moral powers."[6] There was no doubt in Vassar's mind that the best way to obtain good health was physical education, and his commitment to physical education for women was more than just talk. In 1861, the charter year of the institution, Vassar College began constructing a fully equipped gymnasium—the Calisthenium—for conducting physical education classes and recreational activities. It also established a special School of Physical Training to meet the health requirement of the students. From the very beginning of its existence, the college hired a professor of physiology and hygiene and an instructor to carry out the physical education program at the institution.[7]

Following its introduction at influential Vassar College, physical education became an integral part of women's college education. By the mid-1880s, physical education programs came to exist in all eastern women's colleges and coeducational institutions and were soon established throughout the country.[8]

Physical Education and the Rise of College Sports for Women

For the first quarter-century of their existence, college physical education programs for women lacked the leadership of formally trained physical educators. Commonly, medical doctors, hygienists, and physiologists were hired to teach and supervise students' physical activities that emphasized hygiene, health, and "vigorous womanhood." Although this practice lasted well into the twentieth century, a significant change took place in the profession of physical education. During the 1880s, several physical education teacher training schools were formed, including the two most famous, the Sargent Normal School and the Boston Normal School of Gymnastics. Originally opened to both male and female students, these two institutions soon committed themselves to training female professionals only. They produced the first generation of women physical education leaders, who soon influenced the development of women's physical education programs and sport, especially at the college level.[9]

Women physical educators took firm control of physical education for women in higher education from the very beginning. Under the strong influence of the nineteenth-century medical view of the female body as well as Victorian values of the "frailer sex," the women physical educators included in their programs the major ingredients of correct posture, facial and bodily beauty, health, recreation, and the democratic ideal of "sport for all." Their mission was to balance the rigors of intellectual life with healthful physical activities. Similar to a mother's control over her daughters, the women physical educators not only taught their students sport skills, but also determined for them "appropriate" sport behavior and "acceptable" values.[10]

It is ironic that the women physical education leaders, while representing the progressive ideals of independence and freedom, strictly confined their students to the Victorian values of the male-dominated society. Such an irony, nevertheless, needs to be recognized in order to understand the development of physical education and sports for college women in the twentieth century.

The decade of 1890s saw a significant change in college physical education programs—the relatively dull routine of gymnastic exercises was giving way to more exciting games and sports. By the turn of the century, nearly every institution of higher education had a sport program for women. Popular activities included archery, bowling, boating, baseball, track and field, horseback riding, skating, swimming, ice hockey, golf, tennis, and basketball.[11]

When college women's physical activities moved toward games and sports, basketball became the most popular team sport for college women across the nation. This dominance remains today. The importance of basketball was not only that it became the most popular game for women, but that, as sport historian Ronald A. Smith maintained, it "created for the first time a *raison d'être* for women leaders to join together to control physical education activity [for women]."[12] It can be argued that the development of women's basketball in the late nineteenth and twentieth centuries epitomized the growth of intercollegiate athletics for women in America.

Senda Berenson, Basketball, and the Philosophy of Women's Collegiate Athletics

Senda Berenson is almost universally acknowledged as the founder of women's basketball; however, her contribution to the philosophy of women's collegiate athletics has not been duly credited. It is probably true that Berenson "accidentally transformed the world of women's sport" in 1892.[13] It was, however, not coincidental that she designed the women's game based on the philosophy that would later dominate women's athletics for over half a century.

Berenson's philosophical basis for women's sports was formed during her training at the Boston Normal School of Gymnastics. Her belief in "sport for the good of all" was most vividly displayed in the game of basketball she designed for women. To eliminate the roughness common in the men's game, Berenson prohibited ball snatching; to prevent the most skilled players from dominating play, she limited dribbling and divided the court into three sections.[14] To Berenson, the benefit of sport for women was not winning, or the thrill of it, but health—physical health and, more importantly, moral health.[15] "Rough and vicious play seems worse in women than in men," she once wrote. "[Although] a certain amount of roughness is deemed necessary to bring out manliness in our young men, [it] can have no possible excuse in our young women."[16] Berenson may have been a good example of the New Woman of the age—single, independent, successful in her career, and politically progressive; deep inside she was at best a modified Victorian lady. She apparently cared more about a woman's appearance than her health, more about her behavior than her performance, and more about her "womanhood" than her rights.

Basketball soon found itself the center of the philosophical conflict between men's and women's college athletics. Lacking a uniform set of rules for women, many teams simply copied the men's game. Consequently, the women's game was thought to have become too masculine; unwomanly playing style increased; and the desire to win overshadowed the enjoyment and welfare of the players. "Shall women blindly imitate the athletics of men without reference to their different organizations and purpose in life?" asked Berenson. "Unless we guard our athletics carefully in the beginning many objectionable elements will quickly come in . . . [and] the great desire to win and the excitement of the game will make our women do sadly unwomanly things."[17]

Foreseeing the "danger" that the women's game would copy the men's, Berenson modified the game for women at Smith College. The Smith College rules, however, did not become the universal standard. Twenty years after Berenson adapted the men's game, more than half of women's teams were still playing by men's rules or different versions of women's basketball.[18] As Smith has indicated, the lack of uniform rules for women was probably the result of the near absence of intercollegiate basketball contests for women. In order to unify the women's game, the Women's Basketball Committee was formed in 1899, the first national body to regulate sports for women.

"Sports for All": A Women's Approach to Athletics

Ancient Greek philosophers likely would have seen the paradoxical nature of the phrase "Sports for all"—a women's approach to athletics. "Sports for all" is a concept of equal opportunity in play and enjoyment for every participant regardless of one's skill and ability. Instead of separating the weaker and less skilled players from the stronger and more skilled, it protects them from being discriminated against. Athletics, from the ancient Greek word *athlon*, emphasizes competition and winning. In athletics only one is honored, the victor, and the rest are more or less ignored.[19] Nevertheless, American women physical educators of the nineteenth and early twentieth centuries joined the two antithetical concepts together to serve their purpose. That paradox would exist in women's athletics for more than half a century.

The formation of the Women's Basketball Committee in 1899 symbolized the beginning of a collective effort of women physical educators to control women's athletics. Basketball provided them with an effective passage to the whole world of women's sports. Through regulating basketball, women physical educators developed the most efficient means to actualize their belief that athletics should be experienced and enjoyed by all girls and women. They assumed the motherly role over their student-athletes and determined to take firm control of women's athletics as they had done in controlling their physical education programs.[20]

The growth of women's athletics was constantly accompanied by women physical educators' criticism of the men's model, which emphasized winning. As Berenson stated, "The greatest element of evil in the spirit of athletics in this country is the idea that one must win at any cost—that defeat is an unspeakable disgrace."[21] The real danger of this evil element, in the opinion of Berenson and her peers, was that it not only had corrupted men's athletics, but was creeping into the women's separate sphere.[22]

In order to keep women's sports under their own control, the women leaders crafted a unique philosophy and movement that attempted to keep both women from participating in highly competitive athletic competitions and men from controlling women's athletics. The impetus for the movement came in 1922 when Harry Steward organized a U.S. women's track team for the first "Women's Olympic Games" in Paris, France, and the male-dominated Amateur Athletic Union decided to take control of women's track and field.[23] The actions of the men greatly infuriated women physical educators. They felt that they were losing control of women's athletics to men and decided to fight.

In April 1923, a Women's Division of the National Amateur Athletic Federation was established under the leadership of Lou Henry Hoover, president of the Girl Scouts and a vice president of the NAAF.[24] Mrs. Hoover, wife of commerce secretary and future president Herbert Hoover, advocated a separate women's organization because she saw fundamental differences between athletics for men and for women.[25] The first conference of the Women's Division produced the anti-varsity, anti-Olympics philosophy known as the "Platform." It condemned the participation of American women in international contests, emphasized participation over competition, and stressed control of women's sports by women.[26] Under such a climate, the "Play Day"—an alternative recreational model of sport—was born and flourished, excluding most American women from the world of competitive athletics.

"Play Day": An Alternative to the Men's Athletic Model

"Play Day" was a form of organized sport activities in schools and colleges that emphasized participation over competition. It usually consisted of female students from three or more schools gathering together for a day of sports activities. While basketball was usually the most popular event, many other sports were also available, such as archery, baseball, field hockey, soccer, swimming, track and field, tennis, and volleyball. The most unique part of Play Day was that individual schools would not compete under school colors. Rather, mixed teams composed of players from various schools would play. Consequently, winning became less important for the participating institutions because no one school could claim victory.

The Play Day system also discouraged intensive team training or coaching, for they were believed unnecessary. It instead emphasized social interaction and learning of social values.[27] The core of Play Day was the concept of "sport for all," a synonym for "anti-varsity" or "noncompetitive" sport. Its more often quoted version was the slogan "a team for every girl and every girl on the team."[28]

Women physical education leaders often denied that they were opposed to competition; they opposed only the "wrong type" of competition. During the 1920s and 1930s, nevertheless, most intercollegiate contests for women were eliminated and Play Days dominated the women's college sporting scene.[29] Women physical educators also continued to protest the participation of American women in the Olympic Games throughout the decades.

Voices of dissent, however, were also heard outside of this mainstream "anti-varsity, anti-competition" philosophy. Some women physical educators believed that the men's sports were clean, open, skillful, and more interesting to play and watch.[30] Ina E. Gittings, director of physical education for women at the University of Arizona, questioned the sanity of the women's model and challenged the worthiness of the anti-competition philosophy. "[Play Days] are extremely weak and offer little or none of the joy and values of real games played skillfully, willingly, intelligently, and eagerly by well-matched teams," wrote Gittings in 1931. "I picture the girls in a Play Day as sheep, huddled and bleating in their little Play meadow, whereas they should be young mustangs exultantly racing together across vast prairies."[31] Gittings saw nothing wrong with varsity competition for women, which was forbidden by the women leaders, and her position reflected the frustration felt by the younger generation of women physical educators. The true problem, as she perceived instead, lay within the women leaders themselves. "There is something wrong with the directors, who have phobias at the thought of making the same mistakes in intercollegiates as men have made," maintained Gittings. "And there is something wrong with the physical education instructors who cannot coach and conduct such activities without letting them get beyond control."[32]

The challenge against the Play Day by Gittings and others contributed to the eventual adoption of the "Sports Day," a more competitive model of women's inter-institutional sport contest that recognized the representation of individual schools.

The Return of Intercollegiate Competition

The anti-varsity, anti-competition philosophy dominated women's collegiate athletics during the years between the two World Wars. Toward the end of that period, the demand for highly competitive women's athletics increased, and the number of varsity teams grew. One good example was the first college women's national championship, the National Collegiate Golf Tournament in 1941, organized by Gladys Palmer, chairperson of the Department of Physical Education for Women at Ohio State University.

As early as 1936, Palmer had called for the creation of a National Women's Sport Association to regulate competitive intercollegiate athletics for women, but without fruition. Her proposal was presented again in 1941. Both proposals were rejected by the National Section on Women's Athletics of the American Association for Health, Physical Education, and Recreation.[33] In 1941, Palmer also proposed to hold a women's national intercollegiate golf tournament but met strong opposition from the female leaders, who opposed "national tournaments of any sorts" and "any organization to increase competition."[34] Despite the opposition from the NSWA, Palmer and her colleagues at Ohio State University launched the tournament. Some thirty women athletes took part in the contest. The event was so successful that even the NSWA commended Palmer and her staff on their "efficient conduct of this tournament." The NSWA, nevertheless, still disapproved the use of the terms "national" and "intercollegiate" for the event and recommended use of "invitational" and "collegiate" instead.[35] The Women's National Collegiate Golf Tournament was interrupted by World War II, but resumed in 1946.

Indirectly, World War II stimulated the growth of intercollegiate athletics for both men and women in two significant ways. First, women workers of unprecedented numbers entered the labor market to fill the vacancies caused by men drawn into military services. Second, the war demanded strong and healthy individuals, men and women, to carry out military as well as civilian duties. Consequently, physical education classes and competitive sport programs in colleges were used as means to develop fitness for war. With moral and financial support from federal, state, and local governments, physical education and athletic programs on college campuses received a tremendous boost and entered a new era. For the men, whose athletic programs had been under scrutiny since the release of the Carnegie Report in 1929,[36] the newly revived emphasis on athletics' importance in developing fitness undermined university administrators' effort to reform college athletics and reestablish the supremacy of higher education.[37] For the women, it not only legitimized highly competitive athletics as a normal form of physical activity for women, but also provided women physical educators with experience in conducting such activities during and after the war. Probably the most important impact of the war was the change in society's attitudes toward women and their participation in sports. This change, along with increasing interest among women physical educators in competitive sports, forged a supportive environment for competitive sports for women.[38]

The resumption of the Women's National Collegiate Golf Tournament in 1946 reflected this climate change. More and more women physical educators favored varsity competition after the war. Even the women leaders began to disagree among themselves regarding the directions of women's sports. The conflict among the women leaders gradually led to more competitive approaches to the Play Day and Sports Day exercises.

While most white institutions emphasized Play Day and intramural sports in the 1920s and 1930s, African American women in some all-black colleges in the South engaged in varsity competitions. Ironically, these black women, racially segregated from the mainstream white middle-class collegians, were the only group of college women afforded the opportunity for high-level athletic competition. They also became the first group of winning female Olympians for the United States. Toward the end of the 1950s, the traditional anti-varsity, anti-competition model for women's sports was being swept aside.[39]

By the mid-1960s American society had changed dramatically. With both the civil rights and women's movements exerting their influence in almost every aspect of American life, the demand for equality for women's athletics was also gaining momentum. This new social and political environment made women physical education leaders realize that only a well-established national governing body could keep women's sports within the boundaries of women's philosophy and under women's control.[40] In 1966, the women physical educators created the Commission on Intercollegiate Athletics for Women. It became the Association for Intercollegiate Athletics for Women in 1971.

The Association for Intercollegiate Athletics for Women and Its Predecessors

The AIAW was established in 1971 as a structure within the Division for Girls and Women's Sports of the American Association for Health, Physical Education, and Recreation. Its official operation began in June 1972 and ceased in June 1982.

The initial mission of the AIAW was to further women's intercollegiate athletics through: (1) fostering broad programs consistent with educational objectives, (2) assisting member institutions in program extension and enrichment, (3) stimulating the development of quality leadership, and (4) encouraging excellence in performance.[41] As a governing body, one of AIAW's major functions was to hold national championships for women in popular sports not offered by other organizations.

Ideologically, the AIAW can trace its connection back to the 1890s when Senda Berenson adapted basketball for women based on the ideal of "sport for all." Organizationally, AIAW's first predecessor was the Women's Basketball Committee formed in 1899, the first national body in charge of women's athletics. The committee changed its name to the National Women's Basketball Committee in 1905 and became a permanent organ of the American Physical Education Association.[42]

In 1917, the APEA created the Committee on Women's Athletics within its structure. The NWBC soon became one of the five subcommittees of the CWA, joining field hockey, swimming, track and field, and soccer. The CWA became the National Section on Women's Athletics in 1932. During the 1930s and 1940s, the NSWA had almost exclusive authority over women's sports in educational settings. By the mid-twentieth century, the NSWA had become ambivalent about intercollegiate and elite athletic competition for women. It would neither endorse nor sanction competition that the traditionalist women physical educators had firmly opposed.[43] Society was changing, and women physical educators had to adjust their positions. Some did, some didn't. Those who did not were eventually left behind. To some extent, the NSWA and its successors changed reluctantly.

The NSWA became the National Section for Girls and Women's Sports in 1953. Four years later, in 1957, the NSGWS changed its name again to the Division for Girls and Women's Sports.[44] From the very beginning, it was clear that the young leaders of the DGWS had a quite different vision of women's college athletics from that of their predecessors. Although still critical of men's athletics, intercollegiate competition for women was no longer an anathema but rather was becoming desirable. As a result of this change in philosophy, the DGWS established the Commission on Intercollegiate Athletics for Women in 1966 and the AIAW in 1971.[45]

The AIAW's more direct root goes back to the National Joint Committee for Extramural Sports for College Women, formed in 1957 as the first national organization attempting to administer women's intercollegiate athletic programs. Between 1957 and 1965, the NJCESCW developed guidelines for conducting extramural events, sanctioning state and regional intercollegiate competitions, appointing sport committees, and supervising the Women's National Collegiate Golf Tournament.[46]

In 1963, the DGWS revised its policies and procedures for competition by recognizing the needs of highly skilled women athletes. In the following year, the NJCESCW decided to dissolve itself and recommended that the DGWS assume its functions in 1965. The DGWS responded to the NJCESCW's request by establishing the CIAW in 1966.[47]

During its existence between 1966 and 1972, the CIAW established standards and controlled competitions through sanctioning regional tournaments; it promoted the formation and growth of governing bodies of women physical educators at local, state, and regional levels and held national championships in seven different sports.[48] Realizing their limited power and resources as a commission to manage the increasing needs and expanding problems of collegiate athletics, women physical education leaders formed an association of institutional memberships—the Association for Intercollegiate Athletics for Women—in 1971. In June 1972, the AIAW officially replaced the CIAW. Almost as soon as they began their full operation as a national organization, the women leaders discovered that they were not the only group interested in the governance of intercollegiate athletics for women.

Cold War, Olympic Defeat, and Women's Sport as a Pawn

The AAU-NCAA Battle

Now the United States is being challenged and defeated in our strong sports and being eclipsed in sports in which we have had small interest. This condition is tragic since many people of the world have placed the fondest hopes on the image of America's strength and ideals. We have a responsibility to these people as well as to the people of the United States to produce our best. Any effort short of the best is unworthy and unpatriotic.

—Thomas J. Hamilton, Chair,
Development Committee of
United States Olympic Association
(1961)

THIS PASSAGE from Hamilton's speech at the 1961 National Collegiate Athletic Association convention touched upon three interrelated issues in American life: the threat of the Cold War; the disappointing U.S. performance at the Olympic Games; and the renewed power struggle within amateur sports.[1]

In the early 1960s, the conflict between the United States and the Soviet Union created tensions such as the Berlin Wall Crisis and the Cuban Missile Crisis. As sport results at the international level were often considered a reflection of the Cold War, it was important for the Americans to win. It was, however, difficult to win the highest number of medals in the Olympics if American women did poorly—which they did. Because

19

NCAA institutions provided most of the male medal winners in the Olympics, it was only natural that a greater emphasis on women's sports might come from colleges as well. Thus the NCAA came to see women's athletics as part of the puzzle to produce Olympic medal winners and to wrest control of amateur athletics from the Amateur Athletic Union. If colleges were to produce the best athletes, then the NCAA wanted greater control over who would represent athletes in the Olympics, coach at the international level, and administer the programs.

Early Disputes Between NCAA and AAU

The AAU came into existence in 1888 as a result of squabbles within the National Association of Amateur Athletes of America, the first national governing body of amateur sports in the United States. Disagreement over eligibility and rule enforcement within the organization led to the withdrawal of some of the most prestigious members from the NAAAA and eventually to the formation of the AAU. Through successfully sanctioning meets and registering athletes, the AAU soon surpassed the NAAAA and became the most powerful amateur sport organization in the United States.[2]

Within three years of its formation, AAU membership grew tenfold. In the 1890s, the AAU's policies would penalize anyone who competed in non-AAU-sanctioned games by barring them from participating in AAU-sanctioned games. For years, these policies remained the primary methods of controlling amateur athletics and sources of revenue. On the other hand, they also became a major source of conflict with other amateur organizations, particularly the NCAA.[3]

The NCAA was established after the 1905 football season to reform college football by curtailing brutality and unethical conduct.[4] During the first annual meeting of the NCAA in 1906, AAU president James E. Sullivan proposed an alliance between the two organizations. The NCAA, however, took no action on Sullivan's proposal.[5]

Even before the formation of the NCAA, basketball had been a constant source of irritation between colleges and the AAU. Dissatisfied with the AAU's registration requirement, the colleges began to publish their own basketball rules. At the second annual meeting of the NCAA in 1906, NCAA president Palmer E. Pierce made it clear that college basketball teams should not arrange games with any clubs playing AAU rules.[6] Pierce's suggestion, at the very beginning of the new organization, set a firm tone for the NCAA's dealings with the AAU in the future.

The relationship between the AAU and the NCAA would remain hostile with but one significant exception. In 1915 a joint committee representing the AAU, the NCAA, and the YMCA met and reached an agreement for formulating and publishing common basketball rules. This agreement, reflecting the mutual need of each organization to best serve its constituents, lasted for two decades until the AAU and the YMCA broke away from the joint committee in 1936.[7]

Open hostility between the AAU and the NCAA erupted after the 1920 Olympic Games, when the AAU-controlled American Olympic Committee was accused of mismanaging the U.S. Olympic team. Joining the increasing public criticism, the NCAA, along with other organizations, demanded the reorganization of the AOC. The reorganization did take place in December 1921 when the American Olympic Association was formed in place of the AOC. The control of American amateur sports, however, remained in the hands of the AAU.[8]

Dissatisfied with the AAU's continued control of athletes who were members of college teams, the NCAA decided to openly challenge the AAU's authority over all aspects of amateur sports. At its convention in December 1921, the NCAA rejected the invitation to join the AOA under its current form of management. The delegates instead voted to create the National Amateur Athletic Federation.[9] Acknowledging the newly erupted dispute between the two organizations, Frederick Rubien, secretary of both the AAU and the newly formed AOA, stated: "It looks as if [the fight between the AAU and the NCAA] is under full headway now. Well, we're ready for it; prepared to fight to the last ditch."[10]

In May 1922, less than four months after Rubien's public "declaration of war" against the NCAA, the NAAF was formed with a membership of thirteen amateur athletic organizations. The NCAA, having supported its formation, chose not to join the federation as an active member in 1922.[11] The newly established NAAF sought revision of the AOA constitution, especially voting power within the organization. It expressed a willingness to join the AOA, but demanded equal voting privilege with the AAU. Although the AAU argued against the NAAF's demand, AOA president Robert M. Thompson succeeded in having the AOA adopt changes in its constitution. As a result, the NAAF, the army, the navy, and the NCAA joined the AOA in November 1922 with voting power equal to that of the AAU.[12]

From "the Paddock Case" to "Articles of Alliance"

The lull in the battle between the AAU and the NCAA did not last long. Deep-bedded conflict between the two organizations soon re-erupted over the Charles W. Paddock case in 1923. A student and star sprinter at the University of Southern California, Paddock competed in the International University Athletic Games despite the disapproval of the AAU, the governing body of track and field in the United States. Because of his Paris adventure, Paddock was disqualified as an amateur under AAU jurisdiction and declared ineligible for the U.S. team trials for the 1924 Olympic Games.[13] With the Paddock case unresolved, the NCAA declared at its 1923 convention that American colleges and universities should reserve the right to determine their students' eligibility to compete in intercollegiate meets at home and abroad.

The Paddock case was eventually settled with his amateur status reinstated by the AAU. But the incident had profound implications within the organization of U.S. amateur sports, especially for the power struggle between the AAU and the NCAA in the years to come.

The settlement of the Paddock case carried the truce between the AAU and the NCAA through the 1924 Olympic Games. The peace, however, broke up at the end of 1926. At a meeting of the AOA, the AAU and its allies succeeded in electing former AAU president William C. Prout as the president of the AOA, giving the AAU unmatchable power over amateur sports. In protest of the AAU's monopoly within the AOA, the NAAF, the NCAA, and their allies withdrew from the association.[14] Suddenly, the future of a strong U.S. Olympic representation seemed in jeopardy.

The untimely death of William C. Prout in 1927, ironically, paved the way for a compromise between the warring factions. Brigadier General Douglas MacArthur was soon elected president of the AOA. Although the breach between the AAU and the NCAA was far from healed, MacArthur, the charismatic and most decorated American soldier of the Great War, succeeded in getting the defecting organizations to rejoin the AOA for the upcoming 1928 Olympic Games.[15] While the United States retained its dominance at the Amsterdam Games, the NCAA was not satisfied with the management of the AAU-controlled Olympic team. In 1929, the NCAA pressured for the reorganization of the AOA and succeeded in having the AOA constitution and bylaws revised. With the reorganization of the AOA completed in 1930, the war between the AAU and the NCAA over sanctioning meets, registering athletes, and U.S. Olympic participation halted temporarily, and the two organizations coexisted in peace for most of the following three decades. In 1946, cooperation between the AAU and the NCAA reached its peak when the two organizations officially adopted the "Articles of Alliance," a document that recognized the common goals of the two organizations and expressed mutual interest in continued cooperation.[16]

While the NCAA gained more and more power in U.S. Olympic operation, the ultimate control of amateur sport in the United States still rested in the hands of the AAU. In the late 1950s, a conflict between the AAU and the NCAA gradually developed in regard to a consistent amateur code. The NCAA also became increasingly dissatisfied with the "dictatorial attitude of the AAU" in representing U.S. amateur sports in international forums. Soviet entry into the Olympic Games and the relatively inferior U.S. Olympic performances during the Cold War provided ample ammunition for the renewal of a power struggle within U.S. amateur sports and brought an end to the peace between the AAU and the NCAA. In 1960, the NCAA unilaterally canceled the "Articles of Alliance."[17]

The Cold War and U.S. Defeats in the Olympics

The United States dominated the first half-century of the modern international Olympic Games, leading the medal counts in six of the eleven Summer Games between 1896 and 1948. In the 1948 London Games, the Americans captured eighty-four medals, nearly double the number won by the second-place Swedish team. America's dominance, however, would not last long. In late 1948, the Communist Party of the Soviet Union issued a decree aimed at raising sports proficiency and winning in the most important sports in world championships.[18] The Soviet Union joined the International Olympic Committee in 1951 and decided to compete in the 1952 Helsinki Games. Although the Soviets had never competed in the Olympics before, their athletic prowess quickly caught the attentions of the sports world through winning international competitions and setting world records.

With the advent of the Soviets, the Olympic Games suddenly caught the fascination of the world with the anticipation of a Cold War showdown between the United States and the Soviet Union. For many Americans, a Soviet triumph at the 1952 Helsinki Games would be "a tremendous psychological cold war propaganda victory for the Russians and a great blow to American ego and prestige," as one reader expressed his concern to the *New York Times*.[19] The United States barely kept its Olympic dominance by retaining its lead in total medal counts (USA 76, USSR 71). But in reality, U.S. prestige was reduced, and the Soviet challenge was real.

At both the 1956 and 1960 Summer and Winter Olympic Games, the Soviet Union defeated the United States in medal counts by convincing margins.[20] The consecutive U.S. defeats by the Soviets at the Olympics caused great public concern about the international image of the United States. The seriousness of the matter was probably best expressed in the words of Thomas J. Hamilton, chair of the Development Committee of the United States Olympic Association. "It is very evident that the United States must take a new and hard look at its Olympic movement and efforts," stated Hamilton in January 1961. "The cold war and present international climate demands that we make the strongest showing possible to uphold the prestige of the United States."[21]

There is no doubt that the U.S. Olympic performances during the Cold War had a negative impact on the international image of the United States. One needs to realize, however, that the superiority of the Soviets on the Olympic stage had much to do with the performance of U.S. female Olympians. The U.S. teams were defeated primarily because of the relatively inferior performance of American women compared to that of Soviet women. In the 1956 Summer Games, U.S. women trailed their Soviet counterparts in medal counts 19 to 14. Four years later in the 1960 Games, Soviet women out-medalled the Americans 28 to 12.[22] "The United States is outscored badly in women's sports events," Hamilton told his colleagues at the 1961 NCAA annual convention. "Obviously some other nations have outreached us in the women's events and will continue to garner the medals unless we give our girls more opportunities for participation and better training."[23] Such opportunities would soon come in the shadows of the Cold War and in the NCAA's desire to control U.S. amateur sports.

Hamilton, previously an admiral in the U.S. Navy and athletic commissioner of the Pacific Big Five Conference (also known as the Athletic Association of Western Universities), suggested that in order to maximize the effectiveness and efficiency of U.S. participation, the U.S. Olympic organization should be "overhauled, modernized, and enlarged."[24]

The subject of the Cold War and U.S. prestige was in many more people's minds, including those of women physical education leaders. At an April 1962 meeting of the Women's Advisory Board to the U.S. Olympic Development Committee, intense discussion took place on "the crucial problems and issues concerning women's sports and the Olympics." Roswell Merrick, staff liaison of the American Association for Health, Physical Education, and Recreation, addressed "the Russian attitude" toward the United States in the sports world and asked what American women could do to help the international climate in sports. "Today the Olympic Sports in the United States are a political football," he stated. "Russians want to humiliate us in all sports. They are just as vigorous in their sports programs as they are in their sputnic [sic] programs. They are determined to win all major events [at the Tokyo Olympics]." He urged the women to look hard at their traditional noncompetitive programs under the Division for Girls and Women's Sports and suggested that it was time to also give attention to "more motor skilled girls."[25] Giving such attention would mean altering the women's decades-long philosophy against high-level competition. It would not be an easy task for the women, but they would not have a choice.

In the meantime, the NCAA also expressed its dissatisfaction with the U.S. Olympic participation under the auspices of the AAU and urged the United States Olympic Association to review its organization and operations.[26] It openly challenged the AAU's authority over amateur sports through initiating the "federation movement." The timing could not have been better for the NCAA to assert its agenda and to seize power from the AAU.

The NCAA and the "Federation Movement"

In early 1962, the NCAA initiated the notorious "federation movement" in direct confrontation with the AAU. The stated purpose of the movement was to establish sport governing bodies independent of AAU control and subsequently to improve U.S. performance in international athletic competitions, especially in the Olympic Games. The more important goal of the movement, however, was to strengthen NCAA's power in U.S. amateur sports. In March 1962, the NCAA sponsored an "Organizational Meeting of the United States Federations" in the sports of basketball, gymnastics, and track and field in Chicago, with eighty-eight delegates representing national sports organizations, intercollegiate athletic conferences, and state high school athletic associations.[27] As a public gesture, the NCAA invited the AAU to the meetings. The latter, however, declined the invitation of the "outlaw federations," insisting that the NCAA would be satisfied with nothing less than the elimination of the AAU.[28] By the end of 1962, the NCAA had successfully sponsored the formation of four separate federations in basketball, gymnastics, track and field, and baseball. The NCAA Executive Committee also disbanded its Special Committee on AAU-Olympic Relations appointed earlier to conduct negotiations with the AAU.[29]

The NCAA's control of the newly formed federations was beyond doubt. Reverend Wilfred Crowley of Santa Clara University, secretary-treasurer of the NCAA, made that relationship crystal clear when he intended to defend the NCAA from the accusation of its manipulation of the federations. "While the federations . . . are not mere puppets of the NCAA, as has been alleged," stated Crowley, "the NCAA has strongly endorsed and encouraged their formation, and the future of the federations will depend upon strong NCAA support."[30] Small wonder that three of the four federations were chaired by NCAA officials, and the other by an NCAA ally.[31] A year later, Crowley himself would become the president of the United States Track and Field Federation, making it literally a sweeping NCAA control of the federations.

Such a control could not have been possible without NCAA executive director Walter Byers, a genius of organizational management, whose tremendous impact on U.S. amateur sports, especially the commercialization of intercollegiate athletics, was yet to come. As Crowley maintained, Walter Byers "skillfully planned, and well directed organizational work" for the formation of the federations.[32] Crowley was not exaggerating. With Byers at its helm, the NCAA was set to become the superpower in American amateur sports.

The disputes between the AAU and the NCAA intensified with the establishment of the NCAA-backed, anti-AAU federations. Rev. Crowley acknowledged the increasing hostility between the two organizations at the 1963 NCAA convention. Presiding over the General Round Table discussions, Crowley told the delegates that the AAU president had called the NCAA and the federations "power grabbers, un-American, gangsters, power-hungry commissars, destroyers of amateurism in school and college sports." "We note with deep regret," he stated, "that if mud-slinging were a sport there would be no question about who would have jurisdiction over that dishonorable activity."[33]

The fight over the control of amateur athletics eventually led to the intervention of the federal government. In October 1962, U.S. Attorney General Robert Kennedy managed to bring the two warring parties to the negotiation table with a governmental truce proposal, known as the "Washington Alliance" agreement. But the agreement failed at the last minute when the AAU changed its position of compromise.[34] The seriousness of the worsened AAU-NCAA relationship and its political ramifications are probably best summarized in the words of Donald Boydston, president of the U.S. Gymnastics Federation. "The American public, unfortunately, thinks of the federations as parallel organizations to the AAU, primarily interested only in international competitions," Boydston said at the 1963 NCAA convention. "We must change our present public image. . . . By building solid foundations of competition at home, we will reach our goal in track, basketball and gymnastics, by kicking hell out of the Communists."[35] With the way the AAU and the NCAA were conducting themselves, any chance of a U.S. victory over the Soviet Union at the 1964 Olympic Games would have diminished.[36] The prestige of the United States on the Olympic stage was in jeopardy. But options for mediating the AAU-NCAA dispute were running out.

The failure of Robert Kennedy's attempt to unite the warring sports bodies led his brother, President John F. Kennedy, to intervene. In January 1963, Kennedy urged the leaders from both sides to submit their dispute to an arbitration panel headed by General Douglas MacArthur. The president succeeded. Shortly thereafter, an agreement between the AAU and the NCAA was reached, known as "The MacArthur Plan." The agreement essentially formed the basis for providing the thrust for stronger U.S. participation in the Olympics without actually resolving the disputes between the AAU and the NCAA.[37]

Since the 1920s, the relationship between the AAU and the NCAA had followed a cyclical pattern that centered around the Olympics. Their disputes over the control of amateur sports usually became worse during the intervals of the Olympiads. Then, with the Games approaching, public pressure would force the two organizations to resolve their differences for a strong U.S. showing at the Olympics. For over a half-century, the AAU was able to capitalize on its advantage as the controlling body of U.S. amateur sports recognized by international federations. The NCAA, on the other hand, had to give up its struggle in order to allow college athletes to compete in the Games.[38] The glorious quadrennia of the Olympics subsequently formed vicious circles in the relationship between the two organizations. After each Games, the NCAA became more and more resentful of the AAU's jurisdiction over U.S. Olympic organization. The collegiate sport leaders did not believe that the AAU deserved such a privilege and would thus intensify their fight against the AAU authority. "The colleges and high schools historically have been and are principal contributors and developers of amateur sports in the United States," stated Byers. "We believe the nation's educational institutions should have a voice in policies which vitally affect their educational and athletic programs." Rather than "taking-over" amateur sports in the United States, as the NCAA had been accused of, Byers maintained that "we seek only what fairminded people would agree is our right."[39]

During the latter half of the 1960s, there was not only a worsened relationship between the AAU and the NCAA, but also the building of conflict between the NCAA and the United States Olympic Committee. The NCAA viewed the USOC as an organization dominated by the AAU and unwilling to undertake meaningful changes. Dissatisfied with its management in general and with the U.S. participation at the 1972 Munich Games in particular, the NCAA withdrew its membership from the USOC.[40]

In the years following the 1972 Olympic Games, the NCAA challenged the USOC from its structure to its constitution, from protection of athletes to the leadership in the U.S. Olympic effort. In 1975, the NCAA and the NCAA-backed United States Gymnastics Federation even brought the USOC to court. They charged the USOC with violations of its own constitution, resulting in unfair treatments of its members.[41] Testifying at the public hearings of President Ford's Commission on Olympic Sports in late 1975, Walter Byers stated that the USOC was "incapable of internal reorganization to accomplish the ends the NCAA believes are essential" for U.S. Olympic success.[42]

The seven-decade-long disputes between the AAU and the NCAA were finally settled when Congress passed the Amateur Sports Act of 1978. The act essentially stripped the power from the AAU and divided it among the national governing bodies for various Olympic sports. It also changed the course of the NCAA's pursuit for power in U.S. amateur sports. With voting power ultimately vested in the national governing bodies, the control of women's sports, especially at the intercollegiate and interscholastic levels, became extremely important.

The Impact of the AAU-NCAA Power Struggle on Women's Athletics

The direct impact of the AAU-NCAA power struggle on women's athletics was the "invasion" of men into the traditionally separate spheres of women. Shortly after severing its relationship with the AAU in 1960, the NCAA made public its intention to create sports federations independent of the AAU. Such federations would administer women's as well as men's programs.[43] Both the NCAA and the AAU tried hard to lure women's sports organizations into their own camp. Reacting to the NCAA initiatives, the AAU in early 1962 invited the American Association for Health, Physical Education, and Recreation to appoint representatives to all AAU committees in which the AAHPER had an interest. It also offered the AAHPER a vice-chairmanship on its Foreign Relations Committee.[44] While many of its members had assisted with the AAU sports programs, this was the first time that the AAHPER had been invited to serve at the policy-making level of the AAU. In October 1962, the AAHPER board of directors accepted all AAU invitations, sending representatives to nine AAU sports committees including women's basketball, track and field, swimming, and gymnastics. It also endorsed the recommendation that the AAHPER affiliate with the United States Track and Field Federation provided it had voting power on both the governing council and the executive committee of the federation.[45]

The creation of the federations symbolized the beginning of the NCAA's historic move into the separate sphere of women's athletics. Such a move was part of the NCAA's strategic plan to increase its power and control over U.S. amateur sports. Speaking with the tone of a real boss of the federations, Walter Byers told the AAHPER and the Division of Girls and Women's Sports leaders that "we are trying to shape up women's programs for both basketball and track and field."[46] The NCAA did not waste any time in its pursuit. By the fall of 1962, it had successfully established its puppet federations in basketball, gymnastics, and track and field. It had also created a Women's Basketball Association of America within the basketball federation. At a time when the AAU and the DGWS were collaborating on a uniform set of rules for girls' and women's basketball, the creation of the Women's Basketball Association was unmistakably a direct challenge to the AAU's authority. It was also a threat to the women's control of their own destiny.[47]

In 1963, the NCAA proceeded to join with the Division for Girls and Women's Sports and the Women's Board of the United States Olympic Development Committee in sponsoring the Institute for Women's and Girls' Sports. It also established a special Liaison Committee on Girls' and Women's Competition with the charge of informing the NCAA Executive Committee about developments in the area of girls' and women's athletic competition.[48]

At its 1964 annual convention, the NCAA broke its "male" tradition by arranging a roundtable discussion on women's sports and inviting two prominent women college athletic leaders to speak to the convention. In greeting the women speakers, the NCAA secretary-treasurer, Everett D. Barnes, termed the event "an historic first" for the NCAA and pointed out that "it was now time" for the men to actively investigate women's athletics.[49] Thus, nearly a decade before the creation of the Association for Intercollegiate Athletics for Women and the passage of Title IX anti-sex discrimination legislation, the NCAA had openly expressed its concerns about competitive athletics for college women.

The NCAA's motive may be questioned; its interest in and willingness to assist the development of women's athletics at the time should not be doubted. At least by the end of 1964, the NCAA had not made any attempt to control women's athletics. Rather, it positioned itself in a cooperative relationship with the women's organizations. In early 1964, the NCAA Executive Committee, at the request of women sport leaders, amended the Executive Regulation to limit NCAA eligibility to male student-athletes only.[50] The 1965 NCAA convention adopted the executive committee's amendment, which virtually prohibited women student-athletes from be-coming eligible for NCAA championships.[51]

By legislating the "separate spheres," the NCAA soon realized its self-imposed disadvantageous position in the struggle against the AAU. In early 1965, the Long-Range Planning Committee of the NCAA discussed the need for encouraging opportunities for young women to compete in intercollegiate athletics.[52] In the meantime, Walter Byers began to actively recruit women physical educators for a new NCAA initiative—establishing a committee to supervise the development of women's competition, especially women's intercollegiate basketball.[53] The new NCAA initiative was part and parcel of its strategic planning. It became clear by the early 1960s that whoever could control the fast-growing intercollegiate and interscholastic women's athletics would eventually become the most dominant force in U.S. amateur sports.

By the mid-1960s, the NCAA's increasing interest in women's intercollegiate athletics greatly alarmed the leaders of college women's athletics. Under pressure, they formed the Commission on Intercollegiate Athletics for Women in 1966 in order to prevent women's intercollegiate athletics from being taken over by the NCAA.[54]

Less than a year after the CIAW became operational, the NCAA council moved to establish a committee to study the feasibility of the NCAA's controlling women's intercollegiate athletics. Two months later, the NCAA appointed a special committee on intercollegiate athletics for women based on its council's decision.[55] The NCAA council's decision was immediately embraced by one of its closest allies, the National Federation of State High School Athletic Associations. In a letter to Walter Byers, Clifford B. Fagan, executive secretary of the NFSHSAA and president of the Basketball Federation of the United States, praised the NCAA initiative and stated that the NFSHSAA should assume responsibility for women's athletics at the interscholastic level.[56]

In accordance with the NCAA initiative and the NFSHSAA rhetoric, the Iowa Girls' High School Athletic Union, another close ally of the NCAA, was forming a new organization devoted to women's basketball. It would allow college teams to join along with clubs to compete in the public sector; the new organization would virtually chip away the DGWS/CIAW's control of women's intercollegiate competition.[57] While the NCAA denied its involvement, it apparently supported the creation of the new organization, at least through the NCAA-sponsored Basketball Federation of the United States. In a letter to the BFUSA president, Charles M. Neinas, assistant executive director of the NCAA, pointed out that "the new organization is desirous of affiliating with BFUSA." Neinas obviously knew more about the organization than someone who had not been involved. But he was not very subtle in guarding his "ignorance." "The organization apparently was formed because of dissatisfaction with the AAU's administration of women's basketball," continued Neinas. "More needs to be done to develop women's basketball and any new organization designed to accomplish this purpose should be encouraged."[58]

The NCAA and its allies were on a mission to gain control of women's athletics at both the intercollegiate and interscholastic levels. Their goal was to strengthen themselves in the power struggle against the AAU over the control of U.S. amateur sports. Nearly fifteen years later, Donna Lopiano, president-elect of the Association for Intercollegiate Athletics for Women, elaborated on NCAA's potential gain of power through controlling intercollegiate athletics for women. There was "no secret that the NCAA has always aspired to become the pre-dominant force in all of amateur athletics," Lopiano told an AIAW audience in January 1981. "The biggest prize garnered through the successful acquisition of women's athletics," the AIAW leader claimed, "[is] a doubling of NCAA voting power in the non-collegiate amateur sport governing bodies in the United States."[59]

It would take one and one-half decades for the NCAA to acquire the power Lopiano was worried about. In 1967, the long and treacherous journey had just begun.

 Growing NCAA Interest in
Women's Intercollegiate Athletics

1963–1968

> We have been vitally interested in the women's
> program, and we are deeply appreciative of the
> many contributions that they have made to
> athletics, not only intercollegiate but intramural,
> certainly to Pan-American competition, and to
> Olympic competition. . . . It is now time that we
> actively investigate this area.
> —Everett D. Barnes, NCAA
> Secretary-Treasurer

THE NCAA began to take an active interest in the development of women's
intercollegiate athletics in the early 1960s.[1] Between 1963 and 1968, the
NCAA participated in sponsoring the Institute for Women's and Girls'
Sports (an Olympic project), established special committees devoted to
women's athletics, invited women speakers to its annual convention, held
meetings with women sport leaders, and maintained regular communications with women's sport organizations. The growing NCAA interest
caused great concern among college women leaders and, ironically, led to
the formation of the Commission on Intercollegiate Athletics for Women
and the establishment of several national intercollegiate championships
for women.

Early Interactions

The first official interaction between the NCAA and college women athletic leaders took place between late 1962 and early 1963, when an NCAA

representative contacted Katherine Ley, vice president of the American Association for Health, Physical Education, and Recreation. As a result of this communication, Ley called a "study conference" to meet in Washington, D.C., in February 1963. Ten men and women representing various institutions attended the meeting, including officials from both the AAHPER and the NCAA. With a focus on preparing guidelines for intercollegiate athletics for women, the meeting resolved to make recommendations to colleges and to propose governance organizations for eligibility in intercollegiate competitions.[2]

At an April 1963 NCAA Council meeting, Richard C. Larkins, a member of the NCAA Executive Committee and the chair of the NCAA Olympic Development Committee, reported on the Institute for Women's and Girls' Sports.[3] At Larkins' request, the NCAA Council endorsed the proposal to join the Division for Girls and Women's Sports and the Women's Board of the United States Olympic Development Committee in sponsoring the institute to be held in Norman, Oklahoma, in the fall of 1963. The council also appropriated $9,500 to underwrite the costs of the institute.[4]

During the NCAA Executive Committee meeting held in August 1963, it was noted that the United States Olympic Development Committee would subsidize the institute in the amount of $9,500, thus leaving the NCAA's offer to underwrite the institute unnecessary. At the same meeting, a special Liaison Committee on Girls' and Women's Competition was established. Headed by Richard Larkins, the committee was charged with keeping the association's executive committee informed of the developments in the area of girls' and women's athletic competition. Its first major task was to arrange a roundtable presentation of the subject at the 1964 NCAA annual convention.[5]

In January 1964, the NCAA convention hosted a special session on developments in women's athletic competition. Sara Staff Jernigan, past chair of the DGWS and chair of the Women's Board of the United States Olympic Development Committee, and Marguerite Clifton, vice president of the AAHPER and chair of the DGWS, made presentations at the invitation of the NCAA. The purpose of the session was made clear by Richard Larkins' introduction: "There has been an increasing amount of interest within the NCAA, particularly the Executive Committee and the Council, in the progress and development of women athletes," he stated. "I would like to point out clearly that there is no attempt to move into the activities which are very well handled by competent leadership. I think our purpose today is merely to understand what the women are doing."[6]

Jernigan's speech began with a brief review of the women's physical education programs and their close association with the feminine culture in the United States. She pointed out the advantages of the women's programs that emphasized the unique philosophy of "sport for all." She also acknowledged the shortcomings of such a philosophy, which resulted in many women's programs' lacking "stimulus, help, and inspiration of the motor-gifted girl." The athletically gifted young women, according to Jernigan, were "often lost in the mediocrity of the classroom or in the sloppy playing of uncoached intramural teams that are not really teams but a group of individuals playing on the same court." Although the DGWS had been promoting more opportunities and help for skilled women athletes since its establishment, Jernigan stated, "it is a little late in life and still only a meager approach to the problem."[7]

Jernigan also addressed a growing concern of women sports leaders over the practice of allowing women to participate on men's varsity teams. She warned that such a situation, approved by many college coaches, could backfire in that men now could have the right to be members of a women's intercollegiate sports team. Asking the men for help in resolving the critical problem, Jernigan suggested that a policy statement by the NCAA would greatly ease "a most unhappy situation." Finally, using the first Institute for Women's and Girls' Sports as an example, Jernigan attributed the success of the project to "the magnificent support the men gave to the women participants on the state and national levels." She made the appeal that "with the full support, understanding and cooperative effort of each member of NCAA," the women physical educators could and would significantly affect the development of intercollegiate athletics for women.[8]

When it was her turn, Marguerite Clifton first acknowledged the growth of intercollegiate athletics for women as well as the lack of financial resources, experience, and women faculty competent enough to administrate the programs. The emphasis of her speech, however, was on the importance of women's leadership in conducting women's programs. Although men could help women's sport by first learning and understanding women's philosophy and then providing their advice and experience, Clifton believed that women must assume leadership in developing intercollegiate programs for women. "Men are uniquely different from women, therefore, their answers to problems fundamental to sports programs will not always be satisfactory ready-made solutions which can be superimposed upon the women's program," she argued. "Failure to observe this premise is undoubtedly the greatest fear that many women leaders have as they move cautiously ahead with this latest development in competition [for women]."[9] In conclusion, Clifton indicated that it might soon become necessary to create an organization similar to the NCAA in order to manage the growing intercollegiate athletics for women, because the DGWS "does not and should not function in this capacity."[10]

NCAA Eligibility for Men Only

Responding to the request of Jernigan and Clifton, the NCAA Executive Committee in April 1964 amended the executive regulation to limit participation in any NCAA event to male student-athletes only.[11] In 1965, the NCAA convention enacted the executive committee's amendment that virtually prevented women student-athletes from being eligible for NCAA championship meets and tournaments.[12] This new NCAA policy soon encountered challenge from members within the organization. At its meeting in February 1965, some members of the NCAA Long-range Planning Committee indicated "a need for encouraging opportunity for young women to compete in intercollegiate athletics."[13] In April, the NCAA Council authorized the NCAA officers to appoint a Committee on Women's Sports consisting of NCAA members and other leaders in women's athletics. It also requested the committee to define the role of the NCAA in the field of women's sports.[14]

At about the same time, Walter Byers was carrying out the new NCAA initiative through actively recruiting women physical educators. In his correspondence with Ella Corinne Brown, a physical education professor at the University of Maine, Byers indicated that the NCAA was in the process of organizing a committee "to supervise development of women's competition and we want to obtain the names of as many women instructors as possible to have a good nucleus from which to build."[15]

In October 1965, Byers wrote E. Wayne Cooley, executive secretary of Iowa Girls' High School Athletic Union, requesting the names of colleges that conducted intercollegiate competition for women, particularly in the

sport of basketball.[16] Cooley provided Byers with the names of five colleges that had intercollegiate basketball for women but indicated that none
of the schools held membership in the NCAA. He strongly recommended
Mildred Barnes of the University of Iowa to be the NCAA appointee to the
American Women's Olympic Basketball Committee. In supporting Barnes,
Cooley made an interesting analysis of the case, which well reflected the
role of women in the hostile relationship between the NCAA and the Amateur Athletic Union: "Though the DGWS has by and large been somewhat
aligned with the AAU throughout the last three or four years," wrote Cooley, "Mildred [Barnes] had not shared their viewpoint in total and actually
at this time serves as the AAHPER representative on the Federation Basketball Committee."[17] Responding to Cooley's letter, Byers acknowledged
the qualification of Barnes and promised Cooley that "when the time
comes for the NCAA to organize developmental activities involving
women, you may rest assured that we will give her consideration for service on the planning committee."[18]

Byers saw clearly that the control of women's sport would play a crucial role in determining the outcome of the AAU-NCAA power struggle.
His communications with both Brown and Cooley were indicative of the
NCAA's strategic approach to that struggle. While the NCAA's actual control of women's intercollegiate athletics was still years to come, its new initiative concerning women's sports caused great alarm among the women
sports leaders.

In January 1966, leaders of the DGWS and the National Association for
Physical Education of College Women (NAPECW) met in Washington,
D.C., to discuss the possible management of intercollegiate athletics for
women.[19] The meeting recommended that the DGWS establish a commission to assume leadership in women's collegiate athletics. Specifically, the
commission would serve three major purposes: (1) to continue the college
women's golf and tennis tournaments; (2) to keep control of women's intercollegiate athletics and forestall any possible NCAA invasion; and (3) to
be prepared for the possible growth of women's intercollegiate athletics in
the future.[20]

Alerted by the NCAA's recent ambiguous policies regarding women's
sports, however, the women leaders made a cautious move. Before officially forming the Commission on Intercollegiate Athletics for Women, the
DGWS board asked Richard Larkins to ascertain in writing the NCAA's in-

tentions in the area of women's collegiate athletics. Larkins conveyed the DGWS's request via a phone call to Charles M. Neinas, assistant executive director of the NCAA.[21] Neinas responded to Larkins' inquiry in March 1966 by indicating that the "male-only" NCAA policy would prohibit women from participating in its national championship events and that, consequently, the women's organization "would not be in conflict" with the NCAA. He further assured that the NCAA was ready to assist the DGWS in formulating policies and procedures for conducting women's intercollegiate athletics and wished the DGWS well in its endeavor.[22] Two days later, Larkins wrote Neinas thanking him for his prompt reply, which would "help the ladies proceed."[23]

Neinas's response reduced the DGWS's concern of a possible NCAA entry into women's intercollegiate athletics.[24] Within two weeks of Neinas's assurance, the DGWS proposed to establish the commission to sanction and sponsor women's intercollegiate championships at state, regional, and national levels.[25] With final approval from the AAHPER—the parent organization of the DGWS—the CIAW was formed and began operation in June 1966.[26] In August 1966, Larkins wrote all members of the National Association of College Directors of Athletics, informing them of the establishment of the CIAW and asking them to support the women's organization. Larkins also sent copies of the letter to executive directors of all three governing bodies of intercollegiate athletics for men: the NCAA, the National Association for Intercollegiate Athletics, and the National Junior College Athletic Association.[27]

Growing NCAA Interest in Women's Athletics

An early connection between the NCAA and women's intercollegiate athletics was through E. Wayne Cooley, executive secretary of Iowa Girls' High School Athletic Union. For years, Cooley not only provided the NCAA officials with information concerning women's athletic organizations and activities, but was also influential at shaping NCAA's policies on women's sports.

In 1966, just before the formal announcement of the establishment of the CIAW, Cooley wrote Charles Neinas and shared his experience and opinion in dealing with women's athletic organizations. He discredited the notion that the DGWS was in charge of both interscholastic and intercollegiate athletics for women because the DGWS was, wrote Cooley, "a financial pauper."[28] Using the state of Iowa as an example, Cooley indicated that over the years women leaders, despite their pride and ability, had developed "an artificial attitude towards competitive athletics solely because they were without the necessary assets to administer a competitive program." The Iowa experience seemed extremely valuable to the NCAA, a men's organization embarking on administering programs for women. In Iowa, Cooley pointed out, "we were able to bring [the women] into our own financial structure, allow them to administer, promote and control with a very minimum of regulation from the State Athletic Office." By giving the women a token sense of responsibility and importance, Cooley and his male associates were able to have the state of Iowa "one hundred percent under control."[29]

Years of experience certainly had refined Cooley's professional savvy on issues concerning women's sport, and the NCAA was lucky to have his knowledge and him as an ally. Responding to a newspaper article on the growth of women's sports nationwide, Cooley shared with Neinas his perception of the new national trend. He pointed out that the real significance of the article rested in the fact that most sports-minded people, particularly those in positions of administrative responsibility, were not aware of such a trend.[30] Interscholastic and intercollegiate athletics for women were mushrooming, but the key issue, as Cooley warned Neinas, was the lack of administration at the national level. Not coincidentally, Cooley suggested that the obvious solution to the "problem" was to bring the matter under control of a national body, either the AAU or the NCAA and its affiliates.[31]

Neither the NCAA nor the AAU had seized control of women's intercollegiate athletics by 1966. The increasing NCAA interest in the governance of women's athletics, however, did put great pressure on the women leaders. Such pressure was most vividly illustrated in Neinas's letter to AAHPER consultant Roswell Merrick in late 1966. Inquiring whether the DGWS had made any plans to increase the number of national championships for women, Neinas signified that the NCAA had been under pressure to "do something for intercollegiate athletics for women." Despite the NCAA's intention to confine its activities to male student-athletes, Neinas made it clear that the ultimate authority of the NCAA came from the membership. "There is a growing interest in intercollegiate athletics for women in NCAA member institutions," he wrote. "It is inevitable that if this trend continues there will be a demand for national championship competition for women."[32] Trying to soften his tone while retaining a strategic position for the NCAA, Neinas ended his letter with a rather intriguing notion. "Please do not misinterpret this letter," he wrote. "The NCAA has enough problems without irritating the DGWS or the gals. It should be recognized, however, that some of the athletic directors in the NCAA believe that national competition for women will stimulate activity at the grass roots level."[33]

In early 1967, CIAW chairperson Katherine Ley wrote NCAA president Marcus L. Plant of the University of Michigan to advise him of the CIAW's activities. She also brought to his attention the NCAA's position concerning women's athletics as stated in Neinas's March 1966 letter—that a national organization assuming responsibility for women's intercollegiate athletics would not be in conflict with the NCAA.[34] Ley's communication showed clearly the CIAW's concern about the NCAA's interest in women's athletics. The NCAA Council, nevertheless, decided at its May 1967 meeting to appoint a committee "to study the feasibility of establishing appropriate machinery to provide for the control and supervision of women's intercollegiate athletics."[35] The rationale for the action was that high school athletic associations were "in the process of reversing their position to provide the same scrutiny and control over women's interscholastic activities as was then exercised in boys' activities."[36]

The NCAA Council's decision met an enthusiastic welcome from the National Federation of State High School Athletic Associations. Clifford B. Fagan, executive secretary of the NFSHSAA, told Walter Byers that his organization was gratified that the NCAA Council had decided to study developments in women's intercollegiate athletics and to determine the NCAA's responsibility in that area.[37] The NFSHSAA's reaction became even more significant in light of the hostile relationship between the NCAA and the AAU. A member of the NCAA-backed United States Track and Field Federation, the NFSHSAA's response was a clear indication that both the NCAA and the NFSHSAA intended to have intercollegiate and interscholastic athletics, including both men's and women's programs, under their control. As Fagan clearly expressed to Byers: "We believe that it is advantageous for all organizations with administrative responsibilities in athletics in the school college community to have somewhat similar policies whenever possible."[38]

Along with the NCAA initiative and the NFSHSAA rhetoric, the Iowa Girls' High School Athletic Union was collaborating with the Basketball Federation of the United States to develop a new amateur basketball organization for women. The Iowa Girls' High School Athletic Union, under the leadership of E. Wayne Cooley, was planning to allow college women's teams to join along with clubs to compete in the public sector. Such a development would virtually chip away the DGWS/CIAW's control of women's intercollegiate athletics. The plan was shocking news to the women and caused a protest from the DGWS. "[The women in the DGWS] are all upset," Neinas wrote in a memorandum to Byers. "Apparently the DGWS doesn't want anyone involved in women's [basketball] without their blessing. . . . DGWS [says] they have the right to the colleges, without having any program."[39]

Like the NCAA Council's decision on women's intercollegiate athletics, Cooley's basketball organization was apparently part of the undertaking evolved around the struggle with the AAU over the control of amateur sports. "Obviously the AAU has the news by now," Neinas told Byers. "Believe you should inform Troester [executive secretary of the AAHPER] about the Council's plan to study women's athletics and possible NCAA supervision. Rather have it come from here than be picked up and blown out of proportion by some gal."[40]

The NCAA Special Committee on Women's Intercollegiate Athletics

In July 1967, the NCAA appointed a special committee on intercollegiate athletics for women based on its council's decision in May. The committee was chaired by Ernest B. McCoy from Penn State University, secretary-treasurer and chair of the eligibility committee of the NCAA. Among the other six selected committee members were Katherine Ley, the CIAW chair, and Elizabeth (Betty) McCue, chair of the DGWS.[41] Upon reception of her appointment, Ley wrote Byers and expressed her surprise over the establishment of the committee. Indicating that the CIAW would soon become active in September, Ley told Byers that "the whole matter becomes a bit more 'sticky' in view of the fact that Ernie McCoy was called in May and he indicated no change in the [NCAA's] hands-off policy adopted earlier."[42]

Byers responded to Ley a month later. While cordial and professional, the tone of Byers' letter was mostly firm and authoritative on the NCAA's position. "The NCAA has been interested in the intercollegiate aspects of women's competition for some time," wrote Byers, listing NCAA's financial contribution to meetings on the subject and its revised rules at the recommendation of the women. He specifically indicated that an increasing number of NCAA member institutions were administering women's programs under the department of athletics. "I don't know precisely what you mean by our 'hands off' policy or who told you this was the official position of the Association," continued Byers. "I would point out, however, that the NCAA committee is a 'study committee.' "[43]

Little surprise that Byers spoke with such authority. Arguably the most prominent figure in the entire history of the NCAA, Byers was on a mission to build his organization into the most powerful cartel in U.S. amateur sports. While most of his associates were preoccupied with big-time men's college athletics and could care less about the women's program, Byers knew too well its importance in the battle for supremacy within amateur sports. He never lost sight of the prize.

In late October, Ley wrote Byers to counter his defense of the NCAA's official position on women's intercollegiate athletics. She reminded him that the DGWS had based its governance plans for women's athletics on the series of NCAA announcements of the "hands-off" policy. "The whole matter came up when DGWS was considering the formation of a Commission on Intercollegiate Athletics for Women," argued Ley. "We wanted to be sure there was no existing organization concerned with or interested in conducting athletic events specifically for college women."[44] The women in the DGWS were concerned about men's entering the separate sphere of women's sports. Their concern was justified.

At the NCAA Council meeting later that month Ernest McCoy reported on behalf of the NCAA Committee on Intercollegiate Competition for Women. McCoy informed the council that there had been "some feeling that women's athletics should be subject to institutional control, similar to intercollegiate athletics for men, rather than being controlled by professional organizations composed of individuals." He indicated that his committee intended to determine if there were a problem in administration of competitive programs for women.[45] Although appointed in July 1967, the NCAA committee had not formally met prior to McCoy's report to the NCAA Council. However, the NCAA Council was aware that the DGWS had raised some question as to why the NCAA was interested in women's competition.[46]

One day following the council meeting, Byers responded to Ley by reiterating the growing number of NCAA member institutions involved in sponsoring intercollegiate competition for women and the increasing athletic opportunities for girls at the high school level. He also highlighted a key element in the tradition of amateur sports—that organizations, either at the interscholastic or the intercollegiate level, had always been based upon institutional membership."[47]

To the dismay of Ley and other women leaders, Byers not only reserved the NCAA's right as a possible organization to administer women's collegiate athletics, but also questioned the legality of the DGWS as the current governing body. "The question of whether the NCAA is the organization to take on this job is a question yet to be determined," wrote Byers. "Likewise, I presume that the question of whether the AAHPER (through DGWS) is the appropriate organization to supervise and control women's intercollegiate sports has not been determined." One thing seemed crystal clear in Byers' mind. "The organization which is eventually selected or developed must be an organization based upon institutional membership," he concluded, "because I do not believe the governing boards and administrators of the high schools and colleges of the nation are going to be satisfied on any other basis."[48]

After receiving Byers' letter, Ley communicated to Richard Larkins her frustration about what she perceived as the changed NCAA attitude toward women's intercollegiate athletics and requested his response. With obviously a different interpretation of Byers' letter, Larkins told Ley that he was not sure that the issue was becoming clouded. Rather, the NCAA Council "could easily make provisions to cover women's athletic competition," speculated Larkins. "Whether this is the right road, I am not prepared to say."[49]

The CIAW Announces National Championships under NCAA Pressure

Byers' letter, along with the NCAA rhetoric on women's sport, caused great concern among women leaders over the fate of women's intercollegiate athletics. Under the pressure, the DGWS Executive Council rushed to approve the CIAW national championships and announced new CIAW programs at a national press conference on December 7, 1967.[50]

Meanwhile, the AAHPER board of directors established a study committee to develop a long-range plan for financing and operating the CIAW. Invitations for committee membership were extended to key representatives of the NCAA (Walter Byers and Ernest McCoy), the National Association of Intercollegiate Athletics (executive director Al Duer), and the National Junior Collegiate Athletic Association (executive director George Killian).[51] The committee met in mid-January 1968. Byers, McCoy, and Killian did not attend, supposedly because of "bad weather conditions." The meeting centered around the issue of how to finance a full-time staff member and the long-range costs of the CIAW. It also entertained the idea of institutional membership as a source for CIAW's basic operating budget and security. However, the consensus among the women was that the idea of membership dues for schools was "inappropriate" at the time, without further explanation.[52]

Within a week after the AAHPER committee meeting, the NCAA Committee on Intercollegiate Competition for Women met in Chicago. In addition to the official members of the committee, DGWS chair Lucille Magnusson, who worked under McCoy at Penn State University, also attended the meeting and took the minutes.[53] A major achievement of the meeting was "improved communication" between the men and the women. The committee members "shared ideas, asked questions of each other and gained a good deal of understanding of the functioning of NCAA as well as the DGWS Commission."[54]

Despite improved understanding and respect, serious questions arose concerning the validity of the CIAW as a functional organization to govern intercollegiate athletics for women. Committee chair McCoy specifically questioned the sanctioning procedure of the CIAW in relation to "how or by whom the right to do this had been delegated to the Commission." He explicitly pointed out the substructure status of the CIAW under the AAHPER/DGWS and asked whether a different organizational structure would be more reasonable. It was suggested that institutional membership be established so that the CIAW would have the strength of backing by colleges and universities.[55]

Finally, McCoy asked what the NCAA could do to assist the development of intercollegiate athletics for women. As the minutes of the meeting indicated, the men were willing to offer their experience and guidance to the women in relation to all administrative details of an athletic program while avoiding some of the problem areas that the men had encountered. "The men were emphatic in stating that they were not interested in taking over women's athletics but rather in assisting in and supporting the new programs for women."[56]

The meeting ended on the seemingly positive note that "the women expressed their appreciation for being included on the committee and for the assistance the men gave during the course of the meeting."[57] The minutes, however, may not have revealed the true feelings of the women leaders who attended the meeting. Interviewed seven years later, Betty McCue recalled that everyone was very polite to one another during the meeting, but there was no real compromise. She believed that the men did not understand what was going on within the women's programs and would not guarantee that women could set their own policies. "Women and DGWS were demanding the right for their own autonomy," said McCue; "we would welcome any help we could get, but we did not want it to be a takeover."[58]

Lucille Magnusson, then the DGWS chair but not a member of the NCAA committee, believed that there was some problem regarding the men's awareness of the DGWS programs at the beginning of the meeting. "They were not knowledgeable about where the women's program was going or how it was going to get there," she stated. "When they became aware of those things, it was not such a problem."[59]

Katherine Ley, then chair of the CIAW and one of the two female members on the NCAA committee, gave a different impression of the situation from those of McCue and Magnusson. "[The men seemed] very supportive of the CIAW," said Ley. "They just wanted to make sure that the women would be provided for in some way."[60] There was no unanimity among women leaders about a NCAA's conspiracy to take over women's sports as there would be a decade later.

The January 1968 meeting turned out to be the only official gathering of the NCAA committee with participation of its members from both sides. Although at the time a desire for future meetings was expressed, such a desire never materialized. For the next nineteen months, formal communication and cooperation concerning the development of intercollegiate athletics for women stalled between the DGWS and the NCAA. Interactions between the two organizations were not renewed until August 1969. By then, however, the relationship between the two had moved onto a new stage.

Early NCAA Attempts at the Governance of Women's Intercollegiate Athletics

1968–1973

> I think it was part of the whole NCAA-AAU
> battle. The NCAA was fighting for jurisdiction
> over the AAU [but] did not have any female
> athletes so how could it expect to be regarded as
> the controlling organization [of all intercollegiate
> athletics].
>   —Katherine Ley, CIAW Chair

KATHERINE LEY'S comment on the NCAA's growing interest in women's athletics cut straight into the NCAA's vulnerability in its decades-long battle against the AAU.[1] In order to change this unfavorable situation, the NCAA undertook to legitimize itself for administering athletic programs for college women. Toward the end of the 1960s, the NCAA, under the guidance of Walter Byers and its legal counsel, pushed for the formation of the Association for Intercollegiate Athletics for Women (AIAW) as an institutional membership organization. In the 1970s, the NCAA stepped up its involvement by urging the AIAW to affiliate with the NCAA. The plan failed when the women refused to submit to NCAA control.

The Birth of AIAW under NCAA Pressure

In 1968 there was little interaction between the NCAA and the Division for Girls and Women's Sports/Commission on Intercollegiate Athletics for Women except for a January meeting of the NCAA Committee on Women's Intercollegiate Athletics with the participation of Katherine Ley,

Betty McCue, and Lucille Magnusson. The women athletic leaders, however, were moving quietly toward finding a resolution for handling the CIAW championships they had established a year before. With the increased responsibilities, it was no longer realistic for the four part-time commissioners of the CIAW to manage the program. According to the reminiscences of Donna Lopiano, later AIAW president, "CIAW was handicapped administratively and economically by its lack of an identifiable membership to provide a direct communication channel to individual institutions and a source of dues to finance its operations."[2] A partial solution to the problem would be to hire a full-time staff member to manage the CIAW's daily operation. The issue thus became a matter of funding such a position, because the CIAW was not a membership organization with a regular income of membership dues. Although the NCAA had pushed for the adoption of an institutional membership structure, the women in 1968 were not ready to accept the idea of charging membership fees. One could reason, though, that women leaders did not want institutions and their athletic departments, run by men, to have financial control and thus power over women's intercollegiate athletics.

In August 1969, Charles M. Neinas, assistant executive director of the NCAA, and Ernest B. McCoy, chair of the NCAA Committee on Women's Intercollegiate Athletics, met with Lucille Magnusson and Martha Adams, two DGWS officials from Penn State University, in Atlantic City. Neinas and McCoy again suggested to the women that an institutionally oriented organization, rather than one composed of individual educators, would be better qualified to administer a national athletic program for women. The men also stressed that the NCAA was not anxious to become involved in women's intercollegiate athletics, but that it was willing to assist in establishing a national association for women.[3]

Two months after the Atlantic City meeting, the CIAW convened and proposed to establish an institutional membership organization for women's intercollegiate athletics.[4] The DGWS executive board approved the proposal and, in December 1970, presented the proposal to the American Association for Health, Physical Education, and Recreation board of directors. After lengthy discussion on the potential legal and tax difficulties, the AAHPER finally approved the establishment of the Association for Intercollegiate Athletics for Women in October 1971. The AIAW officially replaced the CIAW on June 1, 1972.[5]

It is worth noting that as early as 1967 Walter Byers had urged the women leaders to adopt an institutional membership structure for the proposed women's organization. In 1968 and 1969, the concept of institutional membership became the major topic of discussion at meetings between the NCAA and the CIAW/DGWS and among the women leaders.[6] The acceptance of the concept by the women was an inevitable step in the development of women's intercollegiate athletics toward a more competitive direction. That is, a stable and efficient national organization must depend on the commitment of individual member institutions, ideologically as well as financially. Even though he would soon be considered a chief antagonist of women's sports, Walter Byers probably deserved more credit than anyone else in bringing the idea of an institutional membership organization to reality.

The NCAA's Position on Women's Athletics: A "Legal Opinion"

A copy of the proposal for establishing the AIAW was also sent to the NCAA. The women soon found out that the NCAA was much more difficult to deal with than they had expected. In his response to the receipt of the document, Walter Byers informed the CIAW/DGWS that the NCAA was examining its position on women's intercollegiate athletics and might make changes accordingly. "It appears that the NCAA is in a difficult legal position on the basis of its present posture," wrote Byers. "I suspect that it is quite likely that we will proceed to remove such barriers and, in fact, provide competitive opportunities for women as well as men."[7]

Byers' response was likely to have been shocking news to the women. Only a phone conversation between Lucille Magnusson and Charles Neinas seemed to have assured the CIAW/DGWS leaders that no real threat to the women should be perceived from Byers' letter. "I felt strongly that we should appear neither alarmed [n]or defensive about the letter from Walter Byers to Liz [Hoyt]," wrote Magnusson in a memorandum to other CIAW/DGWS officials. Magnusson did not obtain a definite answer from Neinas regarding Byers' statement. As she concluded, however, "it did not seem from what was said that at this point NCAA was planning to get involved in tournament[s] specifically for women." She urged her colleagues to wait to see what the NCAA might have in mind.[8] Magnusson's response probably reflected the general reactions of the women leaders to the NCAA rhetoric.

In February 1971, seven months before the AIAW was established and sixteen months before the passage of Title IX, Byers sent a memo to the NCAA Executive Committee and Council regarding the NCAA's position relative to female competition. It basically summarized the legal opinion on the subject provided by NCAA legal counsel George Gangwere a month earlier. The theme of the opinion, as outlined by Byers, was that the NCAA constitution and bylaws did not prevent the association from adopting rules applicable to female athletic competition. Therefore, the current practice of prohibiting women from participating in the NCAA events might not stand up to a court challenge. Although Gangwere outlined four possible courses of action to deal with the situation, he believed that the best legal course would be for the NCAA to create a women's division within the organization.[9]

Gangwere's legal opinion was a major subject of discussion at the April 1971 NCAA Council and Executive Committee meetings. As a result, the NCAA Council authorized the NCAA president to appoint a committee to review the organization's position on intercollegiate athletics for women. Law professor David Swank of the University of Oklahoma was appointed to chair the committee. Donald Boydston of Southern Illinois University and Edward Czekaj of Penn State University were also asked to serve on the committee.[10]

In June 1971, Walter Byers requested George Gangwere to supplement his January opinion. In his response to Byers, Gangwere maintained that the NCAA, based on its constitution and bylaws, remained obligated to provide equal opportunities for intercollegiate competitions for women. The NCAA, however, could not actually provide such opportunities by merely permitting qualified women to participate in NCAA events, either with men or against men. The simple reason was, argued Gangwere, that "women cannot in general compete equally with men." Thus, the only way for the NCAA to remove itself from a charge of discrimination would be to create the opportunities for competition "by women among themselves."[11]

Gangwere did recognize that the DGWS was in the process of creating a national organization for intercollegiate athletics for women. He also foresaw that any NCAA attempts to supersede the women's organization might meet strong resentment by women athletic leaders. Nevertheless, the NCAA legal counsel predicted that the effectiveness of the new women's organization, the AIAW, would depend on its financial resources. The key difference between the CIAW and the AIAW was that the latter would be equipped with a full-time, paid professional staff, and that could be costly.[12]

The vital point of Gangwere's letter was his suggestion of actions that the NCAA should take. There was a strategic change in his advice compared to the advice in his January 1971 "legal opinion" as presented by Byers. Instead of simply creating a women's division within the NCAA, Gangwere recommended that the NCAA first try to affiliate with the soon-to-be-formed AIAW. "To take full advantage of the great amount of work done heretofore in the field of women's sport, to avoid resentment and hostility from the leading women athletic administrators, and as the best means of locating the necessary additional female administrators," wrote Gangwere, "it would appear desirable for the NCAA to seek the affiliation as an adjunct of the NCAA of the new National Organization for Intercollegiate Athletics for Women.[13]

It is plausible that Gangwere had much faith in the affiliation, one that would unlikely satisfy both the men and the women. Gangwere's advice was more likely well-thought-through legal preparation for the NCAA's eventual control of women's intercollegiate athletics. The idea of the affiliation was thus probably playacting. Its foreseeable failure would therefore justify the follow-up step the NCAA would take. "If such an affiliation is not possible," concluded Gangwere, "then it will be desirable to ascertain the necessary steps for organizing a separate women's group within the NCAA."[14] The immediate impact of this NCAA initiative was a meeting on women's intercollegiate athletics between the women leaders and key NCAA officials.

Early Attempts at an NCAA-AIAW Affiliation

In July 1971, the NCAA Committee on Women's Intercollegiate Athletics met at NCAA headquarters in Kansas City. Representing the NCAA were Byers, Neinas, Gangwere, and two members of the committee, Donald Boydston and Edward Czekaj.[15] At the invitation of the NCAA, DGWS chair JoAnne Thorpe, CIAW commissioner Carole Oglesby, and DGWS consultant Rachel E. Bryant also attended the meeting. Discussions of the meeting centered around Gangwere's letter of "legal opinion" and on how the NCAA could avoid charges of discrimination against women. The meeting also entertained the idea that the AIAW disassociate itself from the AAHPER/DGWS and affiliate with the NCAA. The major outcome of the meeting was that the NCAA legal counsel would draft an affiliation proposal upon receiving a copy of the proposed AIAW constitution.[16]

Noticeably, the concept of a NCAA-AIAW affiliation was not perceived as a "takeover" but as a solution to potential legal challenges the NCAA might face in the future. The men from the NCAA "were looking for an 'out,' " wrote Rachel Bryant. "They were seeking some sort of affiliation with AIAW so that they could say, 'This [AIAW] is the group officially recognized by NCAA to conduct intercollegiate athletics for women.' "[17] It is at least interesting to note that, at the time, the idea of affiliation between the NCAA and the AIAW seemed to have been well received by both the men and the women.

Bryant completed a revised draft of the "Preliminary Operating Code" for the AIAW ten days after the Kansas City meeting. A copy of the draft was sent to Byers so that Gangwere could draft an affiliation agreement between the NCAA and the AIAW.[18] Four weeks later, Gangwere submitted a proposed amendment to the NCAA constitution to permit the NCAA Council to establish a women's division within the NCAA structure in case an affiliation with the AIAW did not materialize. Gangwere's faith in an NCAA-AIAW affiliation was at best questionable. "We cannot be sure that the AIAW will finally accept our proposal," Gangwere wrote in his letter to Byers accompanying the proposed amendment. "If they do not the Council will be free to make other arrangements." The real merit of the amendment, as Gangwere concluded in his letter, was that it would provide "sufficient flexibility to enable the Council to do the job" in dealing with intercollegiate athletics for women.[19]

A flexible legal position was exactly what the NCAA needed in its attempt to take control of intercollegiate athletics for women and its struggle for power in the world of amateur sports. Six years earlier, at the request of the women leaders, the NCAA had tied its own hands by limiting NCAA eligibility to male students. The male-only status of the organization apparently did not help the NCAA in its pursuit of gaining more power in amateur athletics. An obvious solution to the problem would be to have that gender-biased policy changed so the NCAA could claim its control over all collegiate athletics. Probably no one other than Walter Byers in the entire organization was more aware of the urgent need for such a change. Nor did anyone else deserve more credit in conceiving the policies toward implementing a NCAA program for women. In fact, Gangwere's "legal opinion" would not have been born without the influence of Byers' "personal opinion." Weeks before Gangwere submitted his "legal opinion" in June 1971, Byers had clearly demonstrated to Gangwere his stance on the issue. "As we discussed recently," wrote Byers, "I had been leaning toward the solution of changing the NCAA Executive Regulations to permit women to compete in NCAA championship events if that should prove to be their desire."[20]

Byers' letter to Gangwere was likely a direct response to the women's initiative a week earlier. On May 14, 1971, the AAHPER announced the formation of the first regulatory body for intercollegiate athletics for women, with a tentative name of "Organization for Intercollegiate Athletics for Women." The news release stressed one controversial issue in interscholastic and intercollegiate athletics: Should high school and college girls be allowed to compete on previously all-male sports teams? The answer from the AAHPER/DGWS was an emphatic "No." Speaking for the proposed Organization for Intercollegiate Athletics for Women, Frances McGill, former CIAW chair and professor of physical education at the University of New Mexico, made it clear that "young women have a right to facilities, coaching, and competition compatible with their skills." She argued that by allowing women to compete on men's teams, schools and colleges were dodging a much more important problem—the need to fund adequate sports programs for women.[21] The press release underscored the educational model of women's athletics by reiterating the AAHPER/DGWS's objection to awarding athletic scholarships, financial awards, and financial assistance. "Women do not want copies of men's programs," stated Judi Ford, Miss America of 1969, in the release. "They want their own—to fit their own individual needs and skills [and] this will give us a better chance in international competition, too."[22] Ford was probably speaking from her own experience. Only three years earlier, she was a trampolinist and the only female member of the University of Southwest Louisiana men's gymnastics team. She competed with men because there were not "any kind of women's program or scholarships" for her.[23]

Ford may not have realized the significance of her statement, but Walter Byers surely did. A stronger representation of women on the U.S. teams would certainly better the chance of beating the Soviets, especially at the Olympics. Ford might also have been unaware that control of women's interscholastic and intercollegiate athletics would greatly enhance the NCAA's chance to prevail in its struggle with the AAU. Walter Byers, more likely than Judi Ford, saw clearly the implication of the change in women's athletics. A seasoned administrator for the NCAA for two decades, Byers knew exactly which direction the men's organization should take, and most importantly, he knew how to direct the organization. The executive director believed that the NCAA should change its regulations to permit women to compete in NCAA championships. He told not only the NCAA legal counsel but the entire NCAA Executive Committee and Council what to do by simply sending them a copy of his letter to Gangwere. Like an orchestra, the music of the NCAA was produced by the executive committee, the council, and the membership, but conducted by Walter Byers, the architect of the NCAA's policies for women's sports.

An Affiliation Never Conceived

In September 1971, the AIAW held a meeting with representatives of the NCAA, the National Association of Intercollegiate Athletics, and the National Junior Collegiate Athletic Association in Kansas City to discuss the proposed NCAA-AIAW affiliation.[24] According to CIAW chair Lucille Magnusson, George Gangwere orally presented the NCAA women's division affiliation proposal. "I was sincerely disappointed with the proposal for affiliation which Gangwere presented," Magnusson wrote Charles Neinas. Reiterating the importance of women's programs under the control of women, Magnusson stated that "the gals are not yet ready to be split into three groups [with NCAA, NAIA, and NJCAA]. The fact that we could not come to some workable compromise between the three groups . . . was really disappointing to me."[25]

There seemed to be a significant difference between the interpretations of affiliation by the NCAA and by the AIAW. To the NCAA, at least as Gangwere saw it, the affiliation meant that the AIAW "must be subject to NCAA control." Despite having a "great deal of autonomy," the AIAW was to be merely a subdivision of the NCAA.[26] This was obviously not what the women leaders wanted. Magnusson reported that no real understanding resulted from the meeting, because "NCAA and our interpretation of affili-ation were different." [27] The difference, however, did not necessarily mean a hostile relationship between the two organizations at the time. Instead, the women in 1971 seemed to be sincerely willing to affiliate with the men's or-ganizations. They believed that an AIAW affiliation with the men's groups would be advantageous in terms of good public relations and increased publicity for the AIAW. They wanted a "liaison relationship" with the men's organizations, which would involve "no controls or no ties." [28]

Lacking legal expertise, the women seemed to be baffled by Gang-were's proposal. Magnusson wrote Neinas in September 1971 and wanted to know whether it was ever possible for the AIAW to become an affiliate member of the NCAA according to NCAA regulations. It is unknown whether an official proposal for the affiliation was ever produced by the NCAA. The women seemingly never received any copies of such a docu-ment, adding to their frustration. [29]

Two weeks after Magnusson's request, Neinas responded with a letter that suddenly changed the chemistry of the relationship between the NCAA and the CIAW/AIAW:

> It seems to me that the CIAW (AIAW) could become an affiliate member of the NCAA but it would have no meaning or provide no solution to our problem . . . If the NCAA is going to preclude females from its NCAA events and generally discourage their participation on men varsity squads, then the NCAA must devise a means to provide comparable op-portunities for women enrolled in its member institutions. We hope that your organization would be the vehicle to fill that need, but if you feel that you cannot make the adjustments necessary to accomplish that end, then I suppose that we will have to look to some other solution. [30]

Byers also sent a copy of Neinas's letter to JoAnne Thorpe, the new DGWS chair. Both Magnusson and Thorpe immediately expressed their dismay at the NCAA's new position. [31] A much stronger reaction came from Rachel Bryant, the official consultant to the DGWS. "We were all very concerned with the last line of Mr. Neinas' letter," Bryant wrote Byers. "There is only one inference that can be made from this threat: the AIAW must become the female arm of NCAA, or NCAA will set up a competing program to the AIAW in its member schools. I hope I am wrong in making this interpretation," continued Bryant, "but I would like to advise you that no action the NCAA could take would be a bigger mistake." She summarized the women's philosophy on intercollegiate athletics and elaborated on what the big NCAA mistake might mean. "A group of professional women educators have designed an organization and a program in accordance with their accepted philosophy and standards to meet the needs and interests of college women students," wrote Bryant. "To have it now threatened by an organization designed for men and controlled by men would cause such a furor that the NCAA would have a real battle on its hands. The possibility of one girl instituting a court suit to participate on a male varsity team would be a very pale issue in comparison."[32]

Byers' response to Bryant's letter four days later was much milder, yet with no less assertiveness. Defending Neinas's statement as well as the NCAA's position, Byers wrote: "The issue is whether the colleges are going to have an institutional membership organization to manage intercollegiate athletics for women or a professional individual membership organization attempting to do it." Objecting to Bryant's "intemperate remarks," Byers stressed that the NCAA's objections to an affiliation agreement with the AIAW were related to the latter's structural affiliation with the AAHPER. If Bryant's statement could be seen as a threat, then Byers' response was no soft talk either. "You can rest assured," he concluded, "that the NCAA does not intend to delegate responsibilities and Council-voting positions to an organization over which a third party has veto authority."[33]

In late October 1971, the NCAA Committee on Women's Intercollegiate Athletics apprised the NCAA Council on the possible affiliation with the AIAW. Committee chair David Swank made recommendations that seemed to cause more controversies than to provide solutions. While recognizing that the women preferred to run their own program and wanted minimal involvement from the men, Swank suggested that all students meeting necessary qualifications be allowed to enter NCAA championship competition "regardless of sex." The committee also suggested that the AIAW be encouraged to affiliate with the NCAA, although it had concluded that different eligibility standards for men and women would be unfeasible within one organization.[34] Probably uncertain about what actions to take, the council asked the committee to continue its study of the problem.[35]

If the Swank committee at the end of 1971 were going to seek reconciliation with the AIAW by reducing differences between the two organizations, it apparently did not choose the right time. In October, the DGWS Executive Council passed a resolution on athletic scholarships that was miles apart from the NCAA policy. The resolution was also accepted by the CIAW/AIAW a month later. It read: "It is not to diminish but to protect the continued development of athletics for women that the Division for Girls and Women's Sports does not approve the awarding of scholarships, financial awards or financial assistance designated for women participants in intercollegiate sports competition.[36] Irreconcilable differences between the AIAW and the NCAA appeared to exist.

Pretesting the NCAA Legal Position

The year 1972 was significant for women's sports in the United States even before the passage of Title IX. In January, the NCAA convention devoted unprecedented attention to the issue of women's intercollegiate athletics by providing two roundtable sessions. Invited by the NCAA as a guest speaker, the DGWS chair JoAnne Thorpe addressed both sessions on behalf of the AIAW. She began her speeches by stressing the DGWS' anti-athletic-scholarship position as a core element of the educational model for women's athletics. Apparently Thorpe felt that she could not defend the women's position without actually criticizing the men's athletic model, although she did not point a finger at the NCAA. "We are daily accused of being against athletics," said Thorpe, "whereas in truth we are against the evils that are often associated with athletics, principally the exploitation of talent for notoriety."[37]

While the DGWS was not particularly opposed to the NCAA's intended position of allowing women on men's teams, Thorpe maintained that the AIAW was "better equipped than the various men's organizations to recognize and be sensitive to the needs of women." She asserted that the NCAA's position on women's athletics, although legally tenable, had "little value beyond its good legal ring." Citing George Gangwere's analysis of the NCAA's legal position, Thorpe agreed with the NCAA counsel that "as a class women cannot compete physically with men" and that "the classification of separate male and female athletics is a reasonable one that should be sustained by the courts."[38]

The bad news for Thorpe was that Gangwere did not stop his analysis at that point. Whereas Thorpe indicated that the court thus far had not challenged the NCAA's position, Gangwere looked farther down the road. Pointing out that the NCAA was charged by its constitution to regulate intercollegiate athletics for all students, Gangwere had made his case clear back in June 1971. "[The NCAA] cannot deny that intercollegiate athletics among women exits, yet by failing to regulate such athletics it fosters any existing deficiencies in opportunities for competition among women. If the obligation of the NCAA is admitted, then it seems clear that the NCAA should take steps to organize and regulate female athletics in such a manner that it can be reasonably argued that women have equal opportunities with men within the organization."[39]

Rebutting Gangwere's claim, Thorpe told the NCAA roundtable audience that the deficiencies in women's programs could not be overcome by the NCAA's initiating a program for women in its member schools. Instead, the deficiencies could best be overcome by members of the NCAA's supporting the women's programs that were "already in existence and striving for recognition back home."[40]

The DGWS chair also addressed the exploratory efforts on possible affiliation between the AIAW and men's collegiate athletic organizations. An affiliate relationship, she insisted, should not be at the expense of the AIAW's autonomy. "We refuse to be dominated by outside groups. It is impossible to legislate allegiance. This fact would become very real should NCAA decide to attempt to control women's sports." Echoing what Bryant had stated in her letter to Byers two months earlier, Thorpe proclaimed that if any court cases occurred in regard to women's intercollegiate athletics, "the plaintiffs would probably not be women who want to participate but the women athletic directors and coaches who are already providing appropriate experiences for women."[41] In conclusion, Thorpe told her audience four reasons why the NCAA should not attempt to control women's sports: (1) The NCAA intervention would break down the unity of all women under the leadership of the AIAW; (2) the history and philosophy of women's programs had been under the control of women; (3) competition for women was not ready to be organized in the NCAA; and (4) court decisions had not favored the NCAA to take such an action.[42]

Thorpe did find some allies in the male-dominated organization. Both Edward Czekaj, athletic director of Penn State University and a member of the NCAA Committee on Women's Intercollegiate Athletics, and Edward

Steitz, athletic director of Springfield College and chair of the NCAA Olympic Committee, spoke favorably of the women's position. Using the Penn State program as an example, Czekaj demonstrated not only that men's and women's programs could coexist peacefully, but also that the men could help the women in many areas. All of these, according to Czekaj, could be accomplished "if there is a cooperative attitude." It is very likely that such an attitude existed between the men and the women at Penn State. By 1972, Pennsylvania's major land grant university was not only paving its way toward becoming an athletic powerhouse in men's sports, but was among the leading women's athletic institutions.[43] While Czekaj supported the women's position that the NCAA should not offer intercollegiate athletic programs for women, he did not forget his loyalty to the NCAA. In defending the NCAA's position, he made a rather confusing closing statement. "Today you are darned if you do and darned if you don't," said Czekaj. The NCAA could receive "a justifiable complaint of discrimination" by either "preventing women from competing against each other" or preventing them from "competing in NCAA championships."[44]

Unlike Czekaj's, George Gangwere's response to the issue was crystal clear. The NCAA lawyer from Kansas City obviously knew his craft and what really counted in his profession. Gangwere made his presentation short, precise, and straight to the issue from the legal point of view. Because the NCAA was charged to administer intercollegiate athletics for all of its members, argued Gangwere, the real problem was the fact that women had "no opportunity to compete against each other in intercollegiate athletics." He attributed this lack of opportunity to the fact that the NCAA did not make it available to women. Gangwere was certainly aware of the existence of the CIAW/AIAW and its programs. He simply did not count the women's programs as equal to the NCAA's. He believed that the NCAA would have legal problems ahead, and the solution to the problems would be for the NCAA to adopt a program that would give "the same opportunity" to women who desired to do so to compete in intercollegiate athletics.[45]

Despite Gangwere's legal argument, Thorpe contended that the NCAA's newly developed interest in women's athletics was contrary to the organization's original purpose. "When the Constitution [of the NCAA] was written," asserted Thorpe, "although you did not write it in, you obviously did plan only to regulate for men."[46] Thorpe was certainly correct in her judgment. Six and one-half decades earlier, when the NCAA was formed, regular intercollegiate athletics existed for men only; women's interschool competition was rare and almost unknown to the public. The NCAA never developed any interest in the women's programs until the 1960s.

Unsuccessful arm wrestling with the AAU over the control of U.S. amateur sports, especially since the Cold War, forced the NCAA to turn its attention to programs for women. It was only logical for the NCAA to gain control of women's programs if such a control would enhance its chance of winning the NCAA-AAU battle. Thorpe, and the women physical educators, saw the issue differently. "If women in the United States had no competition provided and had no program and no possibility to have one," reasoned Thorpe, "the NCAA would be wonderful to help us in that respect, but I do not think it is quite a logical statement to assume that the NCAA should do this because it has not been done." [47]

Fortunately for Thorpe, she did not have to work very hard to convince the NCAA audience of her position. Most of those who attended the roundtable sessions agreed that women's athletics were, at the time, beyond the realm of the NCAA. [48] Yet in reality, what was going to make a difference in court was not how the NCAA cared about women's programs but whether equal opportunity was actually provided. When Title IX became the law of the land, intercollegiate athletics for women became a whole new ball game.

NCAA Readies Itself for Women's Athletics

The 1972 NCAA convention took no action to change its executive regulations that limited participation in NCAA national championships to male student-athletes. This decision may have reflected the disagreement on the issue between NCAA's leadership and membership. In April 1972, the NCAA Committee on Women's Intercollegiate Athletics presented a report on the subject to the Council. Speaking on behalf of the committee, David Swank indicated that it was "not appropriate at this time for the NCAA to do more than encourage and offer assistance" to the newly formed AIAW. Objecting to Swank's recommendations, executive director Byers maintained that separate programs for women at the institutional level would not solve the legal problem the NCAA would encounter. [49]

Byers may not have had the support to change the NCAA's position on the issue in April, but he did not have to wait long. Only two months later, the U.S. Congress passed Title IX of the Education Amendments Act. Even though the significance of the legislation was yet to come, the legislation certainly helped Byers and Gangwere to persuade the NCAA leadership to accept their case regarding intercollegiate athletics for women. In October 1972, the NCAA Council voted to recommend that the executive committee amend the executive regulations "to permit women to compete in NCAA Championship competition." [50] Three months later and just one day before the 1973 NCAA convention, the executive committee amended the regulations by simply removing the word "male" from the document.[51] In the absence of any objection from the convention floor, the NCAA Executive Committee action automatically became final under the NCAA constitution.[52] This revision of the NCAA policy opened the door for the NCAA to administer and eventually take control of intercollegiate athletics for women.

The *Kellmeyer* Lawsuit

*Scholarships, Equal Opportunities,
and the Questions of Power and Control*

> However noble the purpose of the DGWS
> scholarship statement, I believe that a court,
> when properly confronted with the question,
> would find that it operates discriminatorily
> and illegally.
> —Joel Gewirtz (1973)

THE PHILOSOPHICAL ACCEPTANCE of high-level competition for women by the Division for Girls and Women's Sports in the early 1960s and the rapid growth of women's sports during the decade paved the way for the formation of the Association for Intercollegiate Athletics for Women in 1971. As the first institutional membership organization for women's intercollegiate athletics at the national level, the AIAW adopted the philosophy of the DGWS and put the educational model of college athletics into practice. The AIAW's pursuit of this model was soon shattered by a legal challenge—the *Kellmeyer* lawsuit—against the AIAW's anti-athletic-scholarship policy in 1973. Foreseeing the inevitable defeat in court, the AIAW changed its policy to allow awarding of scholarships to female students based on their athletic talent. Consequently, the AIAW's commitment to the educational model was jeopardized. In order to maintain its power and control of women's intercollegiate athletics, the AIAW gradually abandoned the educational model. By the end of the 1970s, the AIAW had adopted, with few exceptions, the commercial model championed by men's big-time college athletics.

The *Kellmeyer* Case: Accepting Equality and Power over Education

In early January 1973, a group of women filed a lawsuit against the DGWS/AIAW scholarship policy in the U.S. District Court for the Southern District of Florida. The purpose of the lawsuit, known as *Kellmeyer, et al. v. NEA, et al.,* was to invalidate the DGWS/AIAW rules that prevented women recipients of athletic scholarships from participating in AIAW-sponsored intercollegiate competitions. The plaintiffs consisted of Fern Kellmeyer, director of physical education at Marymount College, eleven female students who were recipients of athletic scholarships at Marymount College and Broward Community College, the women's tennis coaches from both schools, and Marymount College. Named as defendants in the suit were the National Education Association; the American Association for Health, Physical Education, and Recreation; the DGWS; the AIAW; the National Association of Physical Education of College Women; the Florida Association for Physical Education of College Women; the Florida Commission of Intercollegiate Athletics for Women; and the Southern Association for Physical Education of College Women.[1]

The plaintiffs cited five federal statutes in support of their charge, including the Fourteenth Amendment and Title IX of the Education Amendments Act. According to the NEA legal counsel, the two statutes would confer jurisdiction with respect to the plaintiffs' claim that the implementation of the AIAW scholarship rule denied to them equal protection of the law.[2]

The AIAW had adopted the anti-athletic scholarship policy only seven months earlier during the CIAW-AIAW transition meeting in June 1972. Deemed as "one of AIAW's greatest strengths" by the women leaders, the rule stated that an institution would be ineligible for membership in the AIAW if it gave athletic scholarships to women in any sports area. One indication of the policy's strength, claimed the AIAW, was that many schools had changed their regulations on scholarships in order to be eligible for AIAW membership.[3]

The *Kellmeyer* case might have been a shock for many involved in women's intercollegiate athletics. It was, however, no surprise to the women leaders. According to *Update,* the official newsletter of the AAHPER, the *Kellmeyer* lawsuit "brought into the open a concern frequently discussed in DGWS Executive Council meetings in the past few years."

Many members of the council had long been concerned that the DGWS statement on scholarships would be challenged on the very grounds raised in the suit.[4]

In February 1973, representatives of all organizations charged in the *Kellmeyer* lawsuit met in Washington, D.C., to hear the report on the litigation by three NEA lawyers, Robert Chanin, Joel Gewirtz, and Aviva Futorian. Chanin expressed the concerns of the NEA regarding the suit. He maintained that the NEA did not want to have "the publicity of someone claiming it denies equal rights" and intended to have itself dropped from the case. He pointed out, however, that there was legal liability among other groups involved. Instead of providing any advice, Chanin questioned the legality of the DGWS scholarship statement: "Is the statement conceptually sound?" "Is the statement workable?" and "Is it legal?"[5] His colleague Joel Gewirtz provided answers to the questions.

Using a legal outline of the litigation, Gewirtz demonstrated *Kellmeyer*'s possible, immediate, and long-term implications. The key issue at hand, maintained Gewirtz, was whether an organization had any rational reason for treating women differently in the constitutional context. By denying athletic scholarships to women in an institution where men were afforded such opportunities, argued Gewirtz, the school would have violated equal protection of the law. While apparently the school would be liable, contended Gewirtz, it did not mean that the AIAW would be guiltless of discrimination. The AIAW may not have intentionally discriminated against women; the enforcement of the AIAW rules, not the intention, would result in such discrimination. By denying women participation in a sanctioned competition if any woman—not if any student, male or female—received an athletic scholarship, the AIAW itself discriminated against women.[6]

Gewirtz was not too concerned about the immediate impact of the lawsuit, for it was still possible to have the *Kellmeyer* case dismissed. But he argued that the possible avoidance of an adverse judgment in the litigation would not solve the problem the AIAW and other organizations were facing. A similar lawsuit would likely be successful when filed against an AIAW member institution. The plaintiffs could claim that the school denied equal protection to women, either by failing to provide women athletic scholarships or by denying females the same opportunities that were afforded to their male counterparts. The court would then require the school to enforce its rules and benefits that would guarantee equal treatment for men and women. Consequently, a school would face two choices: dropping out of the AIAW or requesting that the AIAW change its scholarship policy. If the AIAW policy remained unchanged, maintained Gewirtz, the effect of a successful lawsuit similar to *Kellmeyer* would be "to diminish substantially AIAW membership." The choice for the AIAW then became obvious. "The legal climate is ripe for such litigation, and now is the time when your organizations must face the practical consequences of their rules," wrote Gewirtz. "However noble the purpose of the DGWS scholarship statement, [a court] would find that it operates discriminatorily and illegally. I therefore urge you to begin whatever procedures are necessary for changing your rule so that when defendants must finally file their answer in the *Kellmeyer* litigation they can declare that no discrimination exists under the rule which will then be in effect."[7]

In conclusion, Chanin pointed out that NEA resources were limited and offered the positions the NEA would take: Should the AIAW change its scholarship statement, the NEA would assist to have the suit dropped; should the AIAW decide to retain its current policy, the NEA would move to be dropped as a defendant.[8]

After the NEA lawyers withdrew, considerable discussion took place regarding the pros and cons of the DGWS/AIAW scholarship policy. Participants at the meeting agreed to obtain further information before making a final decision. It was agreed that the committee, composed of officers of the AAHPER, the DGWS, and the AIAW, should solicit the opinion of legal counsel at individual schools as well as of external lawyers who had expressed concerns about the DGWS/AIAW scholarship statement.[9] One of the external lawyers contacted by the committee was Stewart Udall, former secretary of the Interior in both the Kennedy and Johnson administrations. Udall believed that, ideally, no scholarships should be awarded. However, he reminded the AIAW of its responsibilities to member institutions, namely, whether member schools should be subjected to lawsuits because they were adhering to an AIAW rule that might be discriminatory against women.[10] An antagonist of big-time men's intercollegiate athletics, Udall was well respected among the women leaders, and his advice ought to have been persuasive.[11] Responses from legal counsels at individual schools were also discouraging. Most institutions would not fight a suit brought against them; instead, they would require withdrawal from the AIAW to protect themselves.[12]

Foreseeing the unfavorable legal climate and, more importantly, the inevitable loss of AIAW membership should they accept the court challenge, the participants at the meeting agreed to accept the recommendations of the NEA legal counsel. Copies of a response sheet concerning the revision of the DGWS/AIAW scholarship statement were sent to the DGWS Executive Council, the AIAW Executive Board, and AIAW member institutions for final approval. It read: "RESOLVED THAT THE DGWS Scholarship Statement be modified to reflect that the prevention of possible abuses in the awarding of athletic scholarships to women can be accomplished more appropriately by the strict regulation of such programs than by the outright prohibition of such forms of financial assistance."[13] By the end of March 1973, the resolution was accepted by all three groups. In April 1973, the DGWS/AIAW revised its scholarship statement by removing its discriminatory aspects. Clearly the fear of losing membership outweighed the AIAW's philosophical allegiance. In order to maintain its power and control of women's intercollegiate athletics, the AIAW compromised its commitment to the educational model of intercollegiate athletics.

AIAW Reluctantly Accepts Legal and Social Reality

The educational model may never have been endorsed by most women coaches and student-athletes at the grassroots level. According to an AIAW news release, member institutions in the AIAW gave "a resounding 'yes' " on the question of whether the existing DGWS statement on scholarships for women students should be changed. "This surprisingly high affirmative vote [over 80%]," announced the news release, "reflects the consciousness of member institutions that time for change has arrived."[14] The release attributed women's traditional anti-athletic-scholarship position to their "natural distaste" to see women students exploited in the way some men students had been. It also defended the position of the women educators with the notion that a university was a place primarily for learning. Yet, by reluctantly accepting the social and legal reality and by the thoughtful selection of excuses for the DGWS/AIAW leaders' position, the statement sounded more like the voice of an apologist for conservative

Victorian values. "But times are changing, and we must change with them," read the statement. "The consciousness of women as to their rights and privileges has been raised, and the whole theory of protecting women from exploitation, of paternalistic action 'for their own good,' has been a casualty of the student movement and the women's rights movement."[15]

The "surprisingly high" vote against the AIAW scholarship policy by its member institutions was a clear indication that the general attitude toward women's sports had changed. It certainly reflected the philosophical gap between the women in the leadership and those at the grassroots level. One may also attribute this change to the civil rights movement, to the rapidly growing influence of the second wave of feminism in the early 1970s, and, more directly, to the enforcement of the Civil Rights Act of 1964 and the recent passage of Title IX of the Education Amendments of 1972. The overwhelming vote supporting athletic scholarships for women, however, may not have been such a surprise to some of the women leaders.

One of the key players involved in the *Kellmeyer* suit was Carole Oglesby, the first president of the AIAW. Interviewed two years later in 1975, Oglesby's comments revealed some vital insights into the reactions of the women leaders and the conflict between the DGWS and the AIAW regarding the lawsuit. According to Oglesby, the AIAW was more firm about not changing the scholarship regulation and wanted to fight the decision in court. The DGWS, on the other hand, was not supportive of the AIAW's position. Rather surprisingly, Oglesby did not defend the AIAW's position despite being the former president of the association. "This situation may have occurred because AIAW was working so hard to make the DGWS philosophy and policies come to life," Oglesby believed. "We may have gotten off to an unrealistic stance, while the DGWS leaders were more realistic."[16]

More realistic also was Oglesby's personal position on the issue before her appointment as the CIAW Commissioner of National Championships in 1970. "I went into this position fully believing that girls and women should have parity/equality with men and boys, including the opportunity to have scholarships."[17] Yet Oglesby soon became an avid spokesperson for the anti-scholarship policy after she was persuaded that women would never have the chance to implement their own model of collegiate athletics by copying the men's programs, including scholarship policy. Explaining her role on the issue of awarding athletic scholarships to women,

Oglesby put the matter in perspective: "It wasn't that I didn't believe still that athletic scholarships were great (I did) . . . It wasn't that I didn't believe that women deserved them (I did) but I agreed, very regretfully, that women having charge of their own programs and determining their own destinies was so important (superordinate) as a goal, that the scholarship opportunities had to be sacrificed."[18]

Oglesby was neither the first supporter nor the first opponent of athletic scholarships for women. The issue of awarding athletic scholarships to women went back to the early 1960s. A survey conducted by the DGWS Philosophy and Standards Section in 1961–62 showed substantial evidence that such a practice existed in the country.[19] By the mid-1960s, some women leaders had made clear their acceptance of athletic scholarships for women. Phebe Scott, one of the pioneers in developing competitive athletics for women and a strong advocate of scholarships, often questioned the discriminatory practice of giving athletic scholarships to men but not to women.[20] Katherine Ley, another key leader of the DGWS, also indicated that she was not personally opposed to awarding athletic scholarships to women. What was more surprising was that most of the women leaders had been supportive of athletic scholarships.[21] A question arises: If many women leaders were for athletic scholarships, then how did the DGWS ever adopt a policy that was against such practice?

Few would doubt the influence of the "Play Day" philosophy on the women's anti-scholarship policy. Yet it would be difficult to accept that this policy was a product of male influence. According to Betty McCue, former chair of the DGWS Philosophy and Standards Section, the women's anti-scholarship attitude was set during the Study Conference on Competition for Girls and Women held in Washington, D.C., in February 1965. While Phebe Scott questioned the rationale for not giving scholarships to women, the men at the meeting insisted that athletic scholarships would get women into eligibility and recruitment problems, and eventually financial troubles. They suggested that the women would have nothing to recruit with if they could avoid giving scholarships. By the end of the conference, the men had succeeded in persuading the women to adopt the anti-scholarship position.[22]

The women leaders in the DGWS apparently took the bad experience of the men as a preventive measure and subsequently adopted the anti-scholarship stance. Prohibiting athletic scholarships did not seem to be the best way to deal with the potential problems that the men had encountered. Yet the women obviously had no better alternatives.

It is worth noting that the "men" who influenced the women's decision on athletic scholarships did not necessarily represent the mainstream of intercollegiate athletics. Bill Reed, Al Duer, and Reuben Frost in 1965 more likely represented the minority of those in men's college athletics establishments. They had more in common with the women leaders and believed in the educational model of college athletics. Each of the three had logical reasons to oppose scholarships. Reed was the commissioner of the Big Ten Conference, which only a few years earlier had attempted to ban scholarships. Duer was the executive director of the National Association of Intercollegiate Athletics, dominated by small colleges. Frost was the president of the AAHPER, an organization with a tradition of anti-big-time college athletics. The real representatives of men's intercollegiate athletics ought to be college and university presidents, athletics directors, and NCAA faculty representatives, who shared common interests in "big-time" college athletics. It was unlikely that the "truer" representatives of men's intercollegiate athletics would have agreed with Reed, Duer, and Frost.[23]

Opposing athletic scholarships seemed to be a reluctant choice of the women leaders. This choice in 1965 may have diverted women's athletics from the troubles caused by the practice of giving athletic scholarships in the men's programs. Yet, by the outright prohibition of such a practice, the women began to build their program on an unrealistic foundation and forced themselves onto a battleground of lawsuits. "Scholarships became more of a dominant issue than it should have, as far as the good of the organization was concerned," stated Carole Oglesby. "The issue was also not necessarily for the good of women's sports. We stuck with it beyond the realistic point, and in politics, you have to be more realistic."[24]

The Domino Effect of *Kellmeyer* on AIAW Policies

The *Kellmeyer* suit never went to the court. The case was dismissed as a result of the DGWS/AIAW scholarship statement revision in April 1973. The plaintiffs won the case by default. Technically, the DGWS/AIAW did not lose in the litigation. Yet, in order to avoid a seemingly uphill legal battle and, more importantly, to maintain their power and control of intercolle-

giate athletics for women, the AIAW leaders compromised their philosophical commitment.

The impact of the *Kellmeyer* lawsuit on women's athletics and the
AIAW was immeasurable. For the former, the suit symbolized a major step
toward equal opportunity for women student-athletes. The victory of the
uncontested litigation demonstrated that conceivably any form of discrimination against women would not be tolerated by the court. For the latter,
the lawsuit rocked the century-old sex-separate foundation of women's
sports in the United States, especially within the walls of colleges and universities where women physical educators "reigned supreme." It set the
precedent for potential legal actions against the AIAW. The most significant aspect of the suit was that it was brought by women against women.
For the first time in the history of women's intercollegiate athletics, highly
skilled women athletes challenged women physical education leaders
through a legal course. By exposing the traditional sex-separatist philosophy of women's sports to the law of equal protection, the *Kellmeyer* litigation accomplished probably more than the plaintiffs intended—paving the
way for the NCAA's entry into women's college sports. The *Kellmeyer* case
thus symbolized the beginning of the AIAW's loss of power and control
over women's intercollegiate athletics under the impact of Title IX.

The plaintiffs of the *Kellmeyer* case might not have intended to change
the philosophical commitment of the AIAW. The outcome of the litigation,
however, consequently forced the AIAW into adopting the commercial
model, which women educators had been criticizing since the turn of the
century. In the decade following the *Kellmeyer* case, the AIAW saw itself,
step by step, becoming commercialized. Although the AIAW never officially abandoned the notion of the educational model of intercollegiate
athletics, the women's organization's actual practice of the commercial
model made its noble claim increasingly irrelevant.

After the *Kellmeyer* lawsuit and the revision of its scholarship policy,
AIAW membership soared when it was opened to institutions that had
previously been ineligible because of their practice of awarding women
athletic scholarships. By its first delegate assembly in November 1973,
seven months after the revision of the scholarship policy, the AIAW membership had increased to 379 from its original 278 charter members. By the
end of 1975, the membership had jumped to 757. As women's intercolle-

giate athletics were becoming more and more popular, so was its governing body—the AIAW.

This rapid growth of women's college sports was generally perceived
as a result of the Title IX legislation. Yet from a different perspective, a more
direct contributor to the new phenomenon was the *Kellmeyer* litigation.
Rhetorically, the DGWS/AIAW reaffirmed its concern over the potential
abuses associated with the provision of athletic scholarships. It specifically
deplored "the evil of pressure recruiting and performer exploitation" that
frequently accompanied the administration of financial aid for athletes.[25]
Yet actions often speak louder than words. With the *Kellmeyer* lawsuit
pending in court, there were only two choices for the AIAW: sticking to the
educational philosophy but losing control of intercollegiate athletics for
women, or maintaining the power and control by compromising its principles. The AIAW chose the latter. If there had been integrity in the AIAW's
philosophical commitment, it was torn apart by the *Kellmeyer* lawsuit. As
sport historian Joan Hult stated, the revision of the scholarship policy "immediately placed in jeopardy the philosophical commitment of AIAW to
an educational model."[26]

Changing scholarship policy was the opening of Pandora's box. Earlier in 1972, the AIAW had defined an amateur as one who had not received
and did not receive money other than expenses as a participant in that
sport.[27] Nineteen months later, the AIAW Executive Board adopted the motion that a student would not lose her eligibility for AIAW competition if
she entered professional events.[28] The contingency was that the student
must publicly donate the prize money to "a charity, a school or other organization," such as the DGWS and the AIAW. For decades, the women
leaders criticized the exploitation of student-athletes common in the men's
programs. This male exploitation, however, paled in comparison to the
AIAW's new policy, for the NCAA did not allowed its college students to
compete with or against any professionals. Forced donation of cash prizes,
as the AIAW rules dictated, would not prevent athletes from being exploited by the media and public, because the exploitation would always
have taken place first. Cash prizes, donated or not, would only be the result
of being exploited. The AIAW leaders may have intended to provide more
freedom and opportunities to women student-athletes. This new AIAW
amateur policy, however, apparently chose to ignore the fact that forced

donation itself would be a vivid form of exploitation.[29] To surrender to the prevailing pressure for change may be forgivable, but to subscribe to such policies in the name of preserving amateurism was hypocritical.

This hypocrisy of the so-called "educational model" was also seen in the AIAW's regulations on graduate student participation. Contrary to its claim of equal access to all educational activities, the AIAW Executive Board in May 1975 defeated the motion to permit graduate students to participate in intercollegiate athletics.[30] Two years later, the AIAW delegate assembly changed this rule to grant eligibility to graduate students. Yet the change was almost meaningless in reality. According to the rule, the student must use her eligibility "within four years" of initial enrollment as an undergraduate. The rationale for the new policy was that "students may accelerate and graduate in three years."[31] Few, if any, student-athletes would benefit from such a policy.

From Educational Model to Commercial Enterprise

After changing its scholarship rules in 1973, the AIAW moved rather swiftly away from the educational model. From financial aid to eligibility, to recruiting, to transfer students, to amateur status, and to divisional structure, the AIAW policies became more and more noneducational even though some of them were less commercial than the NCAA ones. By late 1970s, the AIAW had adopted regulations in these areas similar to those in the NCAA, with some exceptions.[32]

Most significantly, the AIAW leadership soon came to agree that the organization's livelihood depended largely on the financial success of women's intercollegiate athletics. In May 1975, the AIAW Executive Board approved the concept of naming All-American players in various sports.[33] Four months later, the board unanimously adopted the idea of "seeking to get Airlines to announce AIAW member school teams as they travel to and from competitions." It also authorized the AIAW to serve as the agent in negotiations of commercial contract of women's intercollegiate athletic programs among member schools.[34] In October 1976, the AIAW board unanimously endorsed the concept of commercial subsidy of AIAW championships.[35] Asked whether the AIAW's commercial approach was any different from that of the NCAA, Joan Hult, former chair of the AIAW Ethics and Eligibility Committee, gave the following answer: "Right then I didn't even think about it. But I was for having All-Americans, I thought it was stupid not to, [although it was] in conflict with my view of what was perfect. But actually, I always felt we might as well do it."[36]

At the 1976 AIAW delegate assembly, AIAW president Laurie Mabry presented a proposal for television revenue and officially announced the AIAW's adoption of commercialism for women's sports. She informed her audience that since its 1975 delegate assembly, the AIAW had actively sought increased television coverage of the AIAW national championships and the efforts had been "partially successful." The Public Broadcasting System broadcast 1975 AIAW swimming and diving and basketball championships. The ABC television network also purchased the rights to the 1975 AIAW national basketball championship for use on a special program of women in sports.[37]

It was good to get national exposure for the AIAW programs. That, however, did not mean that the women got the money they needed to maintain their control of the programs. It came down to an issue of finance, as Mabry clearly stated: "While the PBS coverage expanded AIAW's visibility, it did not enhance its economic condition. Since both exposure and remuneration are vital at this stage of the development of women's intercollegiate athletics, a commercial arrangement was deemed to be a necessity."[38]

In 1975, the AIAW initiated a more systematic commercial TV arrangement through Marv Sugarman Productions. In return for a guaranteed annual payment to the AIAW and equal profit participation, Sugarman Productions would serve as the exclusive agent for the AIAW media efforts. The first product of this agreement was a basketball game between the U.S. national team and the People's Republic of China team that appeared on an NBC program.[39] While some believed that the event provided the AIAW national publicity and promoted goodwill between China and the United States, the debut of this commercial arrangement, to the disappointment of many AIAW leaders, was a financial failure.[40] Sugarman Productions also incurred a loss in the first year under the contract with the AIAW because of "inability to interest the major broadcasting systems or public broadcasting systems to financially support the AIAW National Championships."[41]

Both the NCAA and the AIAW leaders would deny that their models were commercial in nature. But in reality, the commercial model was in operation and had the tacit acceptance of both groups. Pushing further toward the commercial model that the women physical educators had previously condemned, the 1976 delegate assembly established the AIAW as the sole authority over the TV right of intercollegiate athletics for women.[42] The women in the AIAW obviously now knew better that the true control of women's athletics depended on the control of financial success.

In May 1977, the AIAW board approved the formation of a promotions committee to identify endorsement opportunities for the AIAW and to promote the association "through media, publications, education, and business communities."[43] As a result of AIAW's philosophical shift, the Eastman Kodak Company became the first major commercial sponsor of AIAW national championships. The recognition of the Kodak All-American Team at the 1977 AIAW large-college basketball championship symbolized the official endorsement of the commercial model by the AIAW.[44]

Within seventeen months of its approval of the Kodak All-American Team, the AIAW also contracted the sponsorship of Hanes for the Hanes Medalist All-Star Basketball Classic, of Tea Council of the USA for the Small-College Tennis Championship, of Coca-Cola USA for the funding of the High School Brochure and AIAW championships, of Hanes for the Hanes All-American Basketball Classic, and of Broderick for the Broderick Award and Cup for outstanding women college athletes. The AIAW's endorsement of "full" commercialism took place in October 1978 when the board adopted that "the AIAW policy on commercial sponsorship of televised events be modified to permit the advertisement of beverages such as beer and malt liquor."[45] The AIAW's approval of alcoholic advertising came less than a decade after the NCAA first allowed beer advertising in its football telecasts.[46]

With growing commercialism, in 1979 the AIAW surpassed the nine hundred mark in active member institutions and became the largest institutional membership organization in collegiate athletics.[47] But the women's organization had almost no money in the bank.[48] This financial plight became a major concern for the AIAW leadership, especially when in 1979 the association was to become legally and financially separated from its parent organizations, the American Alliance for Health, Physical Education, Recreation, and Dance and the National Association for Girls and Women in Sport.[49] Reacting to the perceived financial reality of the organization, the AIAW Executive Committee resolved to establish a reserve fund, with anticipated income from television and radio rights, to secure the fiscal soundness of the association. The 1979 AIAW delegate assembly also approved the resolution despite significant disagreement between the AIAW leadership and membership on the distribution of potential monetary income.[50] Only one thing became certain in the AIAW: the acceptance of the commercial model was no longer a controversial issue by 1979.

From the revision of athletic scholarship rules in 1973 to the full embracement of commercialism in 1979, the AIAW, in less than six years, changed itself from an idealistic organization to one whose policies were becoming more and more dependent on its commercial potentials. It is no surprise to see the change in AIAW's philosophical commitment. When the power and control of intercollegiate athletics for women were at stake, when the interests of those who controlled women's sports were threatened, the educational model was sacrificed for greater security. Ironically, this sacrifice did not bring the security the AIAW leaders had hoped for. Rather, it put the women's organization in a vulnerable position without the protection of a unique ideology. Like any other conventional commodity, women's athletics was thrown into a marketplace where the laws of economics and cultural customs ruled. When the NCAA and its allies failed to have men's interscholastic and intercollegiate athletics exempted from Title IX compliance, they again turned their attention to the control of women's athletics.

7

Equality over Power

The Impact of Title IX on Intercollegiate Athletics for Women

No person shall, on the basis of sex, be excluded
from participation in, be denied the benefits of, or
be subjected to discrimination under any
education program or activity receiving Federal
financial assistance.
   —"Title IX: Prohibition of Sex
   Discrimination"

HISTORY WILL NOTE that 1972 was a dynamic year for women's sports in the United States. Billie Jean King, at twenty-eight, won her fourth Wimbledon singles title and was named "Sportsperson of the Year" by the popular magazine *Sports Illustrated.* Even more important than her personal achievement was King's leadership in the battle for equality in women's professional sports. The year was also significant for women's athletics on college campuses. In June, the Association for Intercollegiate Athletics for Women began its official operation, becoming the first national governing body of women's intercollegiate athletics with institutional memberships. Weeks later, Congress passed Title IX of the Education Amendments Act, prohibiting sex discrimination in educational institutions.[1] With joined forces of strong individual leadership, growing organizational efforts, and federal intervention, the stage seemed set for the realization of equal opportunities for women's sports.

Title IX: Equality for All, but Not on Women's Terms

Title IX had little immediate legal impact on college sports because of lack of enforceable means. The first official guidelines for Title IX did not become effective until July 1975.[2] At the national level, Title IX did influence the NCAA to change its policy on women's athletics. In October 1972, the NCAA Council voted to amend the organization's executive regulations to allow women to compete in NCAA championships. The 1973 NCAA convention subsequently endorsed the council's amendment, a move seen by the AIAW as a direct challenge to its power and control of women's intercollegiate athletics. Title IX also aided the 1973 *Kellmeyer* litigation against the AIAW's anti-athletic-scholarship policy (see chapter 6). The uncontested triumph of the *Kellmeyer* case and the consequent change of the AIAW's scholarship policy immediately put in jeopardy the fledgling AIAW's commitment to the educational model.

There were, however, exceptions in the early days of the Title IX era. In the same month as the *Kellmeyer* lawsuit and the NCAA legislation, an event at the University of New Mexico offered some much needed comfort to the AIAW leaders. Cathy Carr, a dual gold medalist in swimming at the 1972 Olympics, withdrew her acceptance of a scholarship after the AIAW ruled against her eligibility for AIAW events. Carr had been awarded the scholarship as a result of her performance at the Olympics. "I would call the award a notoriety scholarship," an official of the institution reportedly stated. "We just wanted her name to be associated with the university."[3]

Carr's withdrawal from her scholarship was encouraging news for the women leaders. It showed that the AIAW's anti-scholarship policy could be effective. Yet from a different perspective, the Carr incident can be seen as the lack of Title IX's impact at the time, and the limited legal implication of the event could not possibly compensate for the negative repercussion on the AIAW brought by the *Kellmeyer* lawsuit.

The *Kellmeyer* case was a statement that discrimination against women in sport came not only from the male-dominated society, but also from women physical educators who controlled college women's sports. It was a symbolic revolt of women at the grassroots level against the traditional maternalistic control of women's college athletics. In the name of protecting women from commercial exploitation and male control, the women leaders simply took away the rights of those who wanted equal opportunity in college sports. The so-called protection by the women leaders, as sport historian Ronald A. Smith pointed out, was a different form of exploitation in college sports—exploitation by exclusion—in this case, exclusion by denying athletic scholarships for women.[4]

Title IX was passed to provide inclusion and equal opportunities for women and men in all educational activities, including intercollegiate athletics. While the legislation became a threat to men's college athletics, it ironically assumed the practice of the male model as the standard for equality. Moving toward equality thus meant pushing the women's educational model toward the men's commercial model. This assumption not only frightened the supporters of the male athletic tradition, who feared the eventual need to share "men's money" with women, but also cast dark clouds over the separate sphere of women's college sports.

The first delegate assembly of the AIAW was filled with confusion caused by the anticipated implementation of Title IX and a sense of uncertainty over the future of the association. Puzzled by the outcome of the *Kellmeyer* case and its ramifications, many AIAW delegates wondered whether women must follow what was laid down for men by men. "Are there any protections to ensure different philosophical routes for men and women?" they asked.[5] This sense of confusion may be best explained by Joanna Davenport, former president of National Association for Girls and Women in Sport and a member of the AIAW Executive Board. "When we were sued over the tennis scholarship down in Florida," stated Davenport, "I would dare to say there were many women, the majority, [who] had never even heard of the word 'litigation,' or lawsuit."[6]

The reality of the changing legal climate apparently had little impact on the decision-making process of the AIAW. Its first delegate assembly adopted a resolution to maintain separate programs for women.[7] Voices of dissent, however, were equally noticeable. In a speech entitled "Solomon's Judgment on Women's Sports," Marjorie Blaufarb, editor of AAHPER's newsletter *Update*, delivered the following message for the assembly delegates to ponder: "If individuals or groups consider certain practices to be very harmful, they must try to get their own institution to forbid them for both sexes. *We cannot set double standards.* I believe that those persons, male or female, who have a deep rooted distrust of competitive athletics for women students should not act as dogs in the manger, but accept the last quarter of the 20th century as it is, and not as they wish it would be."[8]

If Title IX were bad news for the NCAA officials, it was not entirely good news for the AIAW leaders either. During the AIAW assembly, Jack Whitaker, a lawyer from Kansas City, was invited to give an interpretation on the proposed guidelines of Title IX. To the disappointment of the women, Whitaker's talk provided little support for the validity of the so-called "educational model" of women's athletics. Whitaker told his audience that whether the women's model was better than the men's was a judgment that was very difficult to make, and that under the circumstances, it was for the U.S. Department of Health, Education, and Welfare, not anyone else, to make such a judgment. One purpose of Title IX, maintained Whitaker, was affirmative action to remedy an imbalance that existed, and the imbalance in this case was the "exclusion of women from competitive intercollegiate athletics on the same scale as men."[9]

It must have been a very difficult reality for the women leaders to comprehend. While Title IX was passed to end discrimination based on sex, it offered hardly any protection to the AIAW's pursuit—keeping women's intercollegiate athletics under the control of women. The membership of the AIAW was growing, and the doors to athletic opportunities for women were opening. Yet, by the conclusion of the first AIAW delegate assembly, the future of the educational model for women's athletics seemed rather gloomy.

Linda Estes—A Radical Voice Within the AIAW

Most people agreed that women were deprived of equal opportunities in college sports. Few recognized that women were also discriminated against by their own women sports leaders. Very few women dared to challenge such discrimination. Throughout the history of the AIAW, one voice epitomized the constant challenges aimed at the fairness and legality of AIAW policies. That voice belonged to Linda Estes, director of women's athletics at the University of New Mexico.

During the decade of the AIAW's existence, Linda Estes was the most vocal internal critic of the women's organization. Her challenge of the AIAW's discriminatory rules against women student-athletes went back as early as 1973. In August of that year, Estes wrote AIAW past-president

Carole Oglesby insisting that the AIAW had all the potential in the world. "I would like nothing better than to whole heartedly support AIAW," stated Estes. "But I cannot do so as long as the officers of AIAW continue to *encourage* discrimination against women in athletics." [10] Estes first disputed the position of the AIAW National Championships coordinator, who supposedly supported an Illinois law that limited women's college teams to six hours of practice per week. [11] She then rebutted the stance of Leotus Morrison, president-elect of the AIAW, who had made the following statement in an AIAW newsletter: "Do we request monies in terms of needs or in terms of envy? Are we more dedicated to financial and equipment problems than to player problems?" Offended by Morrison's remarks, Estes questioned the AIAW leader's true standing on women's athletics. She wrote: "Women's intercollegiate athletic programs have existed for years on a shoestring budget with women coaches, more often than not, coaching without pay, and I know of no group of educators who have been more dedicated to the welfare of their students than women coaches of intercollegiate teams. For the president-elect of AIAW to even insinuate that women are requesting additional funds out of envy and are neglecting the problems of their players is an unforgivable blunder in my eyes." [12]

The different positions of Morrison and Estes on the issue were obvious. Morrison, emphasizing the AIAW's commitment to the educational model, represented the ideological hierarchy of the organization, who saw money as the principal source of evil in men's big-time programs. Estes, on the other hand, spoke for the rank and file of women athletic administrators who experienced on a daily basis the hardship of running their programs without much financial support. She certainly had little patience for entertaining the noble ideals shared by Morrison and the like.

In October 1973, Estes wrote to the three AIAW presidents, protesting the sexist policies and languages in the AIAW handbook. [13] Referring to the policy that required supervision of a woman chaperone for participation in AIAW national championships, Estes pointed out that the gender requirement of the chaperone was "archaic, stupid, and more important[ly], illegal." It was discrimination against men for no rational reasons, argued Estes, because men coaches were "no more likely than women chaperones or coaches to engage in 'immoral' behavior with women athletes." [14] Estes may have been referring to the alleged high degree of lesbianism in college women's sport leadership. [15]

A month later, Morrison responded to Estes' challenge. While agreeing with Estes on certain issues, Morrison stressed the importance of establishing the unique identity of the AIAW. "I see these times as a period in which we can create programs designed for women," wrote Morrison. "Legality is certainly a factor but to opt for 'something' just because a man has it negates my value as a self-determing [sic] female."[16]

Morrison's reply did not please Estes. Quite the opposite, it raised more questions for Estes about the qualifications of the AIAW leader. "Certainly no one wants to negate your value as a self-determining female," Estes fought back, "[but] even self-determining females are not allowed by the law to maintain practices which result in sexual discrimination against other females."[17] To Estes, what the AIAW stood for philosophically was irrelevant as far as women's rights were concerned. "Even women (DGWS, AIAW, women physical educators) are not allowed to discriminate against women [student-athletes]," stressed Estes. "It seems to me that a number of people in AIAW just seem to think they can disregard the law. I suggest you go back and carefully read the advice given by the NEA attorneys regarding the Kellmeyer case."[18]

Evidently Estes did not feel that she should have allegiance to the AIAW simply because she was a woman. Based on her statements, she was more likely to be seen as an ally of the NCAA rather than a supporter of the AIAW. Speculating on the AIAW's intention to pursue a court settlement regarding its present policy on scholarships, Estes wrote: "While the AIAW is going bankrupt fighting a case that they cannot possibly win, the NCAA can take over women's athletics. At this point, that doesn't sound like too bad an idea to me. In my opinion, it is much easier to make progress with men regarding discrimination against women than it is with women who insist on discriminating against other women.[19]

Estes was clearly disgusted by the conservative agenda of the DGWS/AIAW. To her, the DGWS/AIAW's philosophical commitment to the educational model was hardly different from the "anti-competition, anti-Olympics" movement led by women physical educators during the 1920s and 1930s. "I believe that the initials DGWS stand for 'Don't Give Women Sports' and the AIAW means Association for Interfering With Athletics for Women," she told a group of students at the 1974 AAHPER convention.[20] Such "interference" may have caused the resignation of Mary Rekstad, a DGWS consultant and AIAW liaison. Seeing the resignation as a result of the philosophical conflict between Rekstad and the DGWS/AIAW leadership, Estes could not resist a cynical retort to Morrison. Terming Rekstad's resignation as the AIAW's loss, Estes sarcastically suggested replacing her with Phyllis Schlafly, the conservative Philadelphian who started the national campaign to defeat the Equal Rights Amendment. "I am sure," Estes wrote, "that her philosophy is very close to that of DGWS."[21]

The shrill voice of Linda Estes was obviously too radical for the DGWS/AIAW establishment, at least in the early 1970s. A veteran of the AIAW, Estes constantly fought for what she believed to be true equality for women's sports and often found herself at odds with the AIAW leadership. Her straightforwardness and her sometimes confrontational manner of communication did not make her a popular figure among the women leaders. These personal traits may also have alienated her from others who shared her views but could not appreciate her undiplomatic behavior. Whatever others may have thought of her, however, did not prevent her from fighting for her convictions. In later years, the rare and uncompromising voice of Linda Estes was to become, at least, an extra burden for the AIAW leadership.

The NCAA Lobby Against Title IX Implementation

The draft Title IX regulations, issued by the Office of Civil Rights of the U.S. Department of Health, Education, and Welfare in October 1973, caused great confusion among men and women involved in college sports. By the end of 1973, both AIAW and NCAA officials were seeking legal advice concerning the potential impact of the regulations.[22] In February 1974, Robert C. James, chair of the NCAA Legislative Committee, briefed the chief executive officers of NCAA member institutions on the status of Title IX regulations. He maintained that the current development of the regulations should be "a matter of critical concern" and that its final approval would have dramatically negative effects on the present practice of intercollegiate athletics. In his words, these effects would be "frequently disruptive, often destructive and surely counter-productive to the very objectives which Title IX seeks to attain."[23]

Apparently serving more than just an internal news briefing, the memorandum set the tone for the NCAA to deal with Title IX implementation in the years to come. James made it very clear that his committee opposed "imposition of unrealistic administrative and operating requirement, drawn by persons totally unfamiliar with the practical problems of athletic administration, in the name of a non-discriminatory sex policy." He urged each member institution to carefully review the draft regulations whose demands were "either unrealistic or counter-productive" and to respond to HEW immediately.[24]

The correspondence from Robert James symbolized the beginning of a strenuous campaign led by the NCAA against the implementation of Title IX. Responses to the NCAA's call for action came quickly. Within ten days of the mailing of James's memorandum, John A. Howard, president of Rockford College in Illinois, sent a strongly worded letter to Kenneth Cole, assistant to President Nixon for domestic affairs. Howard challenged not only the sections on college sports in the regulations but also the principles of Title IX. "Our government has already seriously and perhaps permanently compromised the potential of American higher education through Affirmative Action programs," he wrote.[25] Saying that quality of education was sacrificed in "trying to find partially qualified minority and women candidates," Howard maintained that the implementation of affirmative action was the opening of "Pandora's Box." What Howard saw as the effect of affirmative action on education in general was apparently no different from the specific effect of Title IX on college sports. He contended: "Equal opportunity is a commendable and necessary objective in this country but, like anything else, if carried to excess it can distort and poison. There is no way that government can make oranges and apples equal. Nor can the government make men and women equal. . . . The proposed extension of the Affirmative Action program to athletics is, I believe, a misguided effort to gain some political advantage at the expense of the character of a very basic function of higher education."[26]

It was likely Howard thought that women did not have much to do with athletics. "I would observe that when everybody had to do chores before going to school, athletics were not needed," he continued. "Since television has replaced the chores, sports and athletics fill a vital need in clearing cobwebs from the brain of the much too sedentary American youth."[27] Howard probably did not think that sedentary American "female" youth could also benefit from playing sports. Or did he believe that they were already too active? Whatever his belief may have been, Howard did a much needed service for the NCAA leadership. "Your March 1 presentation to Kenneth Cole is excellent," Walter Byers wrote Howard ten days later.[28] A simple but definite compliment, Byers' response to Howard's letter reaffirmed the NCAA's position regarding Title IX regulations.

In the meantime, John W. Winkin, president of the National Association of Collegiate Directors of Athletics, wrote directly to President Nixon, expressing "serious concern" about the draft regulations. Repeating the rhetoric in the memorandum of Robert James, Winkin urged Nixon to protect the tradition of intercollegiate athletics, for which the president's interest and support were well known. "We cannot believe," wrote Winkin, "that you wish your administration to destroy the growth of intercollegiate athletics through the interpretations of an act which, when drafted, never intended such an outcome."[29] The strategy of the NCAA campaign was simple: to insert a wedge between Title IX—a legitimate federal law—and the regulations written by HEW—what the NCAA leaders believed a "misinterpretation" of the legislation.

Two weeks after Winkin's letter, NCAA president Alan J. Chapman also wrote Nixon, adding that the implementation of the regulations could cause financial dilemmas for institutions of higher education. Schools would be forced to choose "between massive new costs" or "major reductions in existing programs," argued Chapman, and the victims of the regulations would ultimately be "student-athletes of both sexes." The NCAA president knew that any regulations implementing Title IX must have the approval of the president. So he pleaded: "We earnestly hope you will never grant your approval to regulations of the kind presently considered by HEW."[30]

The president did not respond. Even if Nixon had favored the NCAA's position on the issue, he was otherwise preoccupied. With further disclosure of the Watergate scandal and under public and congressional pressure, Nixon resigned from his presidency in August 1974.

The AIAW Copes with Title IX Pressure

While the anticipated implementation of Title IX was causing chaos within the NCAA, it did not bring any ease to the AIAW either. Realizing the vulnerable position of AIAW's sex-separate policies in light of the law, the first

AIAW delegate assembly adopted a motion calling for the AIAW Executive Board to meet with the NCAA, the National Association of Intercollegiate Athletics, and the National Junior Collegiate Athletic Association. It directed the board to negotiate for "feasible working policies for the governance of athletic competition relative to the implications of Title IX."[31]

Cooperation among the organizations never materialized, at least between the AIAW and the NCAA. In February 1974, AIAW president Carol Gordon told the AIAW Executive Board that the NCAA was no longer interested in meeting with the AIAW after the men met "a dead end" in the HEW office. "It may mean that they feel so threatened that they feel they are going to have to gain a more controlling position," wrote Gordon.[32] The NCAA's encounter at HEW would not do the AIAW any good, as Gordon assessed the situation. "If this is the case, we may have the same problem with NCAA that we are having with the [NJCAA]," she warned the AIAW leaders, referring to the NJCAA's move to establish its own program for women. "We need to be alert to the possibilities that NCAA may be making a move . . . to set up their own women's organization."[33] This was surely disturbing news to her colleagues, and Gordon was not a happy messenger.

The draft regulations of Title IX put the AIAW leaders in an awkward position. They certainly welcomed the spirit of the law, but they did not want it to give men the right to enter the traditional "separate sphere" of women's sports. Fearful of negative consequences of their own actions, the AIAW leaders moved gingerly, avoiding either specific comments or full support of the draft.[34] The women's mixed feelings toward the Title IX regulations were well reflected in a memorandum sent to the representatives of AIAW member institutions by AIAW president Leotus Morrison in June 1974. "As we view the regulations, we feel relieved they are finally out and that HEW has demonstrated good faith by extending the comment time and providing twelve briefings. However, we do feel that the regulations fail to provide substantive standards by which compliance of Title IX can be evaluated. The regulations are written for maximum flexibility [but] provide no measuring stick."[35]

It was no secret that, should the regulations become final, the NCAA would have the right to offer programs to women and the AIAW's sex-separate control of women's intercollegiate athletics would be in jeopardy. It was a dilemma for the AIAW leaders. Supporting the regulations, women's programs would be "equalized" with men's; opposing them, on the other hand, the women could be perceived as both against Title IX and supporting the men's athletic establishment.

The spirit of Title IX and the application of the law could mean quite different things for different people. There was increasing fear among college presidents that the proposed Title IX guidelines would mean the end of all intercollegiate athletic programs when men were forced to share "their" money with women. AIAW president Carol Gordon made an extra effort to quell such fear. She told the presidents of AIAW member institutions that quality programs for both men and women could be put within a reasonable framework without destroying one in order to provide for the other. She may also have made a regrettable promise on behalf of the AIAW. Defending the AIAW from being quoted as insisting on "equal funding" for men's and women's programs, Gordon wrote that as an organization, "our total stress has been on equality of opportunity for participation in quality programs and not on equal funding."[36]

"Equal funding" had been the most sensitive and essential issue concerning the implementation of Title IX in intercollegiate athletics, and Gordon's comment on the issue did not go unnoticed by those in control of men's athletics. During its campaign against the proposed Title IX regulations, the NCAA used Gordon's statement as a significant piece of evidence that women supported the men's position on how to administer college athletics.[37]

In October 1974, the AIAW submitted its official comments on the proposed Title IX regulations to HEW, clarifying speculations of the AIAW's position on the issue. "AIAW strongly supports the letter and the spirit of Title IX and the proposed regulations . . . insofar as they implement the concept of equal opportunity regardless of sex," read the document. However, the AIAW disagreed with various provisions in the regulations concerning athletics. It maintained that the goal of equal opportunity for women could be best attained by "revision . . . modification or elaboration" of the proposed rules, and by "adoption of additional regulations." In a seemingly less friendly tone, the document asserted that the proposed guidelines wholly failed to indicate HEW's rationale as to what constitutes equality. Contrary to what Gordon had claimed seven months earlier, it suggested that equality of athletic opportunities for male and female students be measured by "equal per capita expenditures."[38] The AIAW leaders apparently had come to realize that the best way to measure "equal opportunity" was through actual share of financial resources. This potential share of financial resources was exactly what the men feared. As Walter Byers warned, it could mean the "possible doom of intercollegiate sports."[39]

The Tower Amendment

The NCAA's campaign against the implementation of Title IX regulations gained an enormous boost in Congress in May 1974. The U.S. Senate, in approving the Elementary and Secondary Education Act, adopted an amendment that limited the applicability of Title IX to intercollegiate athletics, sponsored by Republican Senator John G. Tower of Texas. The amendment stated that Title IX "shall not apply to an intercollegiate athletic activity to the extent that such activity does or may provide gross receipts or donations to the institution necessary to support that activity."[40]

The passage of the Tower Amendment prompted Walter Byers to send an official thank-you letter to the Texas senator on behalf of NCAA member institutions. "We thank you for your leadership in protecting the intercollegiate athletic programs of the colleges of this nation," wrote Byers. "Your willingness to pursue this matter, and the success you have achieved, represents a major breakthrough and we know you will continue to follow this matter when it is considered by Senate-House conferees."[41] Four days later, Byers issued a memorandum to the athletic directors of NCAA member institutions in District Six along with a copy of his letter to Senator Tower.[42] Byers urged the directors to extend their appreciation to Senator Tower for his effective leadership in fighting the proposed Title IX regulations. He also promised them that the NCAA leaders were making their best efforts to secure acceptance of the Tower Amendment by the Senate-House conference committee.[43]

Byers' memorandum soon became obsolete. Only one day after the memorandum was sent, the Tower Amendment was eliminated by the Senate-House conference. The congressional action was a blow to the NCAA's months-long lobbying against the implementation of the proposed Title IX regulations. The NCAA blamed "intensive lobby pressure" from the Women's Equity Action League, the National Physical Education

Teachers Association, and the legal assistance of Gwen Gregory, the HEW officer chiefly responsible for drafting the regulations.[44]

The anticipated implementation of Title IX had a new twist not only because of the deletion of the Tower Amendment but because of the adoption of the Javits Amendment. Sponsored by Republican Senator Jacob K. Javits of New York, the amendment required that the portion of regulations concerning college athletics should include "reasonable provisions considering the nature of particular sports."[45] The terms "reasonable provisions" and "particular sports" were language ambiguous enough to cause confusion and furor among NCAA leaders. Two days after the congressional actions, Alan Chapman and Richard Koenig telegraphed the Senate-House conferees on behalf of the NCAA, urging them to "reconsider and clarify" the action of substituting the Javits Amendment for the Tower Amendment. The telegram read: "It is essential that revenue-producing sports be protected to assure the funds necessary to offer non-revenue-producing sports programs to both men and women."[46] Charging that the draft regulations would severely damage college athletic programs, the NCAA officials maintained that HEW was proposing an "unwarranted and deep intrusion of government into institutional management." Such an intrusion would impose "arbitrary rules unnecessary to assure equal opportunity in sport for men and women." They warned that any attempts to manage intercollegiate programs through federal directives "can only lead to chaos for men's and women's athletics."[47]

The NCAA's protest apparently did not have any significant effect on congressional position concerning Title IX implementation. One week after the NCAA's telegram protest, and two years after the passage of the legislation, the Department of Health, Education, and Welfare published the proposed regulations of Title IX in June 1974, without accommodating the NCAA's requests.[48]

Controlling the Women's Program—the NCAA's Best Defense

Both the defeat of the Tower Amendment and the publication of Title IX regulations were indicative that the NCAA's chance was slim to have revenue-producing sports exempted from Title IX. The disappointing congressional effort nevertheless reinforced the belief among NCAA leaders that the best way to protect the men's interests was to take control of the women's programs. While maintaining its lobbying effort for a favorable revision of the regulations, the NCAA leadership also stepped up its pursuit to administer intercollegiate athletics for women.

In February 1974, Walter Byers appointed a new NCAA special committee on women's intercollegiate athletics at the directive of the NCAA Council. Committee members representing NCAA institutions were John Fuzak of Michigan State University, who became NCAA president in 1975; Stanley Marshall of South Dakota State University, who assumed the position of NCAA secretary-treasurer in 1975; Robert Scannell of Penn State University, who soon proved himself a strong opponent of the Title IX regulations; and David Swank from the University of Oklahoma, the former chair of the NCAA special committee on women's athletics. Along with the NCAA representatives were leaders of two longtime NCAA allies, George Killian, executive secretary of the NJCAA, and Clifford Fagan, executive secretary of the National Federation of State High School Athletic Associations. Token representation of women was given to Carol Gordon, AIAW president, from Washington State University, and to Mary Jean Mulvaney from the University of Chicago.[49]

In his letter to the committee appointees, Byers defended the NCAA's past policies on women's athletics and indicated that times had changed. "Circumstances are such now that it is imperative that the NCAA take a leadership role . . . in administration and conduct of intercollegiate athletics for both men and women."[50] Byers pointed out that the rationale for the NCAA's new position was recent challenges in court and the imminent publication of Title IX regulations. He concluded that the NCAA remained vulnerable to possible legal attacks.[51] The seasoned NCAA leader apparently chose not to address a more important reason for the NCAA's initiative, which was to increase its power in amateur sports through first controlling both men's and women's intercollegiate athletics.

The NCAA's initiative was backed with a strong legal argument. Early in the year, NCAA counsel George Gangwere supplied the NCAA leadership with his updated legal opinion on women's athletics. Reiterating his previous position, Gangwere maintained that the NCAA had an unavoidable responsibility to organize and govern intercollegiate athletics for women. "The truth is," argued Gangwere, "that [the AIAW] probably cannot do the job on its own soon enough without the investment of money and administrative effort by the NCAA." But the key point of his argument was that the NCAA could not make such an investment without some control over the program. Furthermore, women's programs would not likely provide equal opportunities for women "if the rules for male and female athletes [were] not highly coordinated."[52] Gangwere did exactly what the NCAA leaders wanted—he portrayed the NCAA as the only capable and legitimate candidate to provide true equal opportunities for women in intercollegiate athletics. "The necessity for substantially equal athletic opportunities for women is no longer a matter of speculation," surmised Gangwere. "The longer the implementation of this purpose is delayed, the less likely the NCAA will be able to determine the nature and extent of the actions which will be ultimately adopted."[53]

Gangwere's preaching might not have convinced the majority of NCAA members in early 1974. His legal expertise, however, was good enough for Byers to persuade the NCAA leadership to accept what he believed the right path for the organization. In May 1974, the NCAA Council endorsed a resolution calling for the development of opportunities for women students to compete in sports programs of NCAA member institutions.[54] In August, Byers told the NCAA Executive Committee that, under the circumstances, "the NCAA eventually will be involved in women's athletics."[55] Days later, at the NCAA Council meeting, David Swank repeated Byers' rhetoric, only with more details. As recommended by the association's long-range planning committee, Swank suggested that the NCAA "immediately pursue an aggressive course including introduction of championship events for women, toward a merger with AIAW."[56] In response, the NCAA Council authorized that the special committee meet at the earliest possible date.[57]

The NCAA Special Committee on Women's Intercollegiate Athletics met in October 1974 in Chicago with four AIAW representatives: AIAW president Leotus Morrison, president-elect Laurie Mabry, DGWS/AIAW consultant Bonnie Parkhouse, and legal counsel Margot Polivy. The meeting centered around the issue of possible merger or affiliation of the NCAA and the AIAW. While the women insisted on the importance of women's involvement in decision making, attendees from both sides agreed that the university administration was going to seek "a single voice and single policy for all athletics."[58] To achieve that, the women suggested that both the NCAA and the AIAW be dissolved to form a third unified organization with equal representation of men and women. David Swank responded that the NCAA Council would be unlikely to accept the idea of equal representation. The women countered that they could not accept anything less than equal representation. The meeting adjourned without substantial reconciliation between the two organizations and with some bad news for the AIAW representatives. During the meeting, George Killian announced that the NJCAA would "inaugurate three championships for women students at its member institutions during the current academic year."[59] The NJCAA initiative was probably the biggest fear of the AIAW leaders at the time: witnessing men "invading" the separate sphere of women's athletics but unable to stop the process with any legal leverage.

The women's fear was revealed in a memorandum issued to the AIAW Executive Board by Leotus Morrison. Pointing out the NJCAA's effort to encourage schools "to go with NJCAA," Morrison wrote, "apparently many athletic directors are making it difficult for the women to stay with or go with AIAW membership."[60] The NJCAA's initiative was penetrating the AIAW's power base. The problem for the AIAW was that, with Title IX becoming the law of the land, the men's "invasion" into traditionally women's territory seemed justified.

Considering the close relationship between the NJCAA and the NCAA, it was doubtful that the former's plan was without the knowledge or consent of the latter. Rather, it was likely part of the NCAA's scheme to take control of women's intercollegiate athletics. If the NJCAA could set a precedent, it would be a tremendous boost for the NCAA's own pursuit in the same direction. With an existing governing model for both men's and women's programs, the NCAA would have a much better chance not only to win the support of its member institutions, but also to defeat any challenges from the AIAW. For the AIAW leaders, the only possible worse fear would be to see the NCAA invading the "big-time" women's programs. This fear soon became a reality.

NCAA Initiates a Pilot Program for Women

In October 1974, the NCAA Council authorized the NCAA staff and legal counsel to examine the "legal, financial and political ramifications" in establishing NCAA championships for women in selected sports.[61] A month later, the NCAA's Washington, D.C., counsel, Philip B. Brown, affirmed to Walter Byers that the NCAA's decision to introduce championships for women "should have a favorable—or at least a neutral—political impact."[62] Brown's response was probably not unexpected. What may really have interested Byers, however, was Brown's analysis of possible consequences from the NCAA initiative. Asserting that the NCAA's move should be favorable both in Congress and with the general public, Brown wrote:

> Such an affirmative step should also strengthen the NCAA's hand in opposing the unreasonable excesses of the current Title IX proposals. It may also have a healthy effect on certain organizations, such as the AIAW, which apparently expect that, as a result of their advocating extreme Federal intervention in the affairs of educational institutions, they will be entitled to receive greatly increased resources for women's athletic programs which they will develop, administer and conduct. Action now by the NCAA may cause such groups to think twice in pushing for Federal regulations, and to adopt a more reasonable approach to cooperative efforts to improve athletic opportunities for women.[63]

In December, the NCAA staff completed its study entitled "The NCAA and Women's Intercollegiate Athletics." The study concluded that the NCAA should provide "the same meaningful services and high-quality National Collegiate Championship competition . . . for the women student-athletes and teams of its member institutions as it does for men student-athletes." It specifically recommended that the NCAA offer pilot programs for women in selected sports beginning in the spring of 1975.[64]

The efficiency of the NCAA staff and timely actions of the NCAA legislative body were at the direction and facilitation of Walter Byers, who wanted to have the issue resolved as soon as possible. Two years after the NCAA changed its male-only eligibility rule in January 1973, Byers believed that the time had come for the organization to officially declare its authority over intercollegiate athletics for women, and the upcoming 1975 NCAA convention seemed to be the right forum to accomplish that goal. Byers undoubtedly showed such an intention in his letter to NCAA president Alan Chapman: "I am enclosing a copy [of the staff report] for you and members of the Executive Committee and Council in the thought that all parties would have a chance to read the report prior to our District of Columbia confabulation."[65]

One day before the 1975 NCAA convention, the NCAA Council approved the concept of the staff report and recommended it to the special committee for implementation "at the earliest possible time."[66] It is worth noting that the council did entertain two different options at its meeting, either to offer championships for women "immediately" or to adopt the concept of the report but proceed with the implementation "at a slower pace, assuring a longer transitional period for the membership." It seems that any doubt on the choices was cleared away when Byers pointed out that the NCAA would become vulnerable if opportunities for women were not offered soon. Interestingly, Byers attributed the NCAA leadership's initiative on women's programs to pressure from the NCAA membership.[67]

The council's proposal caught the membership off guard and met significant opposition from the rank and file.[68] Many were angered by the leadership's secretive handling of the matter. David Swank acknowledged this angry mood when he addressed the issue at the General Round Table session of the convention. "I am not sure based on some of the comments I have heard around the halls how much pleasure I have to be up here this afternoon," stated Swank, "but I do hope it will not be any worse than when I presented the reorganizations proposal a couple or three years ago."[69] The members' dissatisfaction, however, seemed much less significant than Swank's reaction. Questioned by a delegate as to whether the NCAA Council had done any consultation with the women, Swank answered affirmatively, but then explained that it had not done so on the NCAA Council's proposal in question. He was, nevertheless, rather frank about what he perceived as a major consequence of the proposal. "I am sure there will be some opposition [from the AIAW] to this position," Swank admitted. "That may be the biggest understatement made at this Convention."[70] Swank undoubtedly knew how big an understatement it was. Having been NCAA's chief officer on women's intercollegiate athletics for nearly four years, the law professor and member of the NCAA Council could not possibly have miscalculated the implication of the proposal for the AIAW.

On the same day as Swank's talk, NCAA assistant executive director Tom Jernstadt briefed the AIAW delegates of the NCAA Council's proposal at their annual assembly in Houston. According to the reminiscences of Donna Lopiano, Jernstadt was "heatedly and closely questioned by the delegates" after he had read the proposal. Subsequently, the AIAW Executive Board communicated its outrage to the NCAA and urged the NCAA

Council to withdraw its proposal. "AIAW views with grave concern the announced intention of NCAA to commence a pilot program of intercollegiate athletics for women," it stated in an AIAW telegram sent to the NCAA Council. "AIAW has no choice but to view failure to reconsider as an effort by NCAA to undermine the existing women's intercollegiate championship program."[71] Unofficially, individual AIAW members were also encouraged to telephone their male counterparts at the NCAA convention to seek support for the women's position.[72]

The AIAW's protest may have influenced the decision on the NCAA Council's proposal. After lengthy debate, the NCAA membership defeated the original version of the proposal but approved a revised resolution. Both the original and revised versions directed the NCAA Council to prepare a comprehensive report and plan on the subject of administering women's intercollegiate athletics. They also gave the council the authority to conduct pilot programs for women's national championships. The revised version, however, required that the council's report and plan be circulated to all members of the NCAA and the AIAW for comments. It also limited the council's authority on the matter, mandating a joint NCAA-AIAW committee to make recommendations to the council before final proposals were delivered for consideration by the 1976 NCAA convention."[73]

The first month of 1975 therefore saw a partial defeat of the NCAA leaders' attempt to control women's intercollegiate athletics. Ironically, neither the rejection of the NCAA Council's proposal nor the publication of proposed Title IX regulations protected women's intercollegiate athletics from men's "invasion." On the contrary, the NCAA leaders soon renewed their attempt to govern women's intercollegiate athletics. Only this time they were better prepared and more determined to achieve their goals.

Walter Byers, executive director of the NCAA, 1951–87. *Courtesy of Ronald A. Smith.*

Katherine Ley, vice president of the AAHPER in 1962–63 and chair of the CIAW in 1967. *Courtesy of AAHPERD.*

George H. Gangwere, NCAA legal counsel who provided "A Legal Opinion" in 1971, which became the basis for the NCAA to enter the governance of intercollegiate athletics for women. *Courtesy of George H. Gangwere.*

JoAnne Thorpe, chair of DGWS in 1971–72. *Courtesy of AAHPERD.*

Bonnie Lauer, 1973 AIAW Golf
Championship, Mount Holyoke
College. *Courtesy of Archives of the
AIAW, Special Collections, University of
Maryland Libraries.*

Marianne Crawford (no. 23),
member of the 1974 Immaculata
College National Championship
Team. *Courtesy of Robert and Theresa
Halvey Collection, Philadelphia
Archdiocesan Historical Research Center.*

Tina Krah (no. 35), member of
the 1974 Immaculata College
National Championship Team.
*Courtesy of Robert and Theresa Halvey
Collection, Philadelphia Archdiocesan
Historical Research Center.*

Delta State, 1975 AIAW National Basketball Championship. *Courtesy of Archives of the AIAW, Special Collections, University of Maryland Libraries.*

Immaculata College, 1975 AIAW National Basketball Championship. *Courtesy of Archives of the AIAW, Special Collections, University of Maryland Libraries.*

Ann Carr (Penn State Gymnastics), 1977–78 AIAW Broderick Award winner. *Courtesy of Archives of the AIAW, Special Collections, University of Maryland Libraries.*

Nancy Lieberman (Old Dominion University), 1978–79 AIAW Broderick Award winner. *Courtesy of Archives of the AIAW, Special Collections, University of Maryland Libraries.*

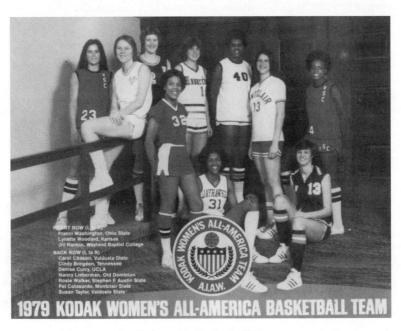

1979 Kodak Women's All-America Basketball Team. *Courtesy of Archives of the AIAW, Special Collections, University of Maryland Libraries.*

California vs. Penn State University, 1980 AIAW Division I Final (field hockey). *Courtesy of Archives of AIAW, Special Collections, University of Maryland Libraries.*

Seven women leaders of the CIAW. *Left to right:* Rachel Bryant, Alyce Cheska, Maria Sexton, Fran Schaafsma, Ann Stiff, Frances McGill, and Katherine Ley. *Courtesy of Archives of the AIAW, Special Collections, University of Maryland Libraries.*

Dr. Rachel Bryant, consultant in physical education and women's athletics. *Courtesy of AAHPERD.*

Linda Estes, former director of women's athletics at the University of New Mexico, who epitomized the voices within the AIAW that constantly challenged the organization's sex-separatist policies, financial priorities, and dependence on its legal counsel, Margot Polivy. *Courtesy of Linda Estes.*

AIAW presidents. *From left, standing:* Laurie Mabry, Leotus Morrison, Charlotte West, Christine Grant, Peg Burke, Carole Oglesby, Carol Gordon. *Seated:* Donna Lopiano, Carole Moshier, Judith Holland. Merrily Baker and Virginia Hunt were not present. *Courtesy of Archives of the AIAW, Special Collections, University of Maryland Libraries.*

The Challenge to AIAW's Solitary Control

1975–1979

The announcement of a program of
intercollegiate championships for women by
NCAA on January 6, 1975 was deemed a betrayal
of AIAW's good faith efforts to work with the
NCAA. It was difficult to interpret the NCAA
announcement as anything but an attempt to take
over the women's intercollegiate program.
                    —Leotus Morrison, AIAW President
                    (1975)

THE NCAA leadership's attempt to establish a women's program failed despite an amicable campaign.[1] By the end of January 1975, the AIAW appeared to have more to celebrate than to worry about. "AIAW was encouraged," wrote AIAW president Morrison, "by the decisive action of the NCAA Representative Assembly in rejecting the Executive Council plan and directing that future study of women's athletics be made in cooperation with the women's governing body, AIAW."[2] There is little doubt that 1975 heralded a new era for women's intercollegiate athletics. In late January, the first nationally televised women's intercollegiate basketball game was held between Immaculata College and the University of Maryland. Immaculata, a small Catholic liberal arts school outside Philadelphia, defeated Maryland 80 to 48. A month later in Madison Square Garden, Immaculata successfully defended its national championship title by defeating Queens College before twelve thousand spectators.[3] In the same month, the AIAW/National Association for Girls and Women in Sport obtained their first commercial sponsorship of $6,000 from Eastman Kodak Company.[4] The wind was clearly blowing in the AIAW's favor. Yet Morrison's reaction to the NCAA convention resolution on women's athletics was overly optimistic.

NCAA Views AIAW as an Unequal Competitor

In March 1975, the AIAW issued a proposal on "Possible Alternatives for Future Governing Structures for Intercollegiate Athletics." The document, sent to chief officers of member institutions of the AIAW, the NCAA, the National Association of Intercollegiate Athletics, and the National Junior Collegiate Athletic Association, recommended three possible alternatives: (1) to maintain the status quo, (2) to merge the existing men's and women's organizations, and (3) to create an entirely new governing body. The premise for the AIAW to pursue any of the alternatives was that there must be "sexual equality" in program opportunities, governance, power, and philosophic expression.[5]

It was doubtful that the AIAW leaders had much faith in the feasibility of their proposal. As they acknowledged in the document, the men's organizations could still choose to initiate programs for women without the women's approval. "We believe [however] that such action[s] undertaken on a unilateral basis would be unpopular and unwise." Any forms of governance without an equal voice and vote for women in the decision-making processes, it elaborated, would add a further inequity to the list of discriminatory conditions that women were currently attempting to overcome.[6]

The women's fear of men's actions was well founded. Within a month of the distribution of the AIAW proposal, the NCAA Council prepared a report concerning the administration of women's intercollegiate athletics. While the AIAW leaders demanded an equal power for women in decision making, the NCAA Council stressed the provision of equal opportunities for women as a legal and moral obligation of the NCAA. It recommended that the NCAA "proceed immediately" to adjust its services and programs to the needs of female student-athletes.[7]

The NCAA Council report was not necessarily a response to the AIAW proposal, for the AIAW claimed that it never received a response. The truth of the AIAW's claim aside, the absence of an official NCAA reply should be no surprise. By early 1975, the positions of the two organizations on the issue of intercollegiate athletic governance were so far apart that the NCAA leaders apparently did not anticipate any compromise from the women. This attitude was clearly exhibited in the council's report. It maintained that integrated or coordinated programs at the national level could not be achieved if separate male and female organizations were left to accomplish them through bilateral agreements. "Recent history of NCAA efforts in this regard," it read, "dramatized the difficulty of reaching such accords in matters of the most preliminary nature." To further justify the council's position, the report also noted the AIAW's inability to assume the role of governing a quality program at the national level, because the AIAW was "dependent upon AAHPER for financial and staff support."[8]

A day after the distribution of the NCAA Council's report, Leotus Morrison wrote AIAW representatives urging them to oppose the NCAA Council's action. Morrison stressed that women must decide upon the future structure of women's intercollegiate athletics, either through maintaining separate governing bodies or through gaining "sexual equity" within any merged organization. "The institution of a women's program by a male sports governing organization," argued the AIAW president, "does nothing to assure women of real program[m]atic or administrative equality."[9]

A more furious response to the NCAA Council's report came from the executive committee of the American Association for Health, Physical Education, and Recreation two weeks later. Terming the report "a mockery of democratic procedures," the AAHPER accused the NCAA Council on five counts of immoral conduct. The most intriguing of them was "the absence of candor regarding the assets which the control of women's sport would provide the NCAA." Such control would enhance the NCAA's struggle to become the key national governing body for international sports, offer potential financial gain, and garner monopolistic power over national collegiate sports.[10] In conclusion, the AAHPER urged the NCAA to withdraw its report and engage in "an honest dialogue between AAHPER/AIAW and NCAA." It stated in an imperative tone: "The AAHPER invites NCAA to participate in such a dialogue immediately. Failure to accept this invitation will provide the basis for continuing distrust."[11]

One can only imagine the effect of the AAHPER communication, which satisfied probably no one but the AIAW leaders. In a memorandum to AIAW members, Morrison referred to the AAHPER's action as the

AIAW's "major hope for survival." She indicated that the AAHPER president, Roger Wiley, had pledged not only complete moral support but also
necessary staff and financial assistance of the AAHPER in the struggle.[12]
Morrison's correspondence may have cheered up those who were dis-
turbed by the NCAA Council's report. It was, however, a strong testimony
as to the AIAW's dependence upon the AAHPER. Was the AIAW independently capable of providing quality athletic opportunities for women?

The AIAW leaders certainly thought so. Trying to nullify the NCAA's
notion of the AIAW's "inability," the official AIAW response claimed that
the AIAW was "financially sound and in 1974–75 reached a self-
supporting status with opportunities for additional income in the immediate future."[13] "A self-supporting status" might have pleased most
presidents of the AIAW member institutions, but the claim that the AIAW
was "financially sound" was simply false.[14] The financial situation of the
AIAW was becoming such a problem that the 1976 AIAW delegate assembly voted to significantly increase the membership dues. "As an infant organization," reported the AIAW treasurer Bev Johnson, "membership
dues did not adequately cover the expenses of operation. The AAHPER accepted the responsibility for the unfunded debts."[15]

Both the AIAW and the AAHPER felt that a self-supporting AIAW was
essential for the survival of the young organization. "Because a substantial
income has not yet been found or developed," Johnson explained, "the majority of the income must be realized from membership dues." Ironically,
Title IX also contributed to the financial burden of the AIAW. Johnson's report listed "legal service" cost as the number one increase in the AIAW
budget and attributed to it the major justification for a membership dues
increase. "The need for legal advice and services has been estimated to cost
at least three times the amount budgeted for 1975–76."[16] Title IX brought
hope of equality for women's intercollegiate athletics. It also brought a
new operational need to the AIAW: legal service. Although such a service
was necessary, it would also prove to be very expensive and financially
detrimental to the AIAW (see chapter 9).

The Enactment of Title IX Regulations

Although the tensions between the AIAW and the NCAA reached a new
high as a direct result of the NCAA Council's report, the event that took

the center stage of intercollegiate athletics in 1975 was the implementation of the Title IX regulations. In February, the U.S. Department of Health, Education, and Welfare submitted its final draft of the regulations to President Ford. In April, AIAW legal counsel Margot Polivy sent her analysis of the regulations to the executive boards of the NAGWS and the AIAW. Comparing the final draft with the June 1974 version, Polivy pointed out that the new draft was bad news for women in its provisions concerning contact sports, affirmative action, athletic scholarships, and the three-year grace period for compliance. Polivy attributed the unfavorable changes to the questionable political and professional qualifications of HEW personnel. "The draft regulations . . . reflect a political rather than knowledgeable approach to the athletics section," wrote Polivy. "It appears that while HEW realizes that women and athletics have become a controversial issue, the Department personnel drafting the regulations have no interest, experience or expertise with respect to the subject matter."[17] Ironically, Polivy's criticism of the regulations was echoed, at least partially, by Walter Byers. In a letter addressed to selected NCAA representatives, Byers maintained that the regulations were "a major assault upon the revenue producing potential of men's intercollegiate athletics." They did not recognize "the need for increased expenditures for those sports which attract greater attendance."[18]

On May 27, 1975, President Ford signed the regulations into law with a forty-five-day review period before they became final. Two weeks later, Byers wrote to the same group of NCAA representatives on the progress of the regulations. In order to change aspects of the law, Byers said that the NCAA would attempt to offset the possible all-out effort from "assorted women's groups" to obtain revisions in the regulations more favorable to their position. "We must counter their efforts," Byers emphasized, "or face the real possibility that the regulations will be changed . . . in a manner more detrimental to intercollegiate athletic programs."[19]

Byers' call for action against Title IX regulations did not go unsupported. Jim Kehoe, athletic director at the University of Maryland, lashed out at the proposed regulations when he was interviewed by the *Washington Post* in June 1975. While agreeing with the spirit of Title IX, Kehoe maintained that the rules were "unrealistic, impractical and unsound [and] more politically motivated" and that his opposition to them was based on business considerations.[20] As with many male athletic officials, ideology did not seem to be important to him when money came into account. "I see no ability of the women to generate income," Kehoe said, "[and] I don't believe in deficit financing, deficit spending."[21] It is questionable that Kehoe, who probably represented most athletic administrators at his level, truly believed in gender equity. In the fiscal year of 1974, the budget for women's athletics at the University of Maryland was reportedly about 1 percent of that of the men's. While he claimed that the numbers were inaccurate, Kehoe apparently did not think there was anything wrong with the reality. To him, the problem with women's demanding equal rights in athletics was that they did not make an effort to earn such rights, while the men had done so for generations. "They want to destroy something desirable just to make a point," said Kehoe. "They are moving too fast: too much is expected too soon. You have to crawl before you walk, walk before you run."[22]

Resistance to Title IX Regulations from Both Sides

The Title IX regulations signed by President Ford met strong resistance from both the NCAA and the AIAW, although for different reasons. In June 1975, Margot Polivy advised AIAW president Laurie Mabry of the negative impact the regulations would have on women's athletics. Speculating on an unlikely congressional veto of the regulations within the forty-five-day review period, Polivy indicated that a lawsuit would be an alternative action against the regulations. "It is a fair guess that the regulations will face court challenge by women's groups, the NCAA and/or institutions and school districts."[23] Strategically, however, Polivy suggested that the AIAW would be better off to remain silent and to take no legal action until HEW enforced the regulations. "Then if we agree with their interpretation, we can support HEW. If we disagree, we can take legal action against HEW's interpretation as being inconsistent with the regulations, the law or the Constitution."[24] Although Polivy had earlier criticized the HEW for its "political approach" to college athletics, her advice to the AIAW leadership seemed to bear an even stronger political motive than a genuine concern for women's equality. Urging the AIAW not to initiate any immediate action, Polivy made it clear that such a "non-action" should be contingent upon how the men responded to the regulations. "If someone such as

NCAA does [challenge the rules]," Polivy wrote, "we must enter the suit to prevent the case from adversely affecting us."[25]

The "all-out effort" by various women's and men's groups to revise or retain the regulations caused such a political upheaval that Congress decided to hold public hearings to settle the matter. Three days before the AIAW and the NCAA were scheduled to testify at the hearings, Polivy urged the women leaders to change the AIAW's position because "the only apparent opposition" to the regulations came from the male athletic establishment. Since there would be substantial press coverage of the hearings, Polivy wrote, "it would be unfortunate if there was not a strong rebuttal of the NCAA position by AIAW."[26] Obviously giving advice based on her political convictions rather than on the merit of the Title IX regulations, Polivy told the women leaders that nothing was more important than being the adversary of the NCAA.

The Title IX regulations became final on July 21, 1975, despite some last-minute attempts to revise the sections in the document concerning "revenue-producing" sports.[27] As one may image, the finalized regulations satisfied hardly anyone. In a statement accompanying the publication, HEW Secretary Casper W. Weinberger admitted that "there was no way to draft regulations for Title IX that will please all of the people all of the time," especially in the area of athletics. The regulations undoubtedly enhanced opportunities for women in athletics. They also gave schools the flexibility, as Weinberger pointed out, "to keep competitive sports alive and well."[28] The major defect of the regulations seems to be the lack of what the document was supposed to provide—clear guidelines for implementing Title IX. The vague language embodied in the regulations may have provided enough flexibility for HEW to deal with various situations, but it nevertheless became a source of confusion and frustration for both men and women involved in intercollegiate athletics in the years to come.

Attempts at an NCAA-AIAW Alliance

As directed by a 1975 NCAA convention resolution, the first joint NCAA-AIAW committee met in September 1975 to make recommendations to the NCAA Council regarding women's athletics.[29] It first reviewed responses of both the NCAA and the AIAW member institutions to the NCAA Council's report on possible establishment of NCAA national championships for women. Only a small number of institutions responded. Data from both sides indicated an unfavorable reaction to the NCAA Council's report.[30] Subsequently, the AIAW team proposed that the AIAW and the NCAA maintain the status quo and continue to provide separate programs for women and men. While acknowledging the possibility of forming an organization or organizations that would offer programs for both sexes, the AIAW side insisted that the premise for any such organizations should be "an equal voice for women."[31] The NCAA members of the committee were disappointed at the AIAW proposal because "it discouraged the ability of the present Joint Committee to be productive."[32] Walter Byers stated that he would press the council to get a resolution on the NCAA convention floor regarding the NCAA's legal liability to provide opportunities for both sexes. The issue at stake, Byers pointed out, was whether the NCAA would be immune from any legal challenges. If the AIAW insisted that both organizations maintain the status quo, Byers suggested that the NCAA would support the AIAW's position only "if the AIAW would indemnify the NCAA" from court costs.[33] The AIAW certainly would not grant Byers' wish either by choice or by ability to pay.

The joint committee reconvened in November 1975, when both sides agreed to continue exploration of a possible NCAA-AIAW affiliation. This exploration on the NCAA's side resulted in the publication of "A Legal Opinion," essentially a revisit to NCAA counsel George Gangwere's legal opinion of 1971. It stated that not only did the NCAA have the obligation to provide equal opportunities for women, but the AIAW lacked "the recognition and stature, the financial and organizational strength, or the breadth of championship opportunities, offered by the NCAA."[34] Citing numerous legal precedents, it pointed out that a separate newly-developed women's organization "simply cannot in fact provide the same tangible benefits and the same intangible rewards" available through the NCAA-sponsored programs. "The NCAA is best advised to administer female intercollegiate programs under a unitary structure," the document concluded. As a practical matter, it urged the NCAA to add to all levels of its operation "individuals having close familiarity and experience with female intercollegiate competition" and that many of these individuals should be "female."[35]

The immediate impact of "A Legal Opinion" was the NCAA Council's decision to recommend that the NCAA adopt the revised NCAA report and to establish NCAA women's championships beginning in 1977. The NCAA Council justified its action with the following reason: "Since the [Joint AIAW-NCAA] Committee was unable to arrive at mutual recommendations, each organization is free to submit its own report at its own Convention."[36]

The 1976 NCAA convention came up short of endorsing two major resolutions based on the council's report on women's intercollegiate athletics. After vigorous debate, the resolution to apply NCAA rules to women was strategically referred to the NCAA Council for further study. The convention also tabled the second resolution that prohibited the NCAA from establishing championships for exclusively female student-athletes prior to the 1977–78 academic year. However, the membership did vote to establish a standing committee on women's athletics.[37] In May 1976, the NCAA Council appointed a new NCAA Committee on Women's Intercollegiate Athletics as authorized by the NCAA convention and unilaterally discontinued the NCAA appointments to the joint AIAW-NCAA committee.[38]

The main charge of the new NCAA committee was to keep the membership informed of developments in women's intercollegiate athletics and of the NCAA's due legal and societal obligations.[39] While the resolution mandated that the committee continue the efforts of bringing "the rules of the AIAW and NCAA more closely together," it is doubtful that the NCAA leadership truly intended to cooperate with the AIAW. More likely, it saw the earlier joint committee as a waste of time and thus needed one that could effectively further its agenda. The members, which included as the only woman Ruth Berkey from Occidental College, were carefully chosen. Berkey, an executive board member of the AIAW, was obviously not chosen to represent the interests of the AIAW leaders. "We are pursuing a separatist approach to women's intercollegiate athletics," Walter Byers wrote in his letter to Berkey. "Incidentally, you were nominated on the basis that you easily would be the match for eight men . . . and probably more."[40] It must have been no accident that Byers and Berkey had more in common than their views on intercollegiate athletics for women. Later they joined their lives together as husband and wife.

NCAA-AIAW Differences Irreconcilable

The 1976 NCAA convention resolution not to initiate championships for women prior to 1977–78 kept the NCAA-AIAW battlefield relatively quiet for the following two years. In May 1977, the AIAW Executive Board established an AIAW Committee on Men's Intercollegiate Athletics as a counterpart of the NCAA committee.[41] Three months later, the two committees convened for the first time. While the meeting made no significant progress toward reconciling fundamental differences, it did recommend that the NCAA not undertake a survey on its member institutions' desire to initiate championships for women.[42] The recommendation was accepted by the NCAA Council when it voted to postpone the survey until after the 1978 NCAA convention.[43]

The relative peace between the NCAA and the AIAW was interrupted before the year elapsed. In December, the AIAW learned that the 1978 NCAA convention agenda would include a motion to establish NCAA Division II women's championships in basketball, gymnastics, and swimming.[44] To the dismay of the AIAW leaders, the motion seemed to have popular support when a straw vote at the NCAA convention resulted in a narrow victory for the sponsors.[45] The AIAW Executive Board protested the motion by sending a message to the NCAA Council, calling upon the council to "go on record as urging NCAA members to vote against the proposal."[46] Although the NCAA Council conveyed the AIAW's message to the Division II steering committee, the sponsors of the motion refused to withdraw.[47] If the NCAA leadership had been conspiring to take over women's college athletics, as accused by the AIAW, it obviously had not been successful. Only the democratic process seemed to be functioning well in the NCAA. After a lengthy debate, the NCAA Division II membership defeated the motion to initiate championships for women in Division II schools.[48]

A month after the convention, the NCAA Special Committee on Women's Intercollegiate Athletics conducted a survey on the desirability of its member institutions' establishing NCAA championships for women.[49] Results of the survey were reported to the NCAA Council in August, with Division II favoring and Divisions I and III opposing the proposal.[50] Despite the opposition, the NCAA committee proposed that the NCAA consider sponsoring women's championships "if no progress toward common rules is made or if the AIAW Executive Board does not exhibit good faith in attempts to negotiate common rules."[51]

To reconcile rules of the NCAA and the AIAW was not an easy task, perhaps an impossible one, even though good faith may have existed among some members of the two organizations. In October 1978, the NCAA-AIAW Joint Subcommittee on Rules met and proposed a few significant rule changes to the NCAA Council and the AIAW Executive Board, such as the eligibility of transfer students and the definition of maximum allowable financial aid. Not surprisingly, the leadership of both organizations rejected the proposals because they required mutual compromise.[52] As members of the NCAA Council expressed clearly after reviewing its subcommittee's report, it was doubtful that any agreement on common rules could ever be reached between the two organizations.[53] The NCAA leadership, however, failed one more time in its attempt to offer a women's program. At the 1979 NCAA convention, the membership defeated a Division III motion to initiate championships for women.[54] The repeated rejections by the membership, however, never seem to have altered the course of the NCAA leadership to establish a women's program, but rather strengthened its determination. The eventual triumph of that determination was only a question of time.

Merger: A Threat to the AIAW's Foundation

The NCAA members' decision on women's athletics at the 1979 convention was undoubtedly a moral victory for the AIAW leaders. But the victory was not a lasting one. Before long, the AIAW leaders found themselves facing a much more difficult reality—the existence and effectiveness of the AIAW were greatly threatened by movements at the institutional level.

Despite the defeat of the Division III motion at the 1979 NCAA convention, the NCAA leadership continued its pursuit of a women's program, but with a modified strategy. Instead of playing a "leading" role on the issue, the NCAA Council chose to "respond" to the needs of the member institutions. Such an approach would certainly exonerate the NCAA leadership from the accusation of conspiring to take over women's athletics.[55] The tone of the NCAA's new approach to the issue was actually set by Walter Byers before the 1979 NCAA convention. In October 1978, AIAW president Charlotte West invited the presidents and executive directors of the National Association of Intercollegiate Athletics and the NCAA to a meeting to discuss future organizational governance structures.[56] Speaking for the NCAA Council, Byers replied that "present conditions do not augur for a meeting of national college athletic organizations to consider questions for national athletic governance." Byers maintained that the issue must be first resolved at the institutional and possibly conference levels "before intelligent answers can be formulated nationally."[57]

One intelligent answer at the national level, however, could be easily prepared. By the end of the 1970s, the decade with the highest inflation rate in the post-World War II era had put most Americans under economic alarm, including college and university presidents.[58] If compliance with the Title IX regulations, especially in intercollegiate athletics, had put the presidents under financial strains, the high inflation certainly made such strains a double jeopardy. It was obviously more difficult to run the men's programs with a budget significantly reduced because of inflation. It would be even harder to provide equal opportunities for women with equal funding, which many administrators believed to be the mandate of Title IX.

William E. Davis, president of the University of New Mexico and a member of the HEW task force for Title IX policy interpretation, probably best illustrated the issue in his speech to the 1979 NCAA convention. He maintained that compliance with the proposed Title IX athletics policies would involve "massive sums of money at a time of fiscal exigencies in higher education." Consequently, few schools would have the resources to maintain the men's programs at their current level and still provide for guideline compliance. Based on financial and legal analysis, Davis concluded that compliance with Title IX policies would force institutions to choose to abide either by the NCAA rules or the AIAW rules if they were both governing bodies in the same institution. Compliance would be "virtually impossible" for an institution to administer with two different sets of rules and two different organizations. As a university president, Davis wanted the option to participate in either the NCAA or the AIAW programs.[59]

Davis may not have represented the views of all administrators of higher education. His speech, however, helped to explain an important phenomenon since the passage of Title IX—the merger of many men's and women's athletics and physical education departments on college campuses. By 1979–80, more than 80 percent of women's intercollegiate programs were administered under a single athletic department structure, where usually a male athletic director oversaw both men's and women's programs.[60] The merger was apparently a sub-merger for women when the power and control ended up in the hands of male athletic directors. The answer to the phenomenon lay in the legal and economic reality of the time. Although Title IX did not require a single administrative structure for men's and women's athletics, it did not forbid one either. Despite the confusion around the true meaning of "equal opportunity," most college presidents saw the single structure as the best available means to handle any potential problems regarding sex discrimination. Consequently, merger of men's and women's departments became the most logical choice.[61] Financial retrenchment and inflationary costs simply helped to accelerate that process.

AIAW Experiences Growing Pains

In the midst of its struggle with the NCAA, the AIAW suffered a severe blow when its longtime ally—the National Association of Intercollegiate Athletics—announced a proposal to initiate programs for women.[62] For years, the NAIA had supported the AIAW, urging NAIA member institutions to join the AIAW and calling the latter an "educationally sound women's intercollegiate athletics program."[63] The reversal of the NAIA's position was "most distressing" for the AIAW leadership, as termed by AIAW president Charlotte West. Speaking to the 1979 AIAW delegate assembly, West used an analogy to describe the impact on the AIAW of the NAIA's action. "The only complement to a newsworthy event in 1978 that I can make is with the natural disasters that have plagued the country from the drought in California to the floods in Kentucky."[64]

While the NAIA did not publicly explain the rationale for its action, the imminent implementation of the Title IX regulations was undoubtedly a primary factor. Between loyalty to an ally and adherence to the law, the NAIA chose the latter. The timing of the NAIA's announcement was probably more telling. Instead of being forced to defend its position in court, the NAIA revealed its proposal just three days before the deadline for Title IX compliance. The NAIA's initiative was also likely influenced by the

NCAA's move toward establishing its women's programs. Rather than watching its members drawn to the forthcoming NCAA events, the NAIA decided to start its own championships for women. In this game of "intercollegiate politicizing," the only loser was the AIAW.

External oppositions were only part of the growing pains for the AIAW. While it had enjoyed a tremendous growth since its inception in 1972 and had surpassed the nine hundred mark in active members in 1979, the AIAW was continually running a financial deficit.[65] In its first six years of operation, the AIAW averaged an annual deficit of more than 8 percent over its income; it only survived with the backing of the American Association for Health, Physical Education, and Recreation and the National Association for Girls and Women in Sport.[66]

The financial and political backing of the AAHPER and the NAGWS was thus indispensable for the AIAW, especially during its early years of existence. The AIAW's dependence on its parent organizations, however, eventually hindered its growth. One major disadvantage of such a relationship was the AIAW's lack of negotiating power with the NCAA. For years, the NCAA refused to treat the AIAW as an equal in the governance of intercollegiate athletics. As Walter Byers asserted in 1971, the NCAA would not delegate responsibilities and council-voting positions to the AIAW over which a third party had veto authority.

Although the women in the AIAW may not have liked the NCAA's attitude, they certainly had taken notice of Byers' words. In spring 1976, the AIAW Executive Board approved the recommendation to separate the operation of the AIAW from the NAGWS, an affiliate of the AAHPER.[67] A year later, the AIAW board further directed the organization's pursuit of independence by approving "the principles of internal and external autonomy, financial and contractual autonomy and educational focus" as the basis for the AIAW's future relationship with the AAHPER.[68] Eventually, in June 1979, the AIAW legally separated from the AAHPER and became the first independent institutional membership association responsible exclusively for the governance of intercollegiate athletics for women.

The independence of the AIAW in 1979 symbolized not only the organization's operational maturity and financial self-reliance but also its philosophical departure from the AAHPER. While the AIAW leaders still claimed their commitment to the educational model of women's athletics, their practice had moved significantly toward the commercial model of the

NCAA. Since 1975, the AIAW had been actively seeking commercial sponsorships, from airlines and automobile dealers to television networks and alcoholic beverage companies. The growth of the AIAW brought recognition and, to some extent, prestige to itself and to women's intercollegiate athletics. It also brought the need of legal protection for the AIAW. The *Kellmeyer* lawsuit in 1973 taught the women an expensive lesson in law, one that cost the integrity of the AIAW's commitment to the educational model. The women leaders learned that noble ideals alone were not enough for the AIAW to survive in the real world, and so they decided to acquire legal expertise for guidance and protection. Little did the women know that such a service would soon impose a financial burden too great for the organization to withstand. It would eventually lead to the division and financial bankruptcy of the AIAW.

Margot Polivy, Legal Costs, and the AIAW's Financial Disaster

Finances appear to be a subject about which
women in athletics know dangerously little.
—Margot Polivy, AIAW legal
counsel (1975)

AIAW LEGAL counsel Margot Polivy's assessment of the situation may have fallen on deaf ears at the time, but would prove to be prophetic.[1] The AIAW leaders' lack of knowledge of finance played a key role in the organization's fiscal desperation in most years of its existence. Eventually, financial confinement prevented the AIAW from offering compatible programs when challenged by the NCAA's initiatives. It also inhibited the AIAW from seeking further legal actions against the NCAA. If the AIAW had attempted to pursue a noble educational model for women's intercollegiate athletics, this noble pursuit was stopped short by a seemingly lesser but more practical matter—lack of money. Ironically, the less educational but more commercial model of men's athletics was much more successful financially and seemed to be the solution to the AIAW's fiscal grief. It soon became clear that the AIAW was facing a multidimensional dilemma: adhere to the educational model but fail financially and risk legal challenges, or abandon it for monetary security and legal protection. A probe into AIAW's financial resources and organizational priorities revealed much insight into the demise of the AIAW.

AIAW Acquires Legal Counsel

Both the establishment of the AIAW and the passage of Title IX were milestones in the development of women's sports. With the AIAW as the sole

110

national body governing women's intercollegiate athletics, one would assume that the passage of Title IX would favor the growth of the AIAW. Reality proved otherwise. Only seven months after Title IX became law, the
AIAW was sued in the *Kellmeyer* case for its anti-scholarship policy. Meanwhile, the NCAA revised its decades-long "male-only" tradition to permit
females to compete in NCAA championships. Both the *Kellmeyer* lawsuit
and the NCAA's coed policy posed great threats to the stability of the
AIAW and to women's power and control over women's college sports.
Although the AIAW avoided an inevitable defeat in court by reluctantly
changing its scholarship policy, the threat from the NCAA's "takeover" of
women's intercollegiate athletics remained. Consequently, the AIAW
needed a lawyer to protect itself from future legal challenges and the
women's separate sphere from the men's invasion.[2] In spring 1974, the
AIAW acquired Margot Polivy of the Washington law firm Renouf,
McKenna and Polivy as its legal counsel.[3] "All of a sudden like a savior
coming in on a white horse," recalled Joanna Davenport, former president
of the National Association for Girls and Women in Sport, "Margot Polivy
. . . came at the right time for an organization that had never in a thousand
years thought they'll be sued."[4] The deal turned out to be the beginning of
a monogamous yet rugged relationship between the AIAW and the lawyer.
The financial costs of the legal service and Polivy's role in the AIAW soon
became major issues for the women's organization.

Early Challenges to Polivy's Power in the AIAW

Margot Polivy had a smooth entry into the AIAW. After seven months'
service on an hourly rate basis, the AIAW and Polivy's law firm reached a
retainer agreement for the fiscal year of 1975–76.[5] While Polivy's service
provided the AIAW a certain degree of legal security, it also had an immediate negative financial impact on the women's organization. In 1974–75,
the AIAW spent $26,087 for the legal services provided by Polivy, nearly a
quarter of its total income of $105,569.[6] Polivy, however, apparently did not
make a profit from her service to the AIAW. According to the AIAW executive secretary Kay Hutchcraft, the association was receiving far more legal
service than it was paying for, because Polivy's firm was operating "at a
minimum of 50% loss."[7] The extraordinary spending on Polivy's service
met little resistance except for a protest from Linda Estes of the University

of New Mexico.[8] The situation soon changed. Laurie Mabry of Illinois State University became the AIAW president in June 1975 and shortly afterward formed an AIAW Executive Board subcommittee to identify problem areas regarding the legal counsel. In early October, the subcommittee presented a report to the executive committee. Among various problems identified, it indicated that the AIAW had been using Polivy as the only legal advisor and was dependent on her opinion on "all matters." Consequently, Polivy had been acting beyond her role as the legal counsel but had been unable to complete all requested work. The report recommended that other legal advice be sought to best meet the needs of the AIAW and that attorneys understand their roles to be "advisory."[9]

Upon receipt of the subcommittee report, Mabry solicited responses from the AIAW Executive Committee. She stressed the significance of the subcommittee report in terms of future operation of the association regardless of any particular president or legal counsel. "I realize that Margot has interest in our association and our causes beyond mere service, which is good," she wrote. "However, I also believe, in this interest and in light of her own self-confidence in her own ability to see the only right way in all instances, she does attempt to force points well beyond her role as legal counsel."[10] Mabry specifically pointed out that the AIAW executive secretary Kay Hutchcraft's sole dependence on Margot in many instances was interfering with the association's normal decision-making process. This dependence and, subsequently, the AIAW's weakened bargaining position with Polivy had also imposed a threat to the association's financial well-being.[11]

The women leaders' lack of legal knowledge and dependence on Polivy resulted in a retainer agreement that would cover neither court action nor work with governmental agencies.[12] Mabry was not happy with the administrative and financial relationship between the AIAW and Polivy. "Legal counsel should be advisory in nature—rather than an individual that most singly [sic] are frightened to differ with," wrote Mabry. As far as legal costs were concerned, "[we should] put the liability on the legal firm rather than the association."[13] The AIAW president was determined to reduce Polivy's power, if not to completely release her service, when she pleaded for support from the executive committee. Responses to Mabry's request, however, reflected the conflict within the AIAW leadership over the employment of Polivy.

Within days of Mabry's request, Charlotte West of Southern Illinois University, then AIAW commissioner of four-year national championships, shared her opinion with Mabry. Referring to the hiring process of Polivy, West maintained that there would be a clearer understanding and acceptance of any contract "if the Executive Committee and/or Executive Board" were involved. It was obviously too late to change the deal. But the AIAW did not have to be dependent solely on Polivy. "I think that AIAW should explore the possibilities of utilizing more than one lawyer," West wrote, "[because] 'two heads are better than one.' "[14] West's major argument was that the AIAW should maintain a clear employer-employee relationship with Polivy, and "retain Margo [Polivy] in areas that we define." Pointing out Polivy's regular attendance at the executive board meetings while charging the AIAW at an hourly rate, West registered her opposition to the practice. "It probably is not necessary to pay a lawyer to sit through the entire Executive Board meeting, but I would always want [her] to be invited to attend, if interested."[15] To West, Polivy was not the boss but a legal expert paid to serve the organization. Such an assumption obviously was not shared by all AIAW leaders.

A response different from West's came from Leotus Morrison, the AIAW past president who had brought Polivy into the association in 1974. Instead of addressing the AIAW's relationship with Polivy, Morrison asserted that the real problems lay within the AIAW leadership itself: "The elected leaders of AIAW are frightened by a different style of leadership," implying that Polivy was a leader rather than a paid lawyer of the AIAW. She criticized the executive board for soliciting the opinions of Polivy "outside the realm of pure legal judgement" and for resenting the opinions that challenged "traditionally held 'conservative' thoughts and practices."[16] The AIAW Executive Board sounded like a company of political hypocrites who cared more about their personal interests than about equal opportunities of intercollegiate athletics for women. Morrison depicted this situation vividly: "Board members expect more from others than from themselves. They want others to meet deadlines but do not themselves; they expect others to refrain from personal situation observations and/or biases but set no positive example in their own behavior; they solicit agreeing opinions; they desire input to all decisions but are wary of making unpopular decisions."[17] Morrison probably felt the pressure of being accused of bringing Polivy into the AIAW and of allowing Polivy to define AIAW policies.

Thus, instead of addressing the issues, Morrison took the opportunity to defend herself by attacking the entire AIAW Executive Board.

If Morrison's reaction did not discourage the AIAW leadership's attempt to restrain or get rid of Polivy, it certainly encouraged Polivy to defend her position in the association. In a letter to Kay Hutchcraft, Polivy indicated that the present arrangement between her firm and the AIAW was "financially inequitable" and demanded a retainer pay raise to $60,000 in 1976–77, a 233 percent increase from $18,000 in 1975–76.[18] While Polivy may have favored working for the AIAW because of her philosophical beliefs, her dealings with the women's organization surely showed that, for her, political persuasions should not limit her financial reward. "I believe we will be better off," concluded Polivy, "if this matter can be resolved and we can all get on with effectuating the purposes of AIAW and meeting the not insignificant challenges ahead together."[19] To Polivy, one of these challenges was to maintain her own position as legal counsel of the AIAW.

Mabry Attempts to Tame Polivy

In November 1975, Nettie Morrison, AIAW Region 8 president and a member of the AIAW Executive Board, wrote Mabry seeking the executive committee's response to the subcommittee report on Polivy. Nettie Morrison, not to be confused with Leotus Morrison, stressed her displeasure with AIAW's priorities. "I must register a very strong complaint about the quality and quantity of services rendered to member institutions by AIAW," wrote Morrison. "Until such time as the necessary services to members can be improved to a more satisfactory level, I find it difficult to approve of continuing our current agreement with Renouf, McKenna and Polivy without considerable modifications."[20]

Nettie Morrison's concern for AIAW services to its membership was also echoed by Catherine Green, AIAW Region 9 representative from the University of Washington. "Something must be done in this next contract [with the legal counsel]," wrote Green, "particularly in light of our tight budget situation and pressing demands in other areas."[21] The tight budget and the discontent of the AIAW regional representatives became the impetus for a direct confrontation between Mabry and Polivy.

In December 1975, Mabry wrote Polivy, addressing mainly two issues:

the AIAW's relationship with the legal counsel and its limited funds for continued legal services. Mabry's concern for the funds seemed well based. By October 1975, only five months into the fiscal year of 1975–76, AIAW legal expenses had exceeded its budget.[22] While Polivy demanded a retainer fee increase from $7,500 to $17,000 for the remaining five months of 1975–76,[23] Mabry maintained that the AIAW would either continue to honor the original agreement or consider a flat-rate basis affordable by the association. She made it clear to Polivy: "To be honest with you, I will be indicating to the executive committee that I believe that the Association . . . should explore and study many possibilities. This recommendation is not to suggest that you and your firm should not be utilized for services, but to encourage the Association to be more informed and less dependent on any single counsel or firm." [24]

Although the monetary expense for legal services was a crucial issue facing the AIAW, Mabry was more concerned about the soundness of the AIAW's decision-making process under the heavy influence of Polivy. The AIAW president reviewed three incidents during the summer of 1975 when she and Polivy were in disagreement about Title IX and the NCAA.[25] The problem, however, was not the disagreement itself, but that Polivy's reaction was "not in the nature of one who was to offer advice as opposed to making the decision." [26] With the support of the subcommittee report, Mabry was determined to sort out the relationship between the AIAW and its legal advisor. She told Polivy that the elected leadership must determine its own policy; that the role of legal counsel must remain advisory; and that once an organizational position was determined, the counsel must support the position, at least publicly.[27]

A key point made in Mabry's suggestions revealed an intriguing aspect of the AIAW leadership. "The President has the right, even responsibility," Mabry stated, "to involve a larger group when she has the time and feels the consensus of opinion of any smaller group is not representing what she believes the total board may feel or the best interest of the Association membership." [28] There was at least one particular "smaller group" that fit the definition. According to Mabry, she often found herself in the minority when the executive committee met on the issues involving the legal counsel during her presidency. Ultimately, Mabry would call for the meeting of a larger group, usually the executive board, and get the support of the majority.[29]

Polivy Counters Mabry's Challenge

Unintimidated by Mabry's letter, Polivy met the challenge of the AIAW president with a prompt response. Instead of addressing the specific issues raised by Mabry, Polivy built her defense on the philosophy of the AIAW and her role as the "general counsel" for the association. "If we cannot ultimately come to agreement on basic principles," contended Polivy, "then we will not, no matter how hard we try, be able to come to agreement on the specific problems either."[30] The basic principle, as Polivy saw it, was the mutual understanding of her role in the AIAW as established at the time she was retained. It later became clear that the hiring of Polivy was without the approval of either the AIAW Executive Board or the Executive Committee; nor was the so-called "mutual understanding" ever established. "Such an assumption—even without hindsight—was foolish," admitted Polivy. Yet it seemed the AIAW was to blame for such a misunderstanding. Compared to the superior organizational structure of the NCAA, Polivy pointed out that the AIAW suffered from its practice of deriving policies from its elected officers, especially with the radical annual change of its presidents. She called the AIAW "hardly a hoary institution like NCAA with a traditional and mutually comfortable working relationship with its general counsel."[31]

The major point of Polivy's letter, however, appeared to be educating the AIAW president about the meaning of "general counsel." Unlike a lawyer hired to resolve particular problems, argued Polivy, the general counsel "is an integral part of the management team, [who] brings legal knowledge and perspective to bear on a continuing basis on all the business of the client." Although Mabry never mentioned the concept of "general counsel" in her letter, Polivy was clearly upset with Mabry's suggestion that the AIAW should use other legal services. She contended that "an organization that sends its general counsel out of the room except when discussing lawsuits has no general counsel" and that the consequence of such practice would be fatal to the AIAW's survival. "It is doubtful that any organization engaged in AIAW's range and type of activities or of its size exists or could long exist without a general counsel (whether or not it employs one or one hundred lawyers for facing particular legal problems),"[32] a strong argument indeed.

On the other hand, it could be equally destructive if the AIAW had more than one general counsel. Disputing Mabry's suggestion to use other legal services, Polivy wrote that "having more than one general counsel is about as workable as having two independent Presidents or two Executive Directors serving at the same time."[33] Sticking to her perception of the retainer agreement and her role as the AIAW's general counsel, Polivy offered a brilliant answer to Mabry's questions. "All the problems of money and of personality in the world are susceptible to resolution," wrote Polivy, "but if we cannot even agree that AIAW needs a general counsel there seems no point in trying to solve them. . . . AIAW cannot have a new general counsel every time it elects officers or it might as well have none; wisdom comes only with understanding and understanding comes only with time and knowledge about AIAW as well as the law."[34]

The fact that Polivy did not officially become the "general counsel" of the AIAW until 1980 added little to her credibility.[35] Regardless of Polivy's argument, it is doubtful that the AIAW could have survived until 1982 without a legal counsel. But it probably could have survived without the service of Polivy. However, the AIAW leadership as a unity never seriously attempted to secure a legal service that could meet the organization's legal and financial needs. By mid-1976, the AIAW had begun the pursuit of "winning-at-all-cost" in the court of law and put its fate in the hands of Margot Polivy.

Legal Service: The Number One Priority of the AIAW

Polivy's service was the most costly item on AIAW's expenses throughout her tenure with the association, second only to the payroll of its entire national office staff. From 1974 to 1982, the AIAW annually spent between 12.7 percent to 41.7 percent of its total income on legal service, averaging 21.5 percent (see table).[36] In comparison, the AIAW national championships—one of the main purposes for which the AIAW was created and existed—had only an 8 percent share of the same resource.[37]

It is doubtful that the AIAW leaders intentionally prioritized the need for legal guidance over other services. Nevertheless, their lack of knowledge in finance and legal matters apparently led to the AIAW's disproportionate spending. For the survival of the AIAW, this lack of knowledge was dangerous. Margot Polivy predicted it. History proved it.

The AIAW leaders' inexperience in financial matters can be seen in its

A Comparison of AIAW Expenses on Legal Services and Championships

Year	Championship Expense Amount	Percent	Legal Expense Amount	Percent	Total Income Amount
1974–75	$7,502	7.1	$26,087	24.7	$105,569
1975–76	$14,944	8.2	$43,647	23.9	$182,926
1976–77	$27,069	8.0	$57,121	16.8	$339,626
1977–78	$24,600	6.4	$75,415	19.5	$386,189
1978–79	$39,845	6.7	$75,000	12.7	$590,835
1979–80[a]	$64,091	7.7	$123,933	14.9	$830,618
1980–81	$73,204	8.9	$161,108	19.5	$824,112
1981–82	$64,183	9.4	$285,114[b]	41.7	$684,246
TOTAL	$315,437	8.0	$847,424	21.5	$3,944,120

Sources: AIAW Papers, "Analysis—Legal Services Expenditures, January 1976," box 309; "Financial Statements" (1974–1982), box 262; "Cash Disbursements, 1981–82," box 419; "Legal Counsel Cost Analysis," box 419; and Ann Uhlir, memo to Cindy Jackson, 13 May 1981, box 309.
[a] 13 months from 1 June 1979 to 30 June 1980.
[b] Information incomplete in AIAW Papers.

first retainer agreement with Polivy's firm for 1975–76. With a budget of $18,800 for legal services, Leotus Morrison and Kay Hutchcraft contracted Polivy with $18,000 for "general legal advice and counsel." It spelled out clearly that the agreement would not compensate for any work requiring the lawyers to be absent from their offices for four hours or more in any one day. Nor would it cover any services performed in connection with governmental agencies or judicial proceedings. Instead, a hourly rate of $50 would be charged to the AIAW for such services.[38] Not surprisingly, the $800 extra would be of little use. By the end of that fiscal year, the AIAW amassed a total of $43,647 in legal service fees, 232 percent of its original budget of $18,800 and 24 percent of the AIAW's income of $182,926. In comparison, the total expense on the AIAW national championships was only $14,944, a mere 8.2 percent of the same income.[39]

The huge legal cost was obviously hurting the AIAW's service to its membership. However, one may find it difficult to comprehend that what was damaging the AIAW was also handicapping Polivy's law firm. Despite a 205 percent increase in its retainer fee in 1976–77, a jump from $18,000 to

$55,000, the new agreement was, according to Polivy, by no means profitable to the firm. "It is anticipated that the retainer fee will fall significantly short of [the firm's] hourly rate for the same services," stated the contract. Nevertheless, the law firm "has agreed to the present arrangement in order to forward the aims of AIAW and because [it] understands that AIAW's present financial situation precludes any other arrangement." [40]

The AIAW's financial situation was not a sound one. By the end of the 1975–76 year, the association had spent $48,143 over its income of $182,926, incurring a 26 percent deficit. The extra legal cost contributed to more than half of the deficit. [41] It could be anticipated that, after the Title IX regulations became effective in July 1975, the AIAW's programs and need for legal services would grow drastically. For legal services, the growth not only materialized but was funded as well. For the AIAW programs, the growth was less visible. The AIAW championships actually suffered a setback in 1977–78. While Polivy's service cost the AIAW $75,415, 19.5 percent of its income of $386,189 and a 32 percent increase from $57,121 in 1976–77, the AIAW national championships consumed only $24,600, a 10 percent decrease from the $27,069 in 1976–77. [42]

The controversy over Polivy's role in the AIAW and the financial impact on the association of her service reached its peak in 1976. At its spring meeting of the AIAW Executive Board, Laurie Mabry led an attempt to get rid of Polivy as the AIAW's legal counsel. The attempt was narrowly defeated when the new AIAW president, N. Peg Burke, broke the tie of the board decision with a favorable vote to retain Polivy. [43] The board also nullified a proposed "management audit" that could have served as a safeguard for the AIAW's financial situation. Ironically, it was noted that "the Association could not financially afford such an audit." [44] After the 1976 board meeting, the challenge to Polivy's role in the AIAW as well as the highly disproportionate legal expense switched from the AIAW leadership to membership.

Linda Estes and the "Anti-Polivy Campaign"

The explosive growth of the AIAW's legal expense encountered a temporary break in 1978–79. With the signing of the annual retainer agreement in July 1978, Charlotte West became the first AIAW president to put a stop to the association's ever-growing expenditure on legal services. By the end of the fiscal year, the AIAW's legal expense was reduced to 12.7 percent of the organization's income, nearly a 7 percent drop from the previous year. The expense for AIAW's national championships, on the other hand, enjoyed a slight increase. For many, the closing gap between the two expenditures might have been a step in the right direction for the organization. For some, the AIAW's actual spending on the legal service was still a scandalous reality.

In September 1978, Region 7 of the AIAW unanimously passed a resolution concerning the issue of the AIAW legal counsel. It demanded that AIAW relieve itself of the services provided by Polivy's firm and secure its legal services from a firm that would serve in a legal advisory capacity and speak for AIAW "only when authorized to do so by the Executive Board of AIAW."[45] The contentions of Region 7 included: (1) The justification for paying 16 percent of AIAW's budget to Margot Polivy, and (2) Polivy's professional behavior and appearance while representing the AIAW at various official functions. One specific incident was Polivy's presence "under the influence of alcohol" during the ethics and eligibility meeting at the AIAW delegate assembly in January 1978.[46] The resolution, however, was defeated a month later at the AIAW Executive Board meeting. In addition, the board also concluded that "the contentions of Region 7 were found to be without substance."[47] Shortly afterward, Linda Estes, president-elect of Region 7, challenged the three AIAW presidents on the board's decision and the justification for locating 16 percent of the AIAW's budget for legal service as well as on the quality of Polivy's work.[48]

The AIAW presidents replied to Estes' request two weeks later. "Whereas the AIAW Executive Board would prefer not to spend so much of the budget for legal counsel," they wrote, "the members of the Board realize that it was a necessity to do so."[49] One justification for the spending was apparently drawn when they pointed out, erroneously, that the NCAA had "spent over a million dollars in one year for legal services."[50] Indicating the AIAW's intense involvement in legal matters, the presidents stated that the AIAW's not being taken to court was "partial evidence of the exceptional service" of Polivy and her law firm. Possibly the most convincing argument presented by the AIAW presidents was that the law firm only charged the AIAW a "reduced rate."[51] According to the recollection of Polivy, her firm had, throughout the years, charged the AIAW for approximately 30 percent of services provided, and that the actual income from the AIAW accounted for about 10 percent of the firm's annual revenue.[52]

Estes' patience expired before receiving the AIAW presidents' response. She continued her lobby against Polivy's service by sending a letter to the AIAW voting representatives. To the dismay of the AIAW presidents, Estes enclosed in her letter a copy of the retainer agreement between the AIAW and Polivy's firm. While indicating that the $75,000 retainer fee was more than most college presidents' salaries, Estes focused her contention on the justification for the 16 percent of AIAW's budget paid to the legal counsel.[53] The distribution of the retainer agreement apparently angered the AIAW leaders, and Estes was questioned for the ethics of her lobbying effort. "I am tremendously disappointed in the unethical action of circulating a copy of the r[e]tainer agreement," wrote Judith Holland, "and would be interested in learning the process by which you obtained [the copy] which even I, as Past-President, do not possess."[54] Bonnie Slatton, acting executive director of the AIAW, shared the view of Holland. The elaboration on her concern, however, displayed a rather intriguing aspect of the issue. "Although AIAW contracts are made available to any member with a legitimate interest," Slatton wrote, "it is totally inappropriate and unethical to distribute them in a wholesale manner."[55] Opposite to what it may have meant to accomplish, Slatton's letter only made Estes feel that her pursuit was completely justified. "I think it is amazing how upset you people are over the membership having a document which they have every right to have," Estes wrote Slatton, "since they are paying the bills, including your salary!" Challenging Slatton's definition of "legitimate interest" and who should decide what was "legitimate," Estes continued: "The fact is that the membership has a right to that information and if you consider it 'totally inappropriate' and 'unethical' to distribute such information to them, then our national office is even worse off than I originally suspected. I think there was a guy by the name of Richard Nixon who felt the same way about the public's right to know."[56]

According, the AIAW president-elect, Carole Mushier, had written Estes charging there were "errors and misrepresentations" in Estes' letter and accusing her of making inflammatory statements to incite those who were uninformed. To these accusations, Estes retorted: "It would be very difficult to misrepresent something when the document to which I referred was included in order for the membership to draw their own conclusions." She proudly claimed that, because of her action, the AIAW members were now better informed of their business than they had ever been.[57] In this internal conflict of the AIAW, the central figure was Margot Polivy, and she was not to remain silent.

Polivy Defeats "Estes and Company"

In late November 1978, Polivy sent Bonnie Slatton a six-page letter unveiling her side of the story and strong personal feelings regarding the issue. Addressing the campaign against her led by Linda Estes and others, Polivy expressed her "shock" that the relationship between the AIAW and her firm had become "the subject of common gossip." However, she quickly pointed out that "while we find this entire spectacle . . . personally distasteful, the real damage is being borne by AIAW as an organization [because] a few destructive and hostile individuals are creating an atmosphere of dissension and discord."[58] Polivy maintained that the Estes campaign had become so detrimental to the AIAW that the current perception at the U.S. Department of Health, Education, and Welfare with respect to the implementation of Title IX was that the women in the AIAW were deeply divided. A divided AIAW certainly would not help to gain support from HEW, the federal agency responsible for implementing Title IX. Yet the external effect of the Estes campaign was only of minor significance. The real damage to the AIAW was internal. Polivy illustrated that clearly. "The shrill nature of the charges, apparently designed to appeal to every possible prejudice and ignorance, will inevitably make those who do not subscribe to Linda's views self conscious about seeking advice from which they previously [benefited] without hesitation. . . . If this kind of indirect 'fall-out' is not affirmatively resisted, the effects of the vendetta launched by Linda Estes and Company will, I believe, be organizationally suicidal."[59] The seriousness of the matter, as Polivy believed, lay in that it was more than a personal issue. She pointed out that the underlying motivations of the Estes campaign represented "a political and ideological disagreement as to: whether AIAW should remain a separate organization dedicated to furthering women's intercollegiate athletic programs or be subjugated or replaced by an existing men's organization."[60]

Yet Polivy also knew that as a practical matter money was indispensable to her and her firm, and she would not let the attack on them pass easily. "We are all of us sick and tired of being accused of dishonorable motivations," Polivy wrote. "In the four years that we have represented AIAW, we have been paid for only 50% of the time devoted to AIAW." The poor economic situation of the women's organization was apparently no secret to Polivy. "AIAW has not been a financially desirable client and the time and effort devoted to AIAW have had a substantial and deleterious effect upon the firm's economic health." Yet the law firm continued its service to the AIAW. According to Polivy: "We have, within limits, been willing to absorb this nondeductible loss because we believe both that women's sport is pivotal to women's efforts for equality and that non-exploitative governance of intercollegiate athletics can be effective and viable." She made it clear, however, that only money, not ideology, could compensate any financial loss. "Nevertheless," Polivy continued, "as AIAW's resources grow, we believe that the percentage of loss that this firm suffers should diminish."[61]

While Estes and her supporters thought it outrageous for the AIAW to pay Polivy's firm such a large amount of money for legal service, the contested lawyer saw it quite differently. "I find it somewhat ironic that such a great hoopla is being made over the 14 percent of AIAW's budget allocated to legal services,"[62] Polivy stated. If the NCAA were by no means a desirable model for the women's athletics, the men's organization, in Polivy's opinion, surely had some merits for the women to look up to. "The $1 million recently paid by the NCAA [for legal services] represents about 20 percent of that organization's budget—a disparity which becomes enormous," argued Polivy, considering the similar legal needs of the two organizations. The fact that the NCAA actually used less than 4 percent of its income on legal expenses did not add to Polivy's credibility.[63]

Finally, Polivy responded to Estes' charges of drunkenness when representing the AIAW during an executive board meeting. "We have no intention of permitting either our personal or our professional reputations to become the object of cheap shots and misplaced apologies," Polivy wrote. "We cannot and will not tolerate a situation in which we are neither vindicated nor allowed a public forum in which to respond." Polivy suggested that "if the pernicious effects of the Estes campaign are to be eradicated, the retraction must be at least as public as the accusations."[64]

The AIAW Executive Board did not openly punish the Estes campaign.

It did, however, squelch the petition. By simply using a parliamentary procedure—"objection to consideration"—the AIAW leaders successfully muffled the dissenting voice of Region 7.[65] Placed at the bottom of the agenda, the petition against the service of Polivy's law firm was never voted on after time expired for the scheduled AIAW delegate assembly.[66] Three weeks later, Arlene Gorton, associate athletic director at Brown University, challenged the AIAW leadership's "manipulative procedure" used in muffling the "Estes petition." "I am most upset that, for the first time at any Delegate Assembly, we refused a delegate the opportunity to be heard," wrote Gorton. "The motion, made in the closing seconds of the meeting, was a very dangerous and disappointing precedent to establish. I am truly SHOCKED that we, as a Delegate Assembly, would deny freedom of speech to any member, regardless of how odious her point of view."[67] The supposedly democratically-run women's organization was testing the extent of that democracy with Estes and Region 7.

The Estes petition was the first and last major membership protest against the AIAW leadership's decision on legal services. Its failure probably symbolized the strengthened position of Polivy as a leader rather than an advisor to the association, and the AIAW leaders had tarnished the educational model through their own act of hypocrisy. Clearly, their devotion to membership service was only secondary to their commitment to legal security through Polivy's service and to their own power and control of college women's athletics.

The Financial Hemorrhage of the AIAW

The year 1979–80 saw another dramatic increase in AIAW's legal expense. The retainer fee for Polivy's firm rose from $75,000 to $100,000, plus "18% of all monies which become payable to AIAW during the retainer year in excess of six hundred seven thousand dollars."[68] The contract clause may not have been an unusual arrangement, considering the changed philosophical commitment of the organization. By 1979, the AIAW had endorsed the commercialization of women's intercollegiate athletics and reduced its commitment to the educational model. Its revenues from sponsorship were becoming a reality. Foreseeing ever-growing legal needs, the AIAW in 1980 established a legal fund of $10,000 in addition to the $130,000 budget for Polivy's service in 1980–81. By the end of the fiscal year, however, the association found itself paying Polivy more than $160,000, nearly 20 percent of the organization's total income. In contrast, the AIAW spent only $73,203 for its national championships.[69]

The AIAW's previous legal expenses became almost insignificant compared to what the association actually spent in 1981–82. With an increased retainer fee and a lawsuit against the NCAA, the AIAW paid Polivy's firm at least $285,000, nearly 42 percent of the AIAW's income, while the expense for AIAW national championships was only $64,182.[70] According to Polivy, her law firm provided a total of 4,746 hours of service to the AIAW during 1981–82.[71] One may question whether this information was trustworthy. The 4,746-hour service can be translated into a year's labor of fifty-two weeks, with an average of 18.25 hours per day's work without holidays. That is equivalent to more than two full-time employees' work for twelve months without vacation time.[72] In the month of April 1982, the firm spent a total of 621.25 hours working for the AIAW. This would have meant that Polivy, very likely with the help of some other lawyer(s), devoted an average of 28.24 hours per day working for the AIAW for each and every twenty-two weekdays of the month.[73] Also according to Polivy's tabulation, the monthly $11,000 retainer fee in December 1981 was paid for only fifteen hours of service, making the hourly rate $733.33, a new high.[74]

In the eight years Margot Polivy served as the AIAW's legal counsel, the women's organization paid Polivy's law firm nearly $850,000, more than 21 percent of the AIAW's total income. The AIAW national championships, in comparison, consumed less than $316,000, merely 8 percent of the same assets. When the AIAW ceased operation in June 1982, it still possessed $83,000. This money, however, invested in the American Security Bank in Washington, D.C., and later added mainly to Polivy's payroll, would not help the AIAW win its antitrust lawsuit against the NCAA, nor would it save the AIAW from its eventual demise.

From NCAA "Governance Plan" to the End of AIAW Operation

> The fundamental issue at stake in the NCAA's unilateral decision to initiate women's championships is whether those directly involved in women's athletic programs have the right (as did those involved in men's athletics) to develop an intercollegiate athletic program and system of governance designed to meet the interests and abilities of women student-athletes, or whether a system designed to serve men's athletic programs should be forcibly imposed upon women.
>
> —Christine H. B. Grant, AIAW President (1980)

THE 1979 NCAA CONVENTION defeated a proposal to establish championships for women among the NCAA Division III member institutions.[1] The defeat, however, did not release the NCAA from its legal obligation to provide programs for both men and women, as many believed. The absence of a NCAA women's program put those NCAA member institutions in jeopardy who chose not to belong to any other organizations. On the other hand, schools that belonged to both the NCAA and the AIAW were faced with the difficulty of administering two sets of athletic rules and regulations.[2] While the women in the AIAW lobbied against the NCAA proposal and applauded its defeat at the NCAA convention, the men in the NCAA who believed in the proposal were not necessarily discouraged. They seemed to become more determined and sophisticated in their pursuit to establish a women's program within the NCAA.

The Formation of the NCAA "Governance Committee"

The sophistication of the NCAA leadership can be seen in its handling of the issue of Title IX compliance. Greatly concerned about the implementation of the law and its financial implications, the NCAA invited the AIAW to a joint committee meeting to discuss women's participation in the governance of the NCAA. The AIAW rejected the invitation, citing that "since NCAA had not accepted AIAW's invitation to meet on the subject, it would be inappropriate for the Committee to do so at this time."[3] The AIAW's rejection did not hinder the agenda of the NCAA, for the invitation had apparently served its purpose as a gesture of "goodwill."

One may argue that Title IX did not require the NCAA to offer programs to women. However, it was not clear what action the court might take. It was also true that the statute did not prevent the men's organization from offering such programs. Many people, both men and women, in collegiate athletics were often led to believe that Title IX was more helpful than damaging to the AIAW. This was simply not true. One may clear up this confusion with the help of a correspondence between Hugh McFadden, president of the University of Wyoming, and AIAW president Charlotte West in April 1979.

Responding to West's lobby against the National Association of Intercollegiate Athletics's initiative to establish a women's program, McFadden took the opportunity to address the issue of Title IX and governance of intercollegiate athletics in general. He stressed that the evolution of Title IX and principles of economy would force an institution to reassess its memberships in national organizations. "While you support cooperation with other 'governing bodies,' " McFadden wrote, "you seem to ignore the fact that governance of intercollegiate athletics is an institutional responsibility for decision making."[4] The institution had to make a choice, argued McFadden, especially when there were no meaningful results from the cooperative effort between the AIAW and the NCAA, and when student-athletes, male or female, were denied equal opportunities because of the conflicting rules of the two organizations. He elaborated:

> If [such] a situation arises on campus, . . .the University will be compelled to establish a single institutional rule. Given the dependence upon intercollegiate athletic income from the men's sports of football and basketball,

there will be little choice as to the rule selected. This could cause withdrawal from AIAW participation and be unfair to women's competitive opportunities for championships. To provide such an opportunity, I would have to urge the sponsorship of women's championships by the WAC Conference and the NCAA.[5]

Since it would be an unwise choice to subscribe to an independent women's or men's program, McFadden believed that schools had to undertake a more positive approach to "force a single association of institutions that provides equal opportunities for men and women."[6] He maintained that the identity of the governing body of intercollegiate athletics should be a sex-neutral factor for an institution's decision making. More importantly, for college presidents like him, it was "a matter of great concern in terms of avoiding duplication of necessary administrative requirements and staffing costs."[7]

Probably not by coincidence, McFadden's view was also shared by a number of other educators including Norman C. Crawford Jr., president of Salisbury State University in Maryland. In July 1979, Crawford wrote to four other university presidents who at the time all served on the AIAW chief executive officers advisory council.[8] Based on his recent conversations with many college presidents and athletic directors, Crawford told his colleagues that the AIAW "probably cannot survive another year." He admitted that it was a very serious statement, but "if my conclusions are valid," contended Crawford, "it suggests that we may need to redirect our efforts, from trying to help AIAW survive to encouraging its graceful consolidation with NCAA or NAIA."[9]

Crawford supported his statement with a few arguments. First, almost all college presidents backed the principle of nondiscrimination based on sex and felt uncomfortable with the different sets of rules for men's and women's intercollegiate athletics. Second, there was an inability on the part of the AIAW to compromise any of its rules because of an apparent division within the AIAW leadership.[10] Third, under the pressure of Title IX, institutions would no longer have any incentive to continue membership in the AIAW as soon as the NCAA or the NAIA approved the sponsorship of women's championships. Finally, many presidents who in 1979 opposed the NCAA proposal to initiate women's championships for Division III members had changed their positions. Crawford's concluding statement would soon be proven insightful, if not prophetic. "It seems likely that one or both of the men's athletic governing groups, made up of *institutional* members, is likely to initiate the sponsorship of championships for women within the next year," he wrote. "Assuming that institutions belonging to an athletic governance group sponsoring championships for both men and women are likely to resign membership in AIAW, I see no other consequence but the demise of AIAW through erosion."[11] Crawford suggested that they should either individually or collectively advise the AIAW to face the reality and act accordingly for the best interest of women athletes. That "best interest" apparently could not be met by the operation of a sex-separate AIAW, as Crawford's letter implied. What the presidents could do to protect that "best interest," recommended Crawford, was to advocate significant representation of women athletic directors in their organizational governance and particularly in the conduct of women's championships.[12]

Crawford's correspondence was significant because it reflected a more favorable climate for the NCAA to move into the governance of women's intercollegiate athletics. The NCAA Committee on Women's Intercollegiate Athletics met in June 1979 and discussed the impact of Title IX, the relationship between the NCAA and the AIAW, and the sponsorship of women's championships by the NCAA.[13] It recommended that women be included in the NCAA Council, the Executive Committee, and other decision-making organs of the organization.[14]

In October, the AIAW Committee on Men's Athletics and its NCAA counterpart met to examine the relationship between the AIAW and the NCAA. The meeting suggested that the AIAW and the NCAA conduct, respectively, in-depth studies of five alternate governance structures for intercollegiate athletics.[15] While the participants seemed to have enjoyed an open and friendly discourse, they nevertheless felt frustrated by the fact that neither of the committees was empowered to do anything "more definitive or constructive than discuss the problems."[16]

Despite its lack of authority, the joint committee meeting served an extremely useful purpose for the NCAA leadership. In late October, the NCAA Council authorized the appointment of a special committee on NCAA governance, organization, and services—the "Governance Committee." Terming its action a response to the outcome of the joint committee meeting, the council directed the special committee to examine and make recommendations regarding "the accommodation of women's interests within the NCAA and the development of programs and services for women's intercollegiate athletics."[17] After years of failed attempts, the formation of the Governance Committee became the first major step in the NCAA's eventual success in entering the governance of intercollegiate athletics for women.

A Five-Year Moratorium

The recommendations of the joint AIAW-NCAA committee meeting received a very different response from the AIAW leadership. Alarmed by the NCAA's renewed interest in women's athletics, the AIAW Executive Board voted to stop potential NCAA initiatives of programs for women. The resolution called for a five-year moratorium on any efforts to devise or explore alternative governance structures for intercollegiate athletics. It particularly called upon the NCAA and the NAIA to cease any efforts to initiate championship programs for women. It also urged AIAW member institutions to "dedicate themselves to the encouragement and perpetuation of assuming equality of opportunity for women in the administration and leadership of athletic programs servicing women," without providing any specific guidelines.[18]

In November, AIAW president Carole Mushier informed NCAA president William Flynn of the moratorium, included in the 1980 AIAW delegate assembly agenda. On behalf of the AIAW Executive Board, Mushier also requested the NCAA Council to support the resolution and place it on the NCAA agenda for endorsement by the NCAA membership. "A five year cooperative mor[a]torium," argued Mushier, "would allow all organizations to expend their efforts where they best belong—to enhance the programs for student-athletes."[19]

Three weeks later, after telephone conversation with Mushier, Flynn reiterated his position in writing that the NCAA leadership did not have the authority to take part in the proposed moratorium. Referring to the upcoming 1980 NCAA convention, Flynn acknowledged the proposals to conduct championships for women in Division II and III member institutions of the NCAA. However, he indicated that the NCAA Council would likely take no action either to support or oppose the motion but would allow the members to make their own judgment.[20] Flynn apparently was well versed in organizational politics and tried not to give the impression that the NCAA leadership had anything to do with the membership's initiatives of women's program.

In early December 1979, the U.S. Department of Health, Education, and Welfare issued the final Title IX Policy Interpretation for intercollegiate athletics. As HEW secretary Patricia Harris indicated, the new interpretation gave colleges and universities "maximum flexibility in developing and maintaining their athletic programs" as long as they were free from sex discrimination.[21] While the new policy interpretation was good news for administrators who needed clearer guidance for Title IX compliance, it did not favor the sex-separatist regulations of the AIAW. The policy's emphasis on institutional flexibility for compliance almost paralleled the NCAA's position of letting colleges and universities choose a single governing organization—the easiest way for compliance. At least, the new interpretation would not discourage or prevent the NCAA from entering the governance of women's intercollegiate athletics.

Unable to stop the NCAA's pursuit of the women's program, AIAW president Mushier expressed her view to the AIAW voting representatives. "It is with disappointment that I must advise you of the fact that NCAA Division II and III institutions have submitted legislation to the 1980 NCAA Convention to begin NCAA women's championships."[22] Mushier must have felt helpless in dealing with the NCAA initiatives, because the action "has not been brought by the NCAA Council but has been placed on the agenda in a manner similar to AIAW petitioned motions." Regardless of the nature of the NCAA initiatives, the interest at stake was the AIAW's exclusive power and control over women's intercollegiate athletics. To protect that power and control, Mushier urged the AIAW members to lobby their institutions' presidents and NCAA representatives to vote against the proposals at the NCAA convention. Her plea sounded extremely weak when she tried to analyze the financial impact on the NCAA should its women's championships become reality. As if she truly cared about the welfare of men's athletics, Mushier wrote: "Are the members of NCAA willing to decrease the amount of funding for their men's teams to championships in order to accommodate women's teams?"[23]

Common sense must have prevailed in the AIAW leadership over such weak actions as Mushier's to keep AIAW member institutions from leaving the women's organization. The AIAW soon announced a number of alternative actions to be voted upon at the 1980 AIAW delegate assembly. While it reaffirmed the AIAW's support of Title IX regulations and the five-year moratorium, the news release revealed proposals aimed at modifying the fundamental policies of the AIAW. They were to change the AIAW's rules on institutional control, recruitment, eligibility, transfer students, financial aid, and commercial sponsorship. Accordingly, institutions would be allowed to have rules that were more restrictive, but not less restrictive than those of the AIAW. The news release also conspicuously admitted that the change in the AIAW's rules on institutional control would be "a major departure from AIAW philosophy" that favored the educational model.[24]

Such a "departure," however, seemed to have become a general trend in the AIAW's conduct. With the final Title IX regulations giving more flexibility to institutions for compliance, many college presidents indicated their preference for a single governing body. Under these circumstances, it was not surprising that the AIAW accelerated its departure from the educational model to that of "big-time" college athletics.[25] The AIAW news release was apparently meant to appeal to the colleges and universities against the NCAA proposals to sponsor women's championships. The current legal climate and the AIAW's financial situation, however, would hinder such an appeal.

NAIA and NCAA Championships for Women

In order to prevent the NCAA from entering women's intercollegiate athletics, the AIAW, on the eve of the NCAA convention, made an overt gesture to colleges and universities of its intention to move closer to the commercial model of men's athletics. One of the proposals even went so far as to "modify AIAW's commercial sponsorship policy to permit sponsorship by beer companies."[26] While endorsing such sponsorship was then no longer inconsistent with the AIAW's philosophy, the measure, publicly pronounced prior to the NCAA convention, was a sign of the desperate AIAW's trying to attract financial sponsors and retain its own members. It was a timely response to the move within the NCAA. Only a week before the AIAW news release, the NCAA Governance Committee met and discussed women's athletics. The most noticeable item on its agenda was whether women should receive the same championship transportation and per diem expense as afforded men.[27] The AIAW leaders' fear of the

NCAA's intent to "take over" women's athletics through "lucrative" financial incentives was well founded.

In late December 1979, AIAW president Carole Mushier wrote all presidents of institutions that held memberships in both the AIAW and the NCAA, seeking their support to defeat the NCAA proposals on women's championships. She offered three reasons for her action. First, the NCAA proposals would diminish rather than increase the opportunities for women because of different rules between the NCAA and the AIAW and because of possible schedule conflict. Second, the NCAA's initiatives were likely to cause an increase in the NCAA membership dues, thus resulting in added financial burdens on its member institutions. Finally, the educational model of the AIAW could also be high quality and competitive and "may well serve as the model for all intercollegiate athletic organizations in the future."[28] Mushier did not explain how the AIAW could finance its highly competitive and quality athletics without having its member institutions paying increased dues.

As the year came to an end, the NCAA Governance Committee issued a "Preliminary Report" that focused on the accommodation of women within the NCAA structure. It confirmed that such an accommodation was economically and administratively feasible. Most significantly, it addressed two seemingly related but separate issues. One was equal opportunities for women to participate in intercollegiate athletics; the other was the representation of women in the governance of the NCAA.[29] Apparently, equal opportunities for male and female student-athletes in all NCAA programs and services would satisfy the Title IX regulations; and limited women representation in the NCAA hierarchy should make peace with a general public more and more aware of the issue of equality, but not enough to threaten the ultimate control by men. If the report had no other merits at all, it would at least prove to many undecided NCAA members that the NCAA "Governance Plan" was not as detrimental to its member institutions as portrayed by the AIAW.

Two days before the 1980 NCAA convention, the AIAW leadership launched its last-minute campaign to block the NCAA and the NAIA initiatives to establish women's programs. The AIAW Executive Board called upon the NCAA representatives to vote against the proposals by the NCAA Divisions II and III member institutions. It also asked the NAIA Committee on Women's Athletics to withdraw its similar proposal.[30] Repeating its earlier call for a five-year moratorium, the AIAW leaders also passed a resolution that women's athletic programs and the principle of equal opportunity would be best served by retaining a separate organization committed to women's collegiate athletics.[31] The appeal of the AIAW did not win the support of the NCAA Council. At its meeting prior to the 1980 NCAA convention, the council discussed the resolution of the AIAW Executive Board and determined that "the AIAW action represents one organization attempting to dictate proper decisions of another organization."[32]

Times certainly had changed. Eight years before, when the NCAA leadership made overtures to include women in its programs, it met strong resistance from the NCAA membership. Edward Steitz of Springfield College, who strongly opposed the NCAA leadership's position in 1972, had reversed his stance by 1980. Representing Springfield College as one of the sponsors for the NCAA Division II women's championships, Steitz argued that the NCAA had not only moral and legal obligations to sponsor programs for women but the financial strength to do so.[33] The ideological change of Steitz and others like him epitomized a new era in the history of women's intercollegiate athletics. The 1980 NCAA convention established five Division II and III women's championships to commence in 1981.[34] Although Division I schools did not take similar action, the establishment of "big-time" women's championships within the NCAA was only a question of time.

AIAW Attains Legal and Financial Independence

Two events that took place in 1979 profoundly impacted the growth of the AIAW. In June, the AIAW formally separated from its parent organization—the American Association for Health, Physical Education, and Recreation/National Association for Girls and Women in Sport—and became an independent legal entity. In August, the NBC television network purchased television rights to the AIAW Division I and open national championships, symbolizing a promising step in the AIAW's financial stability and its pursuit of much-needed commercial dollars.[35]

The independence had both a positive and a negative implication for the association. Legally, the AIAW was freer to pursue its destiny without any direct interference from its former parent organizations. Such a freedom, however, was accompanied by the absence of future assistance and protection previously afforded by the AAHPER. Financially, the AIAW became the sole beneficiary of its own revenues, but there was no guarantee of financial success. Should failure strike, the AIAW must face financial hardship without having the AAHPER absorb its deficit as in the past.

In the fall of 1979, however, a financial failure seemed to be the last thing in the minds of the AIAW leaders. Their success in reaching an agreement with NBC apparently prompted optimism within the AIAW about its commercial potential.[36] Speaking of the AIAW's financial success, AIAW president Carole Mushier told the 1980 AIAW delegate assembly to applaud the one-million-dollar television income and "greater financial capability in our institutional programs."[37] But Mushier did not forget to address the women's commitment to the educational model. If she was a bit confused about the AIAW philosophy, her audience must have been too. "The Big Business model is attractive to many—what is the price?" asked Mushier. "Are we willing to pay? Do we still have the courage to dare to be different? . . . I have said before, and will repeat now, that recognition, money and winning are not incompatible with an educational model of athletics."[38] Referring to Charles Corbin's book *The Athletic Snowball*, which characterized men's "big-time" athletics as a snowball heading toward the cliff, Mushier made an analogy that sounded profound but difficult to comprehend.

> "The only noticeable change other than the increased danger of the snowball falling off the cliff was the small friendly snowball slowly being pushed down an adjacent hill by the Women's Snowball Team" [Mushier quoted from the book]. I suggest that this book written in 1977 is already out of date. The women's athletic snowball is on the edge of its own cliff— the snowball and the cliff are [remarkably] similar to that of the men's but they have the distinction of having been created solely by women.[39]

Being the departing president, Mushier did not have to worry about explaining what she really meant in her speech. Such a luxury was not afforded her successor.

1980: Not a "Year of Roses" for the AIAW

Unlike her immediate predecessor, Christine H. B. Grant, the ninth president of the AIAW, painted a more realistic picture of the association at her inaugural speech to the AIAW delegate assembly. "In December, I had also hoped that 1980 would be our year of roses," said Grant. "But through the action of the NCAA, we have been denied that privilege. This apparently will *not* be the year of the roses."[40] With both the NAIA and the NCAA determined to "invade" women's athletics, Grant knew what the AIAW was facing. Yet as the new president, she also knew her duty to keep the organization running and to boost the morale of its members. "As an organization we are unbelievably strong," declared Grant. "But within *this* organization, I believe we have little cause to warrant an attitude of distrust and the growth of such an attitude would be destructive to our Association. We will succeed if we are together."[41]

The problem was that, by 1980, a united AIAW was only wishful thinking. There were not only members who disagreed with the AIAW leadership on its approach to women's athletics, but also a group of "separatists" who simply formed their own organization. "There was a power war between the two groups," said Karen Fey, associate athletics director at New Mexico State University. One was led by Christine Grant to seek an "alternative model" for women's athletics; the other, including Linda Estes, believed women deserved the same opportunities that were afforded men. An outcome of this power war was the creation of the Council of Collegiate Women Athletic Administrators.[42]

The CCWAA was formed by twelve women athletic directors in 1979, and it soon led women into the NCAA structure.[43] Most of the CCWAA members were known as "the west coast women," a term used unofficially for those who disagreed with the AIAW leadership's approach to women's intercollegiate athletics. The CCWAA, as Karen Fey stated, was more interested in "what was best for women's programs" than in fighting for the AIAW's exclusive control of women's programs.[44]

The AIAW and the CCWAA had different views on how to obtain what was the best for women student-athletes. By the early 1980s, the AIAW leadership apparently had neglected its primary commitment to serve women student-athletes. Instead, the AIAW exhausted itself in the political battles against the NCAA in both direct confrontations and through disputes over Title IX regulations. "So on both battles," recollected Christine Grant, "90 percent of our energies went on those two causes and that only left 10 percent of the energies to do the things that should have been our primary considerations."[45]

The CCWAA, on the other hand, divorced itself from the AIAW philosophy that women's athletics must be controlled by women. They did not see the NCAA as all evil simply because it was controlled by men. The CCWAA embraced the NCAA initiative because, they believed, it provided a better alternative for women's intercollegiate athletics. The 1982 court testimony of former AIAW president Judith Holland on the *AIAW v. NCAA* lawsuit shed light on the philosophical split within the AIAW. A substantial number of schools wanted to participate in "alternative" championships "because of dissatisfaction with the AIAW as a governance organization," wrote Holland. "The AIAW does not devote its financial and other resources to national championships. This lack of attention directly and adversely affects women student-athletes." In comparison, "the NCAA championships are of superior quality to AIAW championships." [46] Not surprisingly, Holland's position got herself in direct confrontation with the AIAW leadership, and she was listed as a "co-conspirator" when the AIAW sued the NCAA for conspiring the "taking over" of women's intercollegiate athletics.

The situation of the AIAW deteriorated quickly after the 1980 NCAA Convention. In February, the AIAW urged members of the presidents' committee of the American Council on Education to instruct their representatives to take "appropriate action to defeat/rescind" proposals for women's championships by the NAIA and the NCAA. [47] The AIAW claimed that it had created a viable alternative for intercollegiate athletics but that unfortunately there was a lack of support from the public, including university presidents. The AIAW admitted that it needed to "clearly articulate the structure and basic characteristics of its alternative approach." It nevertheless complained that its lack of recognition was that "the revolutionary [sic] conditions experienced by those in women's athletics have simply not created a conducive environment for fair consideration of options." The situation was so bad, asserted the women, that they had been forced to direct their effort and energy to "a higher goal—SURVIVAL." [48]

While the AIAW was trying to survive, the NCAA proceeded quite smoothly with its women's program. In January and June, the NCAA Governance Committee twice reported its progress and solicited comments from the NCAA membership. [49] Between July and September, the NCAA held regional meetings to brief and discuss the work of the Governance Committee. These events attracted hundreds of institutional representatives, including AIAW members, who spoke against the NCAA plan. [50] In

November, the NCAA Council adopted the final version of the NCAA "Governance Plan" and recommended its presentation at the 1981 NCAA convention.[51]

In the meantime, the AIAW continued to lobby for the support of AIAW members and other organizations in its "battle for survival against the NCAA."[52] In a letter to Sarah Harder, the co-chair of the National Women's Conference Committee, AIAW president Grant wrote that "those in women's athletics will be most appreciative of any assistance you can give us." Grant told Harder that the AIAW's goal was to convince college and university presidents to instruct their representatives to vote against any proposals to implement women's championships or govern women's programs at the 1981 NCAA convention. "Right now, we believe the CEOs will vote in favor of this blatant take-over of women. We have four months to convince them to adopt the opposite stance."[53] Grant apparently did not want her reader to neglect the seriousness of the matter. "As I am sure you realize, this is a women's issue rather than an athletic issue," she continued. "It is our hope that women generally will rally to our plea for help, since it is unlikely that we can win this David-Goliath battle entirely on our own."[54] Grant, by her statement, had admitted that the sex-separate route pursued by the AIAW and the power and control over women's intercollegiate athletics were more important than service to women student-athletes.

In contrast to her letter to Harder, the AIAW president delivered a quite different message to the AIAW constituents in the fall of 1980. "As we begin a new academic year," stated Grant, "the AIAW is alive, well and vital!" By highlighting the association's growth in regard to its membership, structure, publicity, and national recognition, she concluded that the "roots and beginning development of a sound new model of athletic governance are unquestionably evident." She did admit, however, "the growing pain" the AIAW had experienced in the previous ten years and predicted that "the future will be no less problematic than our past."[55] Grant probably did not expect that the problems would come so soon and be so overwhelming.

Impact on AIAW of NCAA Entry into Women's Athletics

When the annual NCAA convention opened in Miami in January 1981, there was hardly any doubt that the future of women's intercollegiate athletics was at a crossroad. Few, however, were absolutely sure in which direction history was turning. Despite an intense AIAW campaign, the NCAA membership rejected the proposals to rescind or delay the NCAA Division II and III women's championships. After lengthy debate and struggle on parliamentary procedures, the membership also voted to establish Division I championships for women in nine sports, making a total of twenty-nine NCAA divisional and open championships for women, all to commence in 1981–82.[56]

Under separate motions, the NCAA convention also adopted the proposals to implement an overall governance plan for women's athletics. The plan not only provided for a minimum representation of women in major NCAA decision-making organs but also for a championship reimbursement equitable for both male and female individuals and teams. In addition, it outlined a four-year transition period during which an institution could apply either the NCAA rules or any other recognized rules for women while common rules for male and female athletes were being devised.[57]

Contrary to the rhetoric of its opponents, the "Governance Plan" did not require NCAA member institutions to participate in the NCAA women's championships. Schools could remain free to maintain membership in the AIAW or any other governance organizations for women, and they could participate in the championships of these organizations as long as they kept their men's programs in the NCAA.[58]

The impact on the AIAW of the NCAA entry into women's athletics was immediate and substantial. It became clear that the AIAW would have difficulty surviving even before the NCAA commenced its first women's championships in November 1981.[59] In 1981–82, the AIAW lost 213 of its 961 institutional members, mainly to the NCAA and the NAIA, and consequently $124,000 in membership dues, a 15 percent decrease in income compared to the previous year.[60] The combined loss of members and dues was a key factor in determining the future of the AIAW. Unlike the NCAA, whose membership dues counted for less than 1 percent of the organization's revenue, the AIAW basically lived on its dues. From 1974 to 1982, membership fees contributed more than 60 percent of the AIAW's total income of $3,944,000. Even in 1980–81 with its peak television rights revenue of $223,000, the $372,792 membership income was still the AIAW's principal financial resource.[61]

The most damaging blow to the AIAW was the change in its Division I program, which generated about 50 percent of the association's income in 1980–81 and almost all of its television revenues. In 1981–82, many AIAW "big-time" schools chose to participate in the NCAA women's championships, including 80 percent of the top finishers in 1980–81 AIAW Division I championships. The loss of membership was the beginning of the "domino effect." The AIAW soon lost its attraction to television networks and commercial sponsors.[62] Ironically, compromising the educational model did not guarantee the AIAW success in its pursuit of the commercial model. The women's organization was failing because of the failure of its commercial attempts.

In 1979, the AIAW had signed a multi-year contract with NBC for the television rights to all AIAW Division I and open national championships. It also had an agreement with the fledgling sports cable network ESPN for carrying selected Division II and III events. The AIAW received a record-high television revenue of $223,000 and national television exposure for twelve of its national championships in 1980–81. The success of AIAW's commercial endeavor ceased in 1981–82, however, when none of the AIAW's championships received any television exposure. The defection of AIAW members to the NCAA and the NAIA championships caused NBC and ESPN to cancel their contracts with the AIAW, citing that the AIAW championships had deteriorated to the point that the AIAW was no longer in a position to provide the "essence of the contract."[63]

Since 1977, the AIAW had benefited from two major commercial sponsors-the Eastman Kodak Company and the Broderick Company, a sports apparel enterprise. The Kodak Company contributed $6,000 annually to the AIAW for the rights to advertise its products, mainly through the selection of the AIAW/Kodak Women's All-America Basketball Team. Its annual contribution increased to $10,500 in 1980–81. The Broderick Company contributed $5,000 annually to the AIAW. The sponsorship included the most prestigious AIAW presentation-the Broderick Cup award, which recognized the most outstanding female collegiate athlete in the nation. In 1981, both companies withdrew their sponsorship, citing the declined value of the AIAW programs because of the loss of quality and quantity of participants.[64]

In addition to the loss of television revenue and sponsors, the AIAW's efforts to license its logo to commercial entities came to a halt in early 1981. Prospective licensees expressed pessimism toward the AIAW's stature as a result of the NCAA's entry into women's intercollegiate athletics. Even an international event failed to boost either the morale or the finances of the organization. Initiated in 1980, the AIAW committed itself to sponsor a U.S. tour of the national women's basketball team from the Peoples Republic of China in anticipation of "attracting substantial public attention as well as money." When the tour commenced in November 1981, however, several U.S. teams had already withdrawn and the schedule was cut short. Unable to secure any television coverage of the event, the AIAW lost almost $6,000 when the tour ended.[65]

The tangible and intangible negative effects from the loss of members and championship participants were so pervasive that continued normal operation of the AIAW became impossible. "Foreseeing the erosion of its position as accelerating rather than arresting in 1982–83," the AIAW leadership directed that membership renewal applications not be distributed for 1982–83.[66] On June 30, 1982, the AIAW officially ceased business except for concentrating all its energies and resources into a last-ditch effort to save the association: a lawsuit against the NCAA.

The Final Judgment

A Tale of Two Trials

> The decision to fight for survival until all resources
> are exhausted has been made. Our future appears
> no longer to be in your hands or the hands of your
> leaders but in the system of justice of this great
> nation.
>
> —Ann Uhlir, AIAW executive
> director (1982)

ANN UHLIR delivered her executive director's report to the 1982 AIAW
delegate assembly with a highlight on the pending *AIAW v. NCAA* antitrust lawsuit and with a sense of pessimism about the future of the
AIAW.[1] She apparently had good reasons to be pessimistic. By the end of
1981, the AIAW had lost nearly 50 percent of the participants in its Division I championships and, subsequently, television exposure and revenues. At best, the AIAW predicted its 1982–83 membership at
approximately 400 institutions, a decline of nearly 60 percent from 961 in
1980–81. This massive membership loss, along with other factors, would
make the continued operation of the association an "economic impossibil-
ity."[2] It was in such a harsh climate that Uhlir invited the delegates for a
New Year's toast. "May AIAW be more than a fleeting reference in the history of sport textbooks of the next century." For those who truly believed
in the proclaimed AIAW philosophy, the ending could not have been more
depressing. "Here's to survival of the great AIAW experiment. May we
meet again."[3]

AIAW Takes NCAA to Court

When 1981 began, there was a glimpse of hope for peace on the AIAW-NCAA battlefield. In her presidential address to the AIAW delegate assembly, Donna Lopiano made a grand gesture of goodwill toward the NCAA and the NAIA:

> The time for looking back—of fixing blame—of accusations of unwillingness to seek common ground is over. All three organizations [the AIAW, the NCAA, and the NAIA] have been at fault. It is reprehensible for professional educators to ignore the existence of each other—to throw things at each other—to refuse to confront our common problems. We must in the coming year exhaust all human effort to resolve our differences. Only then will we best serve higher education and the future of intercollegiate athletics in our country.[4]

This seeming goodwill gesture quickly evaporated after the NCAA voted to adopt the "Governance Plan" and championship programs for women. To the AIAW leaders, a legal action against the NCAA became imminent, but they had to clean up their own house first.

In February, at the advice of legal counsel Margot Polivy, Lopiano wrote Linda Estes to notify her that the AIAW Executive Committee would "seek action to secure your removal" from the AIAW Executive Board at a special board meeting in March. The AIAW president indicated that Estes' parallel service as a member of the NCAA Executive Committee represented "a conflict of interest inimical to the best interests of AIAW."[5] Evidently, Lopiano's action was in contradiction to the policies of the AIAW. Only nine days earlier, the AIAW Executive Committee had informed the AIAW members that the association did not have any policy that would prohibit dual service on the AIAW and the NAIA or the NCAA committees.[6] Lopiano also advised Estes that an interim bylaw would be recommended to the board "to permit removal of a member of the Board 'for cause' by a two-thirds vote of the Board without referral to any other body."[7]

It was no secret that Linda Estes had often represented the voice of opposition to the AIAW leadership since the beginning of the association.

One of the most memorable activities of such opposition was the campaign led by Estes to relieve the AIAW of legal services provided by Margot Polivy and her law firm. A figure like Estes in the leadership obviously did not help to project the AIAW as a unified entity, nor would it enhance the AIAW's chance to prevail in its legal battle against the NCAA. Estes was no doubt a pest in the eyes of many AIAW leaders, but she was not easy to remove. As an elected official, the veteran of the AIAW had her allies both inside and outside the association.[8] For the AIAW leadership, dealing with Estes had always been difficult because of her determination, resourcefulness, and knowledge of proper legal procedure whenever she challenged the AIAW authority.

Shortly after Estes received the letter from Lopiano, a counter-campaign was launched against the AIAW leadership's intent to remove Estes from the board. One of Estes' strongest allies was William E. Davis, president of the University of New Mexico, at which Estes was the director of women's athletics. Davis sent a letter to presidents of all AIAW Division I and Region 7 member institutions, protesting the "arbitrary [and] capricious action" aimed at Estes.[9] The letter generated at least seventeen telegrams or telephone messages sent to Lopiano before the AIAW special executive board meeting in March. Barbara Hedges of the University of Southern California, also chair of the Council of Collegiate Women Athletic Administrators, telephoned Lopiano and indicated that if the board adopted "the conflict of interest policy" to facilitate the ouster of Linda Estes, the University of Southern California would remove its financial support to the AIAW by not renewing its membership.[10] Betty Miles, the AIAW representative from Drake University, registered her protest of the ethics of the AIAW leadership in a telegram sent to Lopiano. "Linda Estes serves on both boards [of the AIAW and the NCAA] because she is truly interested in the present and future of women's athletics and not because she is as narrow-minded as the Executive Committee seems to be in asking for her resignation," wrote Miles. "I object to this heavy-handed, unethical, and unprofessional act of paranoia as a very unwise and politically detrimental step."[11] In addition to the telegram-telephone campaign, a district judge of the State of New Mexico granted a "Temporary Restraining Order" that forbade the AIAW from instituting proceedings to remove Linda Estes at the special board meeting.[12]

The campaign to prevent Estes' removal worked, at least temporarily.

As Lopiano admitted, "this outpouring of criticism generated by Davis' letter resulted in the Board postponing enactment of a removal 'for cause' provision until its May meeting when such policy was adopted."[13] The AIAW Executive Board, however, was not completely unsuccessful in reprimanding Estes. At the recommendation of the executive committee, the board voted to exclude Estes from the remainder of the March meeting. It also demanded that the remaining board members "bind themselves not to disclose any matter discussed in the executive session." An "oath of confidentiality" was subsequently taken.[14]

Despite the impasse on the Estes issue, the March 1981 AIAW board meeting did manage to advance a proposal of historical significance. After the scheduled adjournment hour and the departure of five members, the board approved the motion that "directs and authorizes the Association's legal counsel to initiate any legal action(s) against the NCAA, and others acting in concert with the NCAA, which Counsel and the Executive Committee deem necessary to protect the interests of the AIAW and student athletes and athletic personnel involved in intercollegiate athletic programs. The Executive Board further authorizes the expenditure of the Association funds for this purpose to the extent they may be deemed necessary by the AIAW Executive Committee."[15]

With Estes out of its way and the authorization in place, the AIAW was poised to take the NCAA to court. It only needed a good excuse to launch the litigation. In late April 1981, the AIAW and the NCAA held a joint meeting for the last time, probably to display their "goodwill" to the public rather than to honestly reconcile their differences. Led by their respective presidents, the AIAW and the NCAA delegations met in a Chicago hotel to discuss the possible development of a unified governing body for men's and women's intercollegiate athletic programs. The meeting, however, never went through its first agenda item because of contradictory interpretations of the purpose of the meeting. After two hours of challenging each other's commitment to the issue, the meeting was forced to adjourn by the departure of the AIAW delegation.[16]

By June 1981, the AIAW Executive Committee had decided to pursue legal actions against the NCAA. After "four months of 12 to 18 hour days" of preparation, the AIAW finally put a lawsuit together. On October 9, 1981, the AIAW filed an antitrust lawsuit against the NCAA in the U.S. district court for the District of Columbia, seeking preliminary and permanent injunctions to enjoin the NCAA from "conducting, sponsoring, cosponsoring or supporting national intercollegiate athletic championship events for women."[17] The fate of the AIAW, thereafter, was placed in the hands of a judge.

The Court Closes the Door on the AIAW

The system of the U.S. justice was not on the side of the AIAW. In February 1982, a district judge denied the AIAW's request for a preliminary injunction on the NCAA's initiatives to offer national championships for women. The AIAW immediately filed a motion of appeal for the reversal of the judgment. A week later, the appeal was turned down by the appeals court.[18] Possibly foreseeing a slim chance of winning the uphill battle, the AIAW voluntarily withdrew from further pursuit of the preliminary injunction, concentrating its effort on the antitrust lawsuit.

In March 1982, the district judge proceeded to mediate between the two warring parties when he ordered the AIAW to submit a plan to the NCAA for merger of the two organizations or other solutions. After exchanging settlement proposals and responses, the representatives of the AIAW and the NCAA met in June 1982 in Washington, D.C., at the directive of the judge. The AIAW proposed that the NCAA either stop offering programs and services for women or restructure itself into two sex-separate autonomous divisions. The NCAA maintained that it could not accept either of the proposals. The alternatives offered by the NCAA were subsequently rejected by the AIAW. Not surprisingly, the meeting concluded without any settlement, relegating the judgment of AIAW's legal action entirely to the court.[19]

Nearly eight months after the suspension of its operation, the AIAW heard the verdict on the antitrust lawsuit from U.S. District Judge Thomas Jackson. He ruled in favor of the NCAA.[20] In forty-six pages the judge rendered his findings, discussions, and conclusions on the various issues pertaining to the case. While the ruling denied the specific charges against the NCAA brought by the AIAW, the deliberation of the decision itself was a strong testimony of the legal reality of American society in general and intercollegiate athletics in particular.

Jackson laid the foundation of his ruling by addressing the evolution of governance for women's athletics. Within a period of slightly over a decade, wrote the judge, the percentage of merged men's and women's intercollegiate athletics under a single administrative structure had increased from only 6 percent in 1972 to approximately 80 percent in 1983. "This trend of integrated, unitary administration of men's and women's athletics at the institutional level" was not a unique phenomenon, argued Jackson. It was rather "consistent with the prevailing pattern at all levels of amateur athletics in the United States."[21] What the judge did not mention was the apparent driving forces behind such a trend—the second wave of the feminist movement during the 1960s and 1970s and the passage of the Title IX anti-sex-discrimination legislation. In sharp contrast to the general trend, Jackson pointed out, the AIAW had distinguished itself as an organization that "consistently advocated, and sought to implement, separate-but-equal as the guiding principle" to determine the governing structure of intercollegiate athletics.[22]

The sex-separatist philosophy did not bring the AIAW defeat in the lawsuit, but the AIAW's failure to substantiate its charges did. While the AIAW established itself as the victim of the NCAA's entry into women's intercollegiate athletics, it could not prove to the court that the NCAA had conspired to destroy the AIAW and to monopolize women's intercollegiate athletics. As the judge clearly demonstrated, "a monopoly is illegal per se only if it is willfully acquired or maintained, as distinguished from grown or developed as a consequence of a 'superior product, business acumen, or historic accident,' . . . for the purpose of the antitrust laws is and has always been the protection of competition, not competitors."[23]

In conclusion, the judge ruled on two major AIAW charges against the NCAA. On the charge of the NCAA leadership's "intent to monopolize," the judge wrote:

> The evidence establishes that defendant's governance plan for women's intercollegiate athletics or[i]ginated with its members rather than its leaders . . . being ultimately given a form which reflects in large part the influence of plaintiff's open hostility to it in any form. The process by which it actually came into being is the antithesis of the conspiratorial plotting of a would-be monopolist to acquire surreptitious control of a market to control prices or destroy competition. The court concludes that plaintiff has failed to prove the specific intent necessary to sustain its claim of attempted monopoly.[24]

On the charge of "anti-competitive economic incentives" by the NCAA leadership, the judge used the testimonies from both sides to support his conclusion. Testifying for the AIAW, Donna Lopiano and Christine Grant, both former AIAW presidents, described the economic incentives offered by the NCAA to its women's championships as "irresistible inducements" that the AIAW could not match. The AIAW leaders were, however, "unable to identify a single institution by name which had succumbed to those inducements." On the contrary, they acknowledged that their own institutions—the University of Texas at Austin and the University of Iowa—had managed to resist the inducements on principle because of their relative affluence.[25]

In contrast to the testimonies for the AIAW, three witnesses for the NCAA presented a different set of "incentives" provided by the NCAA women's championships. All of them were women: Judith Holland of University of California at Los Angeles and former AIAW president, Nora Lynn Finch of North Carolina State University and former AIAW Executive Board member, and G. Jean Cerra of the University of Missouri. They maintained that their institutions opted to participate in the NCAA's championships because of the NCAA's superior management and promotional resources, its philosophic emphasis on competitive excellence as distinguished from the AIAW's maximum participation irrespective of ability, its future promise of a uniform rules structure for both sexes, and championship competitions by conferences rather than by state and region in which teams tended to be of disparate abilities.[26]

If sex discrimination had to be considered as a factor in the judgment of the court, then the NCAA witnesses could not have made a stronger testimony when they addressed the issue of equal opportunities. Responding to the alleged "irresistible inducements" offered by the NCAA, all three NCAA witnesses confirmed that the fact that male and female athletes would receive identical subsidies for championship travel was more important than the reimbursement itself. Consequently, the judge found that the plaintiff's evidence regarding the blandishments offered by the NCAA was "both imprecise and contradictory," and it did not support a conclusion that the NCAA "bought defectors from the AIAW with its superior economic resources."[27]

On February 25, 1983, the court ordered that judgment be entered for the NCAA. Fifteen months later, a U.S. circuit court in the District of

Columbia rejected the AIAW's appeal, thus closing the final chapter of the legal dispute between the AIAW and the NCAA as well as ending the decade-long existence of the women's organization.[28] The finale of the AIAW, however, did not lack the drama of irony.

AIAW Prevails in Out-of-Court Settlement with NBC

The lawsuit against the NCAA completely bankrupted the AIAW. By the end of the thirty-one-month trial that stretched from October 1981 to May 1984, the AIAW had accumulated well over $1.2 million expenses in legal fees from the services provided by the AIAW legal counsel Margot Polivy and miscellaneous court costs.[29] In addition to the litigation cost, the AIAW also paid Polivy's law firm another $142,833 retainer fee for the thirteen-month period from June 1981 to June 1982. A significant amount of the time covered by the retainer fee was devoted to the litigation. As Polivy indicated, "an additional 550 hours of litigation was paid from the retainer fee (350 in 1980–81; 200 in 1981–82)."[30] The AIAW's legal cost in 1981–82 was at least $285,000, nearly 42 percent of the association's total income and more than four times what the AIAW spent on its national championships ($64,183) in the same year.[31] There is no doubt that the AIAW exhausted itself in the political and legal battles against the NCAA in both direct confrontations and through disputes over the Title IX regulations. As former AIAW President Christine Grant recollected, "90 percent of our energies went on those two causes and that only left 10 percent of the energies to do the things that should have been our primary considerations."[32] The AIAW's expenditures certainly verify Grant's perception, that the AIAW spent nearly three times as much on legal fees as on running its championships from 1974 to 1982.[33]

Although the legal cost took a large percentage of the AIAW's total income and became a source of discontent within the membership, the criticism against the AIAW leadership and Margot Polivy may not be completely justified. It is true that "legal fees" had always been the number one expense of the AIAW since Polivy became the legal counsel of the association in 1974. However, it was likely that Polivy was underpaid most of the time based on the market value of legal services, and as a consequence, her law firm may have suffered financially. Polivy always made that clear to the AIAW leadership. In April 1978, Polivy told AIAW president Charlotte West that "for every compensated hour there has been at least one un-compensated hour" for her law firm's service to the AIAW. Seven months later, Polivy told AIAW executive director Bonnie Slatton that "in the four years that we have represented AIAW, we have been paid for only 50% of the time devoted to AIAW. AIAW has not been a financially desirable client and the time and effort devoted to AIAW have had a substantial and dele-terious effect upon the firm's economic health." [34] The law firm seemed to be struck by another huge financial loss when the circuit court turned down the AIAW's appeal. After exhausting its funds, the AIAW still owed the Polivy's firm more than $445,000. [35] In addition, the AIAW also owed the NCAA its legal cost for the *AIAW v. NCAA* lawsuit, but was unable to pay. [36]

A legal dispute with the NBC television network would help to allevi-ate the AIAW's debts. Nearly two years after the court rejected the AIAW's appeal, Polivy managed to win for the AIAW a $400,000 out-of-court set-tlement with NBC. [37] The dispute originated in late 1981 when the televi-sion network declined to honor the AIAW/NBC television rights contract because of the AIAW's inability "to provide Division I Championships of a character which formed the basis of the NBC agreement with the AIAW." [38] The legal action against NBC was likely delayed by the lawsuit against the NCAA—the AIAW's first political and financial priority of the time. With the defeat in court, the AIAW's hope to retain its power and control of women's collegiate athletics and to resurrect its fiscal predicament evapo-rated. A lawsuit against the NBC, regardless of its outcome, certainly would not revive the already doomed AIAW. It could, however, bring some much needed cash to pay for Polivy's service. The successful settle-ment with the NBC seemed to serve exactly that purpose. The NBC money, at the direction of the three AIAW presidents, was instantly used to pay for the AIAW's debt to Polivy.

Most former AIAW members had no knowledge of the event. The dis-position of the "NBC income," however, did cause serious controversy. In June 1987, Joan Hult, AIAW archivist and former chair of the AIAW Ethics and Eligibility Committee, discovered that a staff "Severance Pay Plan" had been approved by the AIAW Executive Committee. Stage 2 of the plan stated that it would be "implemented within 30 days of receipt of an NBC payment or a court settlement in the AIAW vs. NCAA action." [39] Hult would not let the event go down in history unchallenged. "I know the

[NBC] money has been received by the Legal [Counsel], but no payment has been made to AIAW staff," Hult wrote the AIAW Executive Committee. "It would seem to me important that this oversight be corrected without further delay."[40] In August 1987, Merrily Baker responded to Hult on behalf of the executive committee. Disputing Hult's interpretation of the "Severance Pay Plan," Baker maintained that neither of the two conditions—an NBC payment or a court settlement favoring the AIAW—ever occurred as defined in the plan, implying that the out-of-court settlement money was not an NBC payment for its contract with the AIAW. She explained, in part: "When an out-of-court settlement with NBC was reached in March 1986, the Executive Committee met, via telephone conference, and agreed that our first obligation was to satisfy the Association's outstanding debts; the NBC settlement money was utilized to do so. The amount of the settlement was not sufficient to cover all of those debts, but, on behalf of the Association we were able to satisfy at least a portion of the debt."[41]

The telephone conference was without the involvement of another member of the executive committee—Ann Uhlir, the executive director of the AIAW.[42] Likewise, Baker's letter to Hult was only carbon-copied to Donna Lopiano and Virginia Hunt, the "past president" and "president-elect" during Baker's presidency of the AIAW.

In April 1988, Ann Uhlir wrote Baker, disagreeing with the executive committee's decision to use the "entire settlement of the NBC obligation" for the reimbursement of the AIAW legal counsel. "Despite the obligations to Renouf and Polivy incurred after the close of AIAW," Uhlir argued, "staff severance benefits preceded those subsequent legal activities." She urged Baker to take necessary corrective action to see that the AIAW staff be compensated in accordance with the "Severance Pay Plan" without further delay.[43]

A letter from Baker to Uhlir in June 1988 seemed to have put a final seal on the controversy over the out-of-court NBC settlement. Speaking for the presidents, Baker reaffirmed their previous interpretation of the "Severance Pay Plan," and maintained that "stage 2 [of the plan] never became a reality." The conclusion of Baker's letter was a short but full description of the status of the AIAW at its very end. Baker wrote: "We believed then, and continue to believe now, that AIAW's first corporate obligation was to satisfy third-party debts. Even with distribution of a subsequent out-of-court settlement with NBC, the AIAW was unable to satisfy its third-party debts at the time of dissolution. Were AIAW still [in existence], those debts would remain. You asked me to take action, Ann, but there is no action to take. The AIAW does not exist; nor are there any AIAW financial resources in existence."[44]

Six years earlier at the last AIAW delegate assembly, Uhlir told the AIAW representatives that the future of the AIAW was "in the system of justice of this great nation." She also hoped that the AIAW would be "more than a fleeting reference in the history of sport textbooks of the next century."[45] The AIAW executive director probably had never imagined that, in that textbook, the last episode of the AIAW legacy was going to be an act of injustice carried out by the AIAW presidents against their loyal employees, and that she would be one of the victims of such injustice.

Epilogue

Reducing the Gap: Gender Equity in
Intercollegiate Athletics at the Dawn
of the Twenty-First Century

In American college athletics the AIAW
represented not the future, but the past.
—Joan M. Chandler (1985)

THE IMPLICATION of the *AIAW v. NCAA* lawsuit in intercollegiate athletics was profound. From a broader perspective, the AIAW's defeat in a courtroom epitomized the fate of the sex-separatist philosophy that had begun long before the creation of the AIAW. For nearly a century, college sports for women were controlled by women physical educators within the "separate sphere" of college campuses. Unlike men's athletics, which was developed by students as extracurricular activity, women's athletics began as part of the nineteenth-century curriculum for female collegians. Rooted in the medical views of the time and the values of Victorian America, women's athletics in colleges served primarily to alleviate the supposedly excessive strain of intellectual work for women while sustaining their state of "womanhood." Even when women's intercollegiate athletics became more competitive, the idea of "playing nice" remained a trademark.

There is a long history in the development of the "playing nice" philosophy, which began in the 1890s when Senda Berenson adapted basketball for her students at Smith College. Berenson's game was a vivid reflection of that philosophy. To her, the benefit of sport for women was not winning or the display of individual excellence but the promotion of physical and moral health for all. As upholders of societal morality, Berenson implied, women certainly should play nice, because "the great desire to win and the excitement of the game will make our women do sadly un-womanly things." Berenson may have had the right idea for women's athletics. Its broader acceptance by women, ironically, only took place when men began to "invade" the separate sphere of women's sports.

In the early 1920s, the "playing nice" philosophy received a great boost when a U.S. women's track and field team, organized by men, was sent to the Paris "Women's Olympics" and when the male-dominated Amateur Athletic Union assumed jurisdiction over women's track and field. The "male invasion" of women's territory led to the unification of women physical educators in a movement of anti-varsity competition, anti-Olympics, and anti-male control of women's sports. Consequently, women's sport contest was confined to "Play Day" on most college campuses, a form of physical activities emphasizing social interaction over competition. Anti-competitive views dominated women's collegiate athletics during the years between the two World Wars, and the influence of "Play Day" lasted well into the postwar era.

The need for change, nevertheless, became inevitable in the 1960s when American society changed more dramatically. With both the civil rights and women's rights movements exerting their influence in almost every corner of American life, the demand for equality in sports also gained momentum. The increasing importance of women's sports also manifested in the wake of repeated U.S. defeats by the Soviets in the 1956 and 1960 Olympics. The relatively inferior performance of American female Olympians, compared to that of the Soviet women, had much to do with the tarnished international image of the United States. Because colleges provided most male Olympic medal winners, the NCAA came to see women's athletics as part of the puzzle to produce Olympic medal winners and to wrest control of amateur athletics from the AAU.

In the shadow of the Cold War, women physical educators and men in the NCAA were both pursuing their interest in women's intercollegiate athletics, but from different perspectives. The women were responding to the increasing demand for varsity-level competition opportunities while vehemently fighting for women's control of women's athletics. The men were more concerned about their power in amateur sports dominated by the AAU. If these men and women had prayed for divine intervention, the closest answer to their prayers was the passage of Title IX by Congress in

1972. Few, though, could foresee the actual impact on college athletics of the anti-sex-discrimination legislation.

Title IX did not strengthen the NCAA's power, but it certainly weakened the century-old foundation of the sex-separatist philosophy of women's intercollegiate athletics. Under the law of equality, the ideal of "playing nice" seemed outdated. To achieve equality meant to move the women's "educational model" toward the men's "commercial model." Title IX, like a double-edged sword, pointed at the traditional men's athletic establishment at one end and the AIAW at the other. The *Kellmeyer* case of 1973 illustrated that the "playing nice" philosophy of the AIAW, despite its noble appearance, was unfeasible and illegal in the reality of American society. The significance of the *Kellmeyer* case lay in the fact that intercollegiate athletics, when equal opportunity was concerned, was a legal rather than a philosophical matter, that the control of intercollegiate athletics came from institutions, and that the men's athletic model was the norm for equity.

There was a belief among the AIAW leaders that the AIAW could have survived if college presidents had collectively supported the educational model. Such a scenario may have been feasible only in theory. Most schools were unlikely to subject themselves to potential legal challenges by applying different rules to men and women student-athletes. In order to minimize legal challenges as well as financial and administrative obstacles, schools were more likely to choose a single national governing body that would provide equal opportunities for both men and women.

One may argue that the pressure to comply with Title IX and the conflict between the AIAW and the NCAA provided college administrators a golden opportunity to reform the big-time, commercial model of college athletics and to choose an educationally more sound and financially more prudent program. Such an opportunity was at best illusive. The educational model lacked the support of the public as well as of college presidents and governing boards. "Unfortunately," as AIAW president Christine H. B. Grant admitted, "only a handful of Chief Executive Officers [of colleges and universities] in this nation realize what AIAW stands for and how different is our approach to intercollegiate athletics."[1] It is likely that the presidents were aware of and understood the proclaimed philosophy of the AIAW. They either did not believe in it or did not believe that it was feasible. "Governance of intercollegiate athletics is an institutional responsibility for decision making," wrote University of Wyoming president Hugh B. McFadden in 1978. "Given the dependence upon intercollegiate athletic income from the men's sports of football and basketball," argued McFadden, college presidents were more likely to commit themselves to a commercial model than to support the AIAW's educational model, which insisted on the separation of men's and women's intercollegiate athletics.[2]

Whether McFadden's view represented that of most college presidents is hard to ascertain. What can be established, however, is that history seems to tell the same story: The development of intercollegiate athletics in the United States was never the sole product of presidential choices. Sport historian Ronald A. Smith's analysis on the control of intercollegiate athletics may enable us to better understand the issue. "University presidents have a greater problem inherent to the control of intercollegiate athletics," wrote Smith. Because the faculty and the governing board of an institution often differ on the value of athletics, the president is caught between the conflicting demands of the two groups. Hired and fired by the board, college presidents have rarely taken a stance on athletics that differs from the board. "It is likely that presidents have felt their jobs threatened if they chose to diminish the non-educational aspects of big-time athletics."[3]

Ever since the late 1800s, Smith maintained, winning in athletic contests has been the most visible means of bringing prestige to an institution. The reality in American higher learning is that academic philosophy is less important than the public image of the institution. If winning in athletics remains the most effective way to promote a school, then commercialized big-time college athletics would likely out-duel any other models with more educational emphasis.[4] College presidents certainly would not have succeeded in supporting the AIAW philosophy, which, among other things, allowed losers in qualifying events to compete in national championships.[5] Nor could they have saved the AIAW even if they had wanted to.

There was no doubt that the AIAW was a victim of Title IX and the men's organizations' entry into the separate sphere of women's athletics. This fact, however, should not be confused with the fate of intercollegiate athletics for women. Title IX meant greater opportunity for women's participation in sports. The victim was the sex-separatist philosophy that advocated the absolute control of women's athletics by women. It is doubtful that the NCAA cared more about equal opportunity for women than about its power in U.S. amateur sports. It is, however, equally doubtful that the

AIAW leaders cared more about the welfare of those they controlled than about their own power and control of women's intercollegiate athletics.[6] This desire for power and control by both the men and the women was the real obstacle that prevented reconciliation between the AIAW and the NCAA. The AIAW leaders wanted nothing less than equal representation on decision-making positions in any combined organization. The NCAA maintained that it was unrealistic for men to accept an equal share of power with women. The AIAW's stance was idealistically correct but practically unwise. The position of the NCAA, however, was merely a reflection of the men's attitude toward the AIAW. Backed by its experience, stability, and financial affluence, the NCAA never saw the financially and administratively dependent AIAW as an equal. After all, the NCAA's attitude toward the AIAW exemplified the general attitude toward women in most other areas of male-dominated society.

The AIAW's questionable commitment to the welfare of those it controlled can also be seen in the association's order of priorities. For the last eight years of its existence, the AIAW spent nearly three times as much on legal services as on AIAW national championships. Christine Grant acknowledged that disparity eleven years after the demise of the AIAW. In the battles "to uphold Title IX" and to fight "against the NCAA starting women's championships," recollected the former AIAW president, "90 percent of our energies went on those two causes and that only left 10 percent of the energies to do the things that should have been our primary considerations."[7] There may be a slight exaggeration in Grant's estimation. But it was symbolically close to the truth. Toward the end, the AIAW became more a political agency for the women leaders than a national organization devoted to the advancement of women's athletics. The AIAW leaders' devotion to their political agenda and a lesser commitment to membership service led to the division of the AIAW when in 1979 the Council of Collegiate Women Athletic Administrators was formed to lead women into the NCAA structure.

In a relatively short life span, the AIAW experienced a rapid growth in membership and provided invaluable intercollegiate athletic opportunities for women. The accomplishments of the AIAW, however, should not be attributed to the educational model, for the history of the AIAW's growth is rather an antithesis of that model. The AIAW's abandoning of the educational model began with the *Kellmeyer* lawsuit in 1973. Fearful of membership loss and defeat in court, the AIAW changed its anti-scholarship policy. The change, as sport historian Joan Hult maintained, "immediately placed in jeopardy the philosophical commitment of AIAW to an educational model."[8]

The rapid growth of AIAW membership was also a result of the vast athletic opportunities created under the impact of Title IX. Likewise, such a growth can be seen as a natural development of the AIAW, because the AIAW was the only organization to offer national championships for college women. If any colleges or universities wanted to provide athletic opportunity to their women student-athletes at the national level, the AIAW was the only place to go.[9]

Toward the end of the 1970s, the AIAW's educational model, with few exceptions, had actually been replaced by a commercial model.[10] From All-Star to All-American, from Hanes Classic to Louisville Slugger, from NBC to ESPN, from airlines to automobile dealers, and from Coca-Cola to alcoholic beverages, the AIAW pursued the commercial model as hard as it could. If there were any significant difference between the AIAW and the NCAA by the turn of the decade, it was not their philosophical commitments but the degrees of success in their commercial endeavors. At its financial peak in 1979–80, the AIAW generated a total income of $830,618, about 1/25 of the NCAA's $20,220,495. The AIAW's income from commercial sponsorship that year was $207,000, less than 1/65 of the NCAA income of $13,607,000 from its football television assessments and Division I basketball championship alone. If the principles of a market economy should also apply to commercialized intercollegiate athletics, there is little doubt as to which side would prevail in the lopsided battle between the NCAA and the AIAW. When the NCAA began to offer national championships with financial incentives for women, a substantial number of schools abandoned the commercially unsuccessful AIAW in favor of the commercially successful NCAA.

One may wonder: Why did the AIAW leaders continue to claim the AIAW as an educational model while in reality that model no longer existed? Careful observers should find an analogy in the relationship between amateurism and big-time college athletics. Neither the educational model nor amateurism was a careless misnomer for their respective subjects. They were products of hypocrisy. Hypocrisy can serve a useful purpose when it comes down to power and control. When equal opportunity for men and women was the mandate of the law and the men's "invasion" of women's "separate sphere" became inevitable, the only remaining means to justify and defend the existence of the sex-separate organization seemed to be to maintain a noble appearance of its philosophy. The AIAW's justification was less than noble, however, as the real aim of the "noble appearance" was to keep the power and control of women's intercollegiate athletics in the hands of women. Many people, including members of the AIAW, did not understand that it was the sex-separatist philosophy that gave women the power and control of women's sports for a century. Under Title IX, the women's sex-separatist model was forced to conform to the traditional male model. With increasing participation in women's sports, ironically, came the demise of the AIAW as well as women's loss of power and control of women's intercollegiate athletics.

For those who were devoted to and truly believed in the AIAW's proclaimed educational model, the demise of the AIAW and their own loss of positions of power were extremely depressing. That is understandable. It would take tremendous strength and courage for them to face the reality. The reality was apparently not a pleasant one, as noted by historian Joan M. Chandler. "As hypocrisy is a necessary condition for survival among intercollegiate athletic empires," wrote Chandler, "the best we can probably do is to mourn the passing of hope for an alternative."[11] Smith College's Senda Berenson, dead for decades, would most likely turn over in her grave, knowing that the era for women's sex-separate control of women's athletics ended in 1981. Ironically, Smith College converted its 110 years of educational-model athletics to commercial-model athletics by becoming the first all-women's college to join the NCAA.[12] Berenson, however, would likely have agreed with Chandler that "in American college athletics the AIAW represented not the future, but the past."[13] The sex-separatist philosophy pursued by college women sport leaders and by the AIAW was a thing of the past. This philosophy was combined with the NCAA's Cold War policy on women's athletics and the nation's Title IX movement. Together, they contributed to the demise of the AIAW and women's loss of power and control of women's intercollegiate athletics.

NOTES

BIBLIOGRAPHY

INDEX

Notes

1. Introduction: Women's Intercollegiate Athletics in a Male-Dominated Society

1. "Testimony of Donna A. Lopiano," *AIAW v. NCAA*, Civil No. 81–2473, Walter Byers Papers, box "Testimony and Affidavits," pp. 31–32, NCAA Library, Indianapolis, Indiana.

2. *Gender Equity—Men's and Women's Participation in Higher Education* (Washington, D.C.: U.S. General Accounting Office, 2000).

3. The mandate, issued by the U.S. Department of Education's Office for Civil Rights in 1998, requires that the proportion of scholarship aid colleges and universities give to women must be within one percentage point of the proportion of women on varsity teams. In 1999–2000, female athletes, who represented 41.5 percent of varsity athletes, received 43 percent of athletic scholarship money. Welch Suggs, "Scholarships for Women Exceed Federal Guidelines," *The Chronicle of Higher Education*, 18 May 2001.

4. In 1998–99, the NCAA spent nearly $37 million on these two accounts for its national championships. "Championships Financial Reports," in *1998–99 NCAA Annual Reports* (Overland Park, Kans.: The National Collegiate Athletic Association, 1999).

5. "Women's Basketball Stays with ESPN in 11-Year Deal," *NCAA News*, 16 July 2001; and "1999 NCAA Financial Report," in *1998–99 NCAA Annual Reports*.

6. Welch Suggs, "College Presidents Urged to Take Control of College Sports," *The Chronicle of Higher Education*, 6 July 2001.

7. "Gender Equity," *1999–2000 NCAA Gender-Equity Report* (Indianapolis, Ind.: National Collegiate Athletic Association, 2000), p. 20; and Lena Williams, "Women Play More, but Coach Less," *New York Times*, 3 May 2000.

8. Nearly everything written about the AIAW has been laudatory. See, for instance, Randi J. Greenberg, "AIAW vs. NCAA: The Takeover and Implications," *Journal of the National Association of Women Deans, Administrators, and Counselors* 47 (1984): 29–36; Bonnie Slatton, "AIAW: the Greening of American Athletics," in *The Governance of Intercollegiate Athletics*, ed. James H. Frey (West Point, N.Y.: Leisure Press, 1982), pp. 144–54; Gail F. Maloney, "The Impact of Title IX on Women's Intercollegiate Athletics" (Ph.D. diss., State Univ. of New York at Buffalo, 1994); Dale E. Plyley, "The AIAW vs. the NCAA: A Struggle for Power to Govern Women's Athletics in American Institutions of Higher Education 1972–1982" (M.A. thesis, Univ. of Western Ontario, Canada, 1997); and Suzanne C. Willey, "The Governance of Women's Intercollegiate Athletics: Association for Intercollegiate Athletics for Women

(AIAW) 1976–1982" (P.E.D. diss., Indiana Univ., 1996). Mary Jo Festle, in her book *Playing Nice: Politics and Apologies in Women's Sports* (New York: Columbia Univ. Press, 1996), gives ample discussion on the NCAA-AIAW power struggle in the context of Title IX legislation. Although her research of the issue relies much more substantially on the primary sources found in the AIAW Papers and official NCAA documents, her general interpretation of the conflict still represents a pro-AIAW point of view.

9. See, for instance, Donna A. Lopiano, "Presidential Address," 6 Jan. 1982, Minutes of AIAW Delegate Assembly, AIAW Papers, box 418, Special Collections, University of Maryland Libraries, College Park, Maryland; L. Leotus Morrison, "The AIAW Governance by Women for Women," in *Women in Sport: Issues and Controversies,* ed. Greta L. Cohen (Newbury Park, Calif.: Sage Publications, 1993), pp. 59–66; Ann Uhlir, "Political Victim: The Dream That Was the AIAW," *New York Times,* 11 July 1982; and Elizabeth Wheeler, "NCAA vs. AIAW," *Women's Sports* 2 (June 1980): 20–23, 59.

10. Donna A. Lopiano, as quoted in Willey, "The Governance of Women's Intercollegiate Athletics," p. 225.

2. The Background of Women's Intercollegiate Athletics: 1890s–1960s

1. For historical background on the development of higher education and sport for women, see, for instance, Dorothy Sears Ainsworth, *The History of Physical Education in Colleges for Women* (New York: A. S. Barnes, 1930); Susan K. Cahn, *Coming on Strong: Gender and Sexuality in Twentieth-Century Women's Sport* (Cambridge, Mass.: Harvard Univ. Press, 1994); Roberta Frankfort, *Collegiate Women: Domesticity and Career in Turn-of-the-Century America* (New York: New York Univ. Press, 1977); Allen Guttmann, *Women's Sports: A History* (New York: Columbia Univ. Press, 1991); Cindy Himes, "The Female Athlete in American Society: 1860–1940" (Ph.D. diss., Univ. of Pennsylvania, 1986); Mabel Lee, *A History of Physical Education and Sports in the U.S.A.* (New York: John Wiley and Sons, 1983); Kathleen McCrone, *Playing the Game: Sport and the Physical Emancipation of English Women, 1870–1914* (Lexington: Univ. Press of Kentucky, 1988); Carroll Smith-Rosenberg, *Disorderly Conduct: Visions of Gender in Victorian America* (New York: Alfred A. Knopf, 1985); Barbara Miller Solomon, *In the Company of Educated Women: A History of Women and Higher Education in America* (New Haven, Conn.: Yale Univ. Press, 1985); Betty Spears, *Leading the Way: Amy Morris Homans and the Beginnings of Professional Education for Women* (New York: Greenwood Press, 1986); Martha H. Verbrugge, *Able-Bodied Womanhood: Personal Health and Social Change in Nineteenth-Century Boston* (New York: Oxford Univ. Press, 1988); and Patricia Vertinsky, *The Eternally Wounded Women: Women, Doctors, and Exercise in the Late Nineteenth Century* (Manchester, England: Manchester Univ. Press, 1990).

2. Carroll Smith-Rosenberg and Charles Rosenberg, "The Female Animal: Medical and Biological Views of Women and Their Role in Nineteenth-century America," in *From "Fair Sex" to Feminism: Sport and the Socialization of Women in the Industrial and Post-Industrial Eras,* ed. J. A. Mangan and Roberta J. Park (London: Frank Cass, 1987), pp. 19–20; Vertinsky, *The Eternally Wounded Woman,* pp. 37–108; and Roberta J. Park and Joan S. Hult, "Women as Lead-

ers in Physical Education and School-Based Sports, 1865 to the 1930s," *Journal of Physical Education, Recreation, and Dance* 64 (Mar. 1993): 35–36.

3. Smith-Rosenberg and Charles Rosenberg, "The Female Animal."

4. Smith-Rosenberg and Rosenberg, "The Female Animal," p. 14.

5. Ellen W. Gerber, "Catherine Esther Beecher," in *Innovators and Institutions in Physical Education* (Philadelphia: Lea and Febiger, 1971), pp. 252–58; and Patricia Vertinsky, "Women, Sport, and Exercise in the Nineteenth Century," in *Women and Sport: Interdisciplinary Perspectives*, ed. D. Margaret Costa and Sharon R. Guthrie (Champaign, Ill.: Human Kinetics, 1994), pp. 64–66.

6. As quoted in Richard A. Swanson and Betty Spears, *History of Sport and Physical Education in the United States*, 4th ed. (Madison, Wisc.: William C. Brown and Benchmark, 1995), p. 141.

7. Ibid., pp. 141–42.

8. University of Wisconsin in 1873, Wellesley College in 1874, and Radcliffe College in 1881 all established physical education programs similar to that of Vassar College. Ibid., pp. 141–44; and Joan S. Hult, "The Story of Women's Athletics: Manipulating a Dream 1890–1985," in Costa and Guthrie, *Women and Sport*, p. 85.

9. Spears, *Leading the Way*, pp. 41–62; and Swanson and Spears, *History of Sport and Physical Education*, pp. 181–83.

10. Hult, "The Story of Women's Athletics," p. 85.

11. Swanson and Spears, *History of Sport and Physical Education*, pp. 184–85.

12. Ronald A. Smith, "The Rise of Basketball for Women in Colleges," in *The American Sporting Experience: A Historical Anthology of Sport in America*, ed. Steven A. Riess (Champaign, Ill.: Leisure Press, 1984), p. 248.

13. Betty Spears, "Senda Berenson Abbott, New Woman: New Sport," in *A Century of Women's Basketball: From Frailty to Final Four*, ed. Joan S. Hult and Marianna Trekell (Reston, Va.: AAHPER, 1991), p. 22.

14. Smith, "The Rise of Basketball for Women," p. 241.

15. Spears, "Senda Berenson Abbott," p. 27.

16. Senda Berenson, "The Significance of Basketball for Women," in *Basket Ball for Women* (New York: American Sports Publishing, 1900), pp. 164–65.

17. Ibid., p. 164.

18. Smith, "The Rise of Basketball for Women," p. 242.

19. James G. Thompson, "Athletics vs. Gymnastics in Classical Antiquity," in *History of Sport and Physical Activity*, ed. Ronald A. Smith and James G. Thompson (University Park, Pa.: privately printed, 1991), pp. 67–72.

20. Hult, "The Story of Women's Athletics," pp. 86–88; and Joan S. Hult, "The Governance of Athletics for Girls and Women: Leadership by Women Physical Educators, 1899–1949," in Hult and Trekell, *A Century of Women's Basketball*, pp. 54–55.

21. Berenson, "The Significance of Basketball for Women," p. 162.

22. Ibid., p. 164.

23. Responding to the invitation of the newly formed Fédération Sportive Féminine In-

ternationale, Dr. Harry Stewart of the New Haven School of Physiotherapy created the National Women's Track Athletics Committee, which organized a U.S. women's track and field team for the Paris games. John A. Lucas and Ronald A. Smith, *Saga of American Sport* (Philadelphia, Pa.: Lea and Febiger, 1978), p. 350.

24. The NAAF was formed in 1922 to promote sport for everyone and to address dissatisfaction with U.S. Olympic programs.

25. Joan S. Hult, "Women's Struggle for Governance in U.S. Amateur Athletics," *International Review for the Sociology of Sport* 24, no. 3 (1989): 251.

26. The sixteen-point "Platform" was adopted at the First Annual Meeting of the Women's Division, NAAF, held in Chicago on April 22, 1924. See Bulletin A (Women's Division, National Amateur Athletic Federation of America, Nov. 1927), in Katherine Ley Papers, box 4, Archives of the AAHPER, Reston, Virginia.

27. Margaret M. Duncan and Velda P. Cundiff, *Play Days for Girls and Women* (New York: A. S. Barnes, 1929), pp. v–vii, 1–5; and Hult, "The Story of Women's Athletics," pp. 89–90.

28. "A Team for Every Girl and Every Girl on the Team," Women's Division, N.A.A.F., Dec. 1927, Katherine Ley Papers, box 4; and Lee, *A History of Physical Education and Sports*, pp. 158–59.

29. Ellen W. Gerber, "The Controlled Development of Collegiate Sport for Women, 1923–1936," *Journal of Sport History* 2 (spring 1975): 23–27.

30. Smith, "The Rise of Basketball for Women," pp. 244–45.

31. Ina E. Gittings, "Why Cramp Competition?" *Journal of Health and Physical Education* 2 (Jan. 1931): 10–12, 54.

32. Ibid., p. 54.

33. Hult, "The Governance," pp. 64–65; and Minutes of the Legislative Board and the Policy and Finance Committee, NSWA, Dec. 1941, NSWA Papers (1932–1953), Archives of the AAHPERD, Reston, Va., box 1, p. 17.

34. Resolutions, 29 Apr. 1941, in Gladys Palmer, "Diary," Apr. 26–29, 1941, Unprocessed Women's Athletics Papers, accession no. 84/94, 9/3–51/8, "College Directors' Convention: 1941," Ohio State University Archives, Columbus, Ohio.

35. Minutes of the Legislative Board and the Policy and Finance Committee, NSWA Papers, Dec. 1941, p. 17.

36. The report, "American College Athletics," showed that corruption was widespread in college athletics, which failed "to utilize and strengthen such desirable social traits as honesty and the sense of fair play." Carnegie Foundation for the Advancement of Teaching, *Twenty-Fourth Annual Report of the President and of the Treasurer* (Boston: Merrymount Press, 1929), p. 117.

37. Jennifer Marien, "An Analysis of the History of Women's Intercollegiate Athletics," unpublished paper, Branford College, Yale University, 1994, pp. 17–18.

38. Hult, "The Story of Women's Athletics," p. 93.

39. Ibid., pp. 93–94; Cindy Himes Gissendanner, "African-American Women and Competitive Sport, 1920–1960," in *Women, Sport, and Culture*, ed. Susan Birrell and Cheryl L. Cole (Champaign, Ill.: Human Kinetics, 1994), pp. 81–92; and Paula D. Welch, "Tuskegee Institute, Pioneer in Women's Olympic Track and Field," *The Foil* 7 (spring 1988): 10–13.

40. Virginia Hunt, "Governance of Women's Intercollegiate Athletics: An Historical Perspective" (Ed.D. diss., Univ. of North Carolina at Greensboro, 1976), pp. 115–21; and Hult, "The Story of Women's Athletics," pp. 94–95.

41. *AIAW Handbook of Policies and Interim Operating Procedures, 1971–1972* (Washington, D.C.: AAHPER, 1971), p. 6.

42. Katherine Ley and Sara Staff Jernigan, "The Roots and the Tree," *Journal of Health, Physical Education, and Recreation*, Sept. 1962, pp. 34–36, 57; Joanna Davenport, "The Historical Development of AIAW," *Proceedings of North American Society for Sport History*, 1979, p. 35; and Hult, "The Governance," pp. 55–56.

43. Hult, "The Governance," pp. 56–74.

44. Ibid., p. 74. DGWS later became the National Association for Girls and Women in Sport (NAGWS) in 1974.

45. Joan S. Hult, "The Legacy of AIAW," in Hult and Trekell, *A Century of Women's Basketball*, p. 282.

46. Ley and Jernigan, "The Roots and the Tree."

47. Ibid.; and Phebe M. Scott and Celeste Ulrich, "Commission on Intercollegiate Athletics for Women," *Journal of Health, Physical Education, and Recreation*, Oct. 1966.

48. The seven sports for which national championships were offered by 1972 were badminton, swimming and diving, basketball, gymnastics, track and field, golf, and volleyball. Minutes of CIAW and AIAW (Regional Representatives), Nov. 12–14, 1971, AIAW Papers, box 418, p. 5.

3. Cold War, Olympic Defeat, and Women's Sport as a Pawn: The AAU-NCAA Battle

1. Hamilton was speaking at the 1961 annual convention of the National Collegiate Athletic Association as part of the report of the NCAA Youth Fitness Committee. *1960–1961 Yearbook of the National Collegiate Athletic Association*, pp. 251–58.

2. The NAAAA, established in 1879, assumed jurisdiction over amateur sports, primarily track and field, in the United States. The withdrawal was led by the Philadelphia-based Athletic Club of the Schuylkill Navy and the New York Athletic Club, which were to become the backbone of the AAU. In the summer of 1889, the NAAAA was disbanded and its members were assimilated into the AAU. Ronald A. Smith, "Amateur Athletic Union," in *Encyclopedia: USA* (Gulf Breeze, Fla.: Academic International Press, 1983), pp. 157–59.

3. Ibid.; and Arnold William Flath, *A History of Relations Between the National Collegiate Athletic Association and the Amateur Athletic Union of the United States, 1905–1963* (Champaign, Ill.: Stipes Publishing Co., 1964), pp. 16–17.

4. The NCAA, when conceived in 1905, was called the National Intercollegiate Football Conference. From 1906 to 1910, it was known as the Intercollegiate Athletic Association of the United States. Ronald A. Smith, *Sports and Freedom: The Rise of Big-Time College Athletics* (New York: Oxford Univ. Press, 1988), pp. 191–208, 272 n.52.

5. Flath, *A History of Relations*, p. 26.

6. Ibid., p. 27.

7. Ibid., pp. 28–29.

8. The AAU possessed a dominant voting advantage and controlled the executive committee and other key positions in the AOA. Ibid., pp. 50–58.

9. The formation of the NAAF was proposed by Secretary of War John W. Weeks. In November 1921, Weeks wrote AOC president Gustavus T. Kirby stating that the constitution and bylaws of the AOA prepared by the AOC were too limited. He proposed instead the formation of the NAAF to be composed of all existing amateur sport organizations in the United States. Flath, *A History of Relations,* p. 59.

10. "Secretary Defends the Athletic Union," *New York Times,* 18 Apr. 1922, p. 6.

11. Flath, *A History of Relations,* pp. 60–61.

12. Technically, the AAU, the NCAA, the NAAF, the army, the navy, and another dozen sports governing bodies each had three votes within the AOA. The YMCA also joined the AOA with one vote. In reality, however, the AAU, with its jurisdiction over the major Olympic sports of track and field, swimming, boxing, wrestling, gymnastics, and the large number of voting affiliates within the AOA, was still the most powerful organization in the AOA. Flath, *A History of Relations,* pp. 61–64.

13. Ibid., pp. 65–67; and *The Final Report of the President's Commission on Olympic Sport 1975–1977* (Washington, D.C.: U.S. Government Printing Office, 1977), p. 398.

14. Flath, *A History of Relations,* pp. 82–85; and *The Final Report of the President's Commission,* p. 398.

15. Flath, *A History of Relations,* pp. 82–85; and *The Final Report of the President's Commission,* p. 398.

16. Flath, *A History of Relations,* pp. 98, 114–15; Jack Falla, *NCAA: The Voice of College Sports: A Diamond Anniversary History, 1906–1981* (Mission, Kans.: NCAA, 1981), pp. 80–82; and *The Final Report of the President's Commission,* p. 399.

17. Flath, *A History of Relations,* pp. 129–32.

18. *New York Times,* 29 Apr. 1951, p. E2.

19. Ibid., 21 Dec. 1951, p. 26.

20. In the 1956 Winter and Summer Games, the USSR led the medal counts over the USA by 16 to 7 and 98 to 74, respectively. In the 1960 Winter and Summer Games, the USSR increased the margins by 21 to 10 and 103 to 71. David Wallechinsky, *The Complete Book of the Olympics* (New York: Penguin Books, 1984), pp. xii-xvi.

21. *1960–1961 Yearbook of the NCAA,* pp. 251–58.

22. Wallechinsky, *The Complete Book,* pp. xiii-xiv, 126–461.

23. *1960–1961 Yearbook of the NCAA,* p. 254.

24. Ibid., p. 252.

25. Sara S. Jernigan, AAHPER past vice-president, letter to Katherine Ley and Marguerite Clifton, 1 Oct. 1962, Katherine Ley Papers, box 6.

26. Formerly the American Olympic Association, the organization changed its name to the United States of America Sports Federation in 1941 in order to gain jurisdiction over the Pan-American Games, held in Buenos Aries, Argentina, in 1942. The United States of America Sports Federation changed its name to the United States Olympic Association in 1945. Finally, the United States Olympic Association became the United States Olympic Committee in 1961. Flath, *A History of Relations,* pp. 111–13; and *The Final Report of the President's Commission,* p. 400.

27. "Organizational Meeting of the United States Federations in the Sports of Basketball, Gymnastics, Track and Field," Conrad Hilton Hotel, Chicago, Ill., 4–6 Mar. 1962, Katherine Ley Papers, box 4; *1962–1963 Yearbook of the NCAA*, p. 173. The Chicago meetings were mistakenly dated as "October of 1961" in *The Final Report of the President's Commission*, p. 400.

28. Louis J. Fisher (AAU President), "A Letter to Amateur Sportsmen in the U.S.," *Amateur Athlete*, Mar. 1962, p. 8., as quoted in Flath, *A History of Relations*, p. 145.

29. *1962–1963 Yearbook of the NCAA*, pp. 169, 126; and Flath, *A History of Relations*, pp. 151–52.

30. *1962–1963 Yearbook of the NCAA*, p. 181.

31. The president of the Basketball Federation of the United States was A. C. "Dutch" Lonborg, athletic director at the University of Kansas, a member of the NCAA Executive Committee and former chair of the NCAA Basketball Tournament Committee; the president of the United States Gymnastics Federation was Donald Boydston, athletic director at Southern Illinois University; the president of the United States Baseball Federation was Everett D. Barnes, athletic director at Colgate University and the elected secretary-treasurer of the NCAA (1963–64); and the president of the United States Track and Field Federation was William B. Russell from the California Interscholastic Federation. Notably, the executive director of the USTFF was another collegian, Charles D. Werner of Penn State University, past president of the National Collegiate Track Coaches Association. *1962–1963 Yearbook of the NCAA*, pp. 174–75.

32. Ibid., p. 176.

33. Ibid., pp. 169, 182.

34. *The Final Report of the President's Commission*, pp. 400–401.

35. Donald Boydston was also the director of athletics at Southern Illinois University. His speech at the 1963 NCAA convention was part of the "General Round Table" session titled "Development Related to the National Sports Federations." *1962–1963 Yearbook of the NCAA*, p. 181.

36. The noncompromising positions of the AAU and the NCAA meant that some of the best American athletes could be declared ineligible for the Olympic competitions.

37. "The MacArthur Plan," Katherine Ley Papers, box 4; and *The Final Report of the President's Commission*, pp. 400–401.

38. Arnold William Flath, "A History of Relations Between the NCAA and the AAU, 1905–1968," in *A History of Physical Education and Sport in the United States and Canada*, ed. Earle F. Zeigler (Champaign, Ill.: Stipes Publishing Co., 1975), pp. 212–14.

39. *New York Times*, 24 Oct. 1961, p. 4.

40. Four major reasons accounted for the NCAA's withdrawal. First, the NCAA was opposed to the Sulger and Greenbrier Amendments, which basically restricted the NCAA's (and its allies') voting power in the USOC and the potential to seek affiliation with any international sport federation. Second, the NCAA was opposed to the action taken by the USOC Board of Directors in early 1972 that recognized the AAU as the franchise holder for wrestling. Third, the NCAA viewed the USOC as unresponsive to meaningful change, dominated by the AAU, and unwilling to give the NCAA and its allies in the school/college community appropriate representation. Finally, the apparent mismanagement of U.S. Olympic interests at Mu-

nich provided the needed catalyst for the NCAA's withdrawal. *The Final Report of the President's Commission*, pp. 401–2.

41. Ibid., pp. 402–3.

42. As quoted in ibid., p. 403.

43. Minutes of the Meeting of the Committee of the Board of Directors to Study Relationships of AAHPER to Various National Organizations for Sports and Athletics, 26 June 1962, Katherine Ley Papers, box 6, p. 2.

44. Donald F. Hull, executive secretary of the AAU, to AAHPER executive secretary-treasurer, 7 May 1962, Katherine Ley Papers, box 4.

45. "Progress Report of the Committee of the Board of Directors to Study Relationships of the AAHPER to Various National Organizations for Sports and Athletics," 4 Oct. 1962, Katherine Ley Papers, box 4, pp. 14–15; and "Reports of the Committee of the Board," 28 Mar. 1963, Katherine Ley Papers, box 4, pp. 1–2.

46. Walter Byers to Roswell D. Merrick, 18 July 1962, Katherine Ley Papers, box 4.

47. A. C. Lonborg to Roswell D. Merrick, 30 Oct. 1962; and Katherine Ley to Arthur S. Daniels, 14 Dec. 1962, Katherine Ley Papers, box 4.

48. *1963–1964 Yearbook of the NCAA*, pp. 132, 144.

49. Ibid., p. 189.

50. *1964–1965 Yearbook of the NCAA*, p. 148.

51. Ibid., appendix-regulations section.

52. Jim Sours, memorandum to members of the Long-Range Planning Committee, 1 Mar. 1965, Walter Byers Papers, box 51, "Women's Athletics."

53. In a letter to Ella Corinne Brown, a physical education professor at the University of Maine, Byers wrote: "The NCAA is in the process of organizing a committee to supervise development of women's competition and we want to obtain the names of as many women instructors as possible to have a good nucleus from which to build." Months later, Byers also sought information about women's intercollegiate basketball through E. Wayne Cooley, executive secretary of Iowa Girls' High School Athletic Union. A close ally of the NCAA, Cooley provided not only the information Byers requested but an insightful analysis of the hostile relationship between the NCAA and the AAU. The significance of Byers' initiatives lies in the fact that they were tied to the functions of the NCAA-backed sports federations. Walter Byers to Ella Corinne Brown, 16 Mar. 1965, Walter Byers Papers, box 51, "Women's Athletics"; Walter Byers to E. Wayne Cooley, 13 Oct. 1965, Walter Byers Papers, box 51, "Women's Athletics"; E. Wayne Cooley to Walter Byers, 11 Nov. 1965, Walter Byers Papers, box 51, "Women's Athletics".

54. Virginia Hunt, "Governance of Women's Intercollegiate Athletics: An Historical Perspective" (Ed.D. diss., University of North Carolina at Greensboro, 1976), p. 56.

55. *1966–1967 Annual Reports of the NCAA*, p. 168; and Walter Byers to Donald N. Boydston, Carl E. Erickson, Katherine Ley, Ernest B. McCoy, Elizabeth McCue, Peter F. Newell, and Dean S. Trevor, 25 July 1967, Walter Byers Papers, box 51, "Women's Athletics."

56. Clifford B. Fagan to Walter Byers, 25 May 1967, Walter Byers Papers, box 51, "Women's Athletics."

57. Charles M. Neinas, memorandum to Walter Byers, 19 May 1967, Walter Byers Papers, box 51, "Women's Athletics."

58. Charles M. Neinas to Clifford B. Fagan, 20 May 1967, Walter Byers Papers, box 39, "NFSHSAA."

59. Donna A. Lopiano, speech given at the "NCAA-NAIA Governance of Women's Athletics Workshop," 7 Jan. 1981, AIAW Papers, box 319, p. 8.

4. Growing NCAA Interest in Women's Intercollegiate Athletics: 1963–1968

1. The epigraph at the beginning of this chapter was part of the introduction given by Everett D. Barnes to the General Roundtable session of the 1964 NCAA National Convention, where two women sports leaders, Sara Staff Jernigan and Marguerite Clifton, past chair and chair of the Division for Girls and Women's Sports, were invited to give speeches to the NCAA delegates. *1963–1964 Yearbook of the NCAA*, p. 189.

2. Attendees of the meeting were Katherine Ley, AAHPER vice president; Phebe Scott of the University of Illinois; Betty McCue of Duke University; Marguerite Clifton of University of California at Los Angeles; Frances Schaafsma of California State University at Long Beach; William R. Reed, commissioner of Big Ten Athletic Conference; Clifford Fagan of the National Federation of State High School Athletic Associations; Roswell Merrick, AAHPER staff; AAHPER president; and an unidentified NCAA representative. The information on the meeting was based on the written statement by Frances Schaafsma dated 24 Nov. 1980. NCAA, "Summary of NCAA Meetings Concerning Women's Athletics Matters, 1963–1980," in AIAW Papers, box 70, "Appendix to Affidavit of AIAW President Donna A. Lopiano," appendix 5, p. 1.

3. The idea of the Institute, according to Sara Staff Jernigan, chair of the Women's Board of the United States Olympic Development Committee and the first director of the Institute, was conceived by the WBUSODC in order to provide more instruction, more coaching, and more practice for the development of women's sports. Over two hundred representatives from every state of the Union attended this first National Institute on Girls' Sports, held in November 1963 at the University of Oklahoma, Norman. *1963–1964 Yearbook of the NCAA*, pp. 200–201.

4. Ibid., pp. 132, 144; and NCAA, "Summary of NCAA Meetings," p. 1.

5. *1963–1964 Yearbook of the NCAA*, pp. 200–201; NCAA, "Summary of NCAA Meetings," p. 1.

6. *1963–1964 Yearbook of the NCAA*, pp. 197–207.

7. Ibid., pp. 198–99.

8. Ibid., pp. 201–2.

9. Ibid., pp. 204–5.

10. Ibid., p. 206.

11. *1964–1965 Yearbook of the NCAA*, p. 148.

12. NCAA, "Summary of NCAA Meetings," p. 2.

13. Jim Sours, memorandum to members of the Long-Range Planning Committee, 1 Mar. 1965, Walter Byers Papers, box 51, "Women's Athletics," p. 2.

14. *1964–1965 Yearbook of the NCAA*, p. 156.

15. Ella Corinne Brown to Walter Byers, 2 Mar. 1965; and Walter Byers to Ella Corinne Brown, 16 Mar. 1965, Walter Byers Papers, box 51, "Women's Athletics."

16. Walter Byers to E. Wayne Cooley, 13 Oct. 1965, Walter Byers Papers, box 51, "Women's Athletics."

17. E. Wayne Cooley to Walter Byers, 11 Nov. 1965, Walter Byers Papers, box 51, "Women's Athletics."

18. Walter Byers to E. Wayne Cooley, 24 Nov. 1965, Walter Byers Papers, box 51, "Women's Athletics."

19. In 1965, the National Joint Committee on Extramural Sports for College Women (NJCESCW), the first national body attempting to guide and administer women's intercollegiate athletic programs, decided to dissolve itself and recommended that the DGWS assume its functions.

20. Frances McGill, chairperson of the DGWS special committee to study the transition, recalled the rationale for establishing the CIAW when she was interviewed by Virginia Hunt in 1975. See Virginia Hunt, "Governance of Women's Intercollegiate Athletics: An Historical Perspective" (Ed.D. diss., Univ. of North Carolina at Greensboro, 1976), p. 56.

21. Hunt, "Governance," p. 186; AIAW, "CIAW-AIAW-NCAA Organizational Relationships Chronology, 1959–1980," Walter Byers Papers, box 1, "NCAA and Women's Athletics," folder "NCAA's Early Involvement with Women's Athletics, 1975," p. 1.

22. Charles M. Neinas to Richard C. Larkins, 8 Mar. 1966, Walter Byers Papers, box 51, "Women's Athletics."

23. Richard C. Larkins to Charles M. Neinas, 10 Mar. 1966, Walter Byers Papers, box 51, "Women's Athletics."

24. Interviewed by Virginia Hunt in 1975, Rachel Bryant, then DGWS consultant, stated: "After receiving this information, the DGWS felt free to go ahead and organize the CIAW without feeling that there was a concern with the NCAA." Hunt, "Governance," p. 187.

25. Minutes of the DGWS, 18–22 Mar. 1966, as cited in Hunt, "Governance," p. 57.

26. Ibid., pp. 58–59.

27. Richard C. Larkins to Members of NACDA, 30 Aug. 1966, AIAW Papers, box 70, "Appendix to Affidavit of AIAW President Lopiano," appendix 7; and Hunt, "Governance," p. 187.

28. E. Wayne Cooley to Charles Neinas, 12 July 1966, Walter Byers Papers, box 51, "Women's Athletics."

29. Ibid.

30. Ibid.

31. Ibid.

32. Charles M. Neinas to Roswell D. Merrick, 22 Dec. 1966, "Appendix to Affidavit of AIAW President Lopiano," appendix 8.

33. Ibid.

34. Katherine Ley to Marcus Plant, 27 Jan. 1967, "Appendix to Affidavit of AIAW President Lopiano," appendix 9.

35. *1966–1967 Annual Reports of the NCAA*, p. 168.

36. NCAA, "Summary of NCAA Meetings," p. 2.

37. Clifford B. Fagan to Walter Byers, 25 May 1967, Walter Byers Papers, box 51, "Women's Athletics."

38. Ibid.

39. Charles M. Neinas, memorandum to Walter Byers, 19 May [1967], Walter Byers Papers, box 51, "Women's Athletics."

40. Ibid.

41. Walter Byers to Donald N. Boydston, Carl E. Erickson, Katherine Ley, Ernest B. McCoy, Elizabeth McCue, Peter F. Newell, and Dean S. Trevor, 25 July 1967, Walter Byers Papers, box 51, "Women's Athletics."

42. Katherine Ley to Walter Byers, 4 Aug. 1967, "Appendix to Affidavit of AIAW President Lopiano," appendix 10.

43. Walter Byers to Katherine Ley, 21 Aug. 1967, "Appendix to Affidavit of AIAW President Lopiano," appendix 11.

44. Katherine Ley to Walter Byers, 6 Oct. 1967, "Appendix to Affidavit of AIAW President Lopiano," appendix 12.

45. *1967–68 Annual Reports of the NCAA*, p. 126.

46. NCAA, Council Minutes, 23–25 Oct. 1967, NCAA Papers, box "Permanent Memorandum, Sept.-Dec. 1967," p. 7.

47. Walter Byers to Katherine Ley, 26 Oct. 1967, "Appendix to Affidavit of AIAW President Lopiano," appendix 13.

48. Ibid.

49. Richard C. Larkins to Katherine Ley, 18 Dec. 1967, as quoted in Hunt, "Governance," p. 190.

50. Hunt, "Governance," pp. 62–63, 191.

51. Ibid., p. 66; "Affidavit of Donna A. Lopiano," NCAA Papers, box "Testimonies and Affidavits," p. 39.

52. DGWS, "Minutes of Commission on Intercollegiate Athletics for Women," 19–23 Aug. 1968, Katherine Ley Papers, box 6, p. 1.

53. Ernest McCoy to members of the NCAA Committee on Women's Intercollegiate Competition, 22 Feb. 1968, "Appendix to Affidavit of AIAW President Lopiano," appendix 14.

54. NCAA, "Minutes from NCAA Committee Meeting—Jan. 21, 1968," "Appendix to Affidavit of AIAW President Lopiano," appendix 14, p. 1.

55. Ibid.

56. Ibid., p. 2.

57. Ibid.

58. Betty McCue, as quoted in Hunt, "Governance," pp. 193–94.

59. Lucille Magnusson, as quoted in Hunt, "Governance," p. 193.

60. Katherine Ley, as quoted in Hunt, "Governance," p. 193.

5. Early NCAA Attempts at the Governance of Women's Intercollegiate Athletics: 1968–1973

1. As quoted in Virginia Hunt, "Governance of Women's Intercollegiate Athletics: An Historical Perspective" (Ed.D. diss., University of North Carolina at Greensboro, 1976), p. 194.

2. "Testimony of Donna A. Lopiano," in *AIAW v. NCAA*, 9 Oct. 1981, NCAA Papers, box "Testimonies and Affidavits," p. 22.

3. NCAA, "Summary of NCAA Meetings Concerning Women's Athletics Matters," p. 3; and "Testimony of Donna A. Lopiano," p. 41.

4. Minutes of the CIAW, 30 Oct.–2 Nov. 1969, as cited in Hunt, "Governance," p. 75.

5. Hunt, pp. 80–82.

6. See "Minutes from NCAA Committee Meeting—Jan. 21, 1968," in "Appendix to Affidavit of AIAW President Donna A. Lopiano," pages between appendixes 14 and 15, AIAW Papers, box 70; and Hunt, "Governance," pp. 66–67, 75.

7. Walter Byers to Elizabeth Hoyt (CIAW representative in the AAHPER national office), 2 Feb. 1971, AIAW Papers, box 37.

8. Lu [Lucille Magnusson], CIAW Chair, memo to [CIAW] Commissioners and Consultants, 8 Mar. 1971, "Appendix to Affidavit of AIAW President Lopiano," appendix 16.

9. Walter Byers, memo to members of the NCAA Executive Committee and Council, 26 Feb. 1971, AIAW Papers, box 37.

10. NCAA, "NCAA Meetings on Women's Athletics," p. 4; 1970–71 Annual Reports of the NCAA, p. 72; and "Affidavit of Donna A. Lopiano," p. 45.

11. George Gangwere, NCAA legal counsel, to Walter Byers, 17 June 1971, AIAW Papers, box 37.

12. Ibid.

13. Ibid.

14. Ibid.

15. The NCAA committee chair, David Swank, was absent from the meeting. He later apologized to the women. "Unfortunately, the meeting was called by Mr. Byers and somehow I was never notified of the time and place of the meeting," wrote Swank. "I think this was probably through a foul-up in the mail service." David Swank to Rachel Bryant, JoAnne Thorpe, and Carole Oglesby, 29 July 1971, "Appendix to Affidavit of AIAW President Lopiano," appendix 24.

16. NCAA, "NCAA Meetings on Women's Athletics," p. 4; and Rachel E. Bryant, memorandum to Troester, Anderson, and Merrick, 15 July 1971, "Appendix to Affidavit of AIAW President Lopiano," appendix 22.

17. Ibid.

18. Rachel E. Bryant to Walter Byers, 16 July 1971, "Appendix to Affidavit of AIAW President Lopiano," appendix 23.

19. George Gangwere, NCAA legal counsel, to Walter Byers, 14 Aug. 1971, "Appendix to Affidavit of AIAW President Lopiano," appendix 26.

20. Walter Byers to George E. Gangwere, 21 May 1971, Walter Byers Papers, box "Title IX 1970–80," folder "Correspondence to Parties External to the NCAA."

21. "New Organization to Protect Women Athletes and Regulate Competition," AAHPER news release, 14 May 1971, Walter Byers Papers, box "Title IX 1970–80," folder "Correspondence to Parties External to the NCAA."

22. Ibid.

23. "Trampoline Star Competes with Men—Judi Ford Eyes U.S. Berth," Rockford Morning Star, 26 Jan. 1968, p. B3.

24. Minutes of CIAW and AIAW (Regional Representatives), 12–14 Nov. 1971, AIAW Pa-

pers, box 418, p. 9; and NCAA, "NCAA Meetings Concerning Women's Athletics," p. 5. The CIAW/AIAW source indicates that the NAIA was absent from the meeting.

25. Lucille Magnusson to Charles Neinas, 7 Sept. 1971, AIAW Papers, box 37.

26. Gangwere to Walter Byers, 14 Aug. 1971.

27. Minutes of CIAW and AIAW (Regional Representatives), 12–14 Nov. 1971, p. 9.

28. Ibid., pp. 9–10.

29. See Lucille Magnusson to Charles Neinas, 7 Sept. 1971 and 1 Oct. 1971; Rachel Bryant to Walter Byers, 8 Oct. 1971, AIAW Papers, box 37; and JoAnne Thorpe to Walter Byers, 6 Oct. 1971, in "Appendix to Affidavit of AIAW President Lopiano," appendix 31.

30. Charles Neinas to Lucille Magnusson, 23 Sept. 1971, AIAW Papers, box 37.

31. Magnusson to Charles Neinas, 1 Oct. 1971; and Thorpe to Walter Byers, 6 Oct., 1971.

32. Bryant to Walter Byers, 8 Oct. 1971.

33. Walter Byers to Rachel Bryant, 12 Oct. 1971, AIAW Papers, box 37.

34. *1970–71 Annual Reports of the NCAA*, p. 88.

35. NCAA Council Minutes dated Oct. 25–27, 1971, Minute no. 7, as cited in "NCAA Meetings Concerning Women's Athletics," p. 6.

36. Minutes of CIAW and AIAW (Regional Representatives), 12–14 Nov. 1971, p. 6.

37. *Proceedings of the 66th Annual Convention of the NCAA* (Overland Park, Kans.: NCAA, 1972), pp. 78–79.

38. Ibid., p. 80.

39. George Gangwere to Walter Byers, 17 June 1971, AIAW Papers, box 37, p. 2.

40. *Proceedings of the 66th Annual Convention of the NCAA* (1972), p. 80.

41. Ibid.

42. Ibid., pp. 80–81.

43. According to Edward Czekaj, by January 1972 Penn State University had established "an intercollegiate program in eleven sports for women." *Proceedings of the 66th Annual Convention of the NCAA* (1972), p. 81.

44. Ibid., pp. 81–84.

45. Ibid., p. 84.

46. Ibid., p. 86.

47. Ibid.

48. Ibid., pp. 85–86, 91–93; and "NCAA Concerned about Legality of Its Exclusion of Women," *The Chronicle of Higher Education,* 17 Jan. 1972, pp. 1, 4.

49. *1971–72 Annual Reports of the NCAA*, p. 77.

50. Ibid., p. 121.

51. *1972–73 Annual Reports of the NCAA*, p. 81; and *Proceedings of the 67th Annual Convention of the NCAA* (1973), p. 172.

52. "Affidavit of AIAW President Donna A. Lopiano," p. 56.

6. The *Kellmeyer* Lawsuit: Scholarships, Equal Opportunities, and the Questions of Power and Control

1. *Fern Kellmeyer, et al. vs. National Education Association, et al.* (U.S. District Court, Southern District of Florida, no. 73, 21 Civ NCR), 17 Jan. 1973, AIAW Papers, box 67, p. 2; and "Women Win Right to Scholarships," *New York Times*, 20 Apr. 1973, p. 66.

2. Joel Gewirtz, NEA legal counsel, memorandum to Carl Troester, AAHPER executive secretary, 21 Feb. 1973, AIAW Papers, box 67.

3. Minutes of CIAW and AIAW Transition Meeting, 1–4 June 1972, AIAW Papers, box 418, p. 6.

4. "NEA and AAHPER Challenged in Courts on AIAW Scholarship Policy," *Update* (AAHPER), Apr. 1973, p. 1. The DGWS Scholarship Statement (accepted by the DGWS Executive Council in Oct. 1971) was endorsed by the CIAW/AIAW in November 1971. Minutes of CIAW and AIAW (Regional Representatives), 12–14 Nov. 1971, AIAW Papers, box 418, p. 6.

5. AIAW, "Minutes of Special Committee to Discuss Course of Action Regarding Suit: *Fern Kellmeyer, et al. v. NEA, et al.*," 6–7 Feb. 1973, AIAW Papers, box 67, p. 2.

6. Gewirtz, memorandum to Carl Troester, 21 Feb. 1973. The memorandum was a summary of the report that the NEA legal counsel presented to the special committee meeting held in Washington, D.C., on 6 Feb. 1973. AIAW Papers, box 67, p. 2.

7. Ibid., p. 5.

8. AIAW, "Minutes of Special Committee to Discuss Course of Action Regarding Suit," p. 3.

9. Ibid., pp. 3–4; Mary E. Rekstad and Elizabeth Hoyt, "*Kellmeyer, et al. v. NEA, et al.*, Summary of Action Taken from January 11, 1973 to February 22, 1973," AIAW Papers, box 67, p. 2; and AAHPER, *Update*, Apr. 1973.

10. AAHPER, *Update*, Apr. 1973, p. 1.

11. Only weeks before his meeting with the representatives of the special committee on the *Kellmeyer* suit, Udall reportedly attacked "anything-to-win attitudes" of big-time college athletics before members of the NCAA at its annual honors luncheon. Despite being one of the five recipients of awards given by the NCAA for "athletic achievement in college" and "career achievement," the former secretary lashed out his criticism with little restraint. He even singled out Adolph Rupp, Woody Hayes, and Tom Osborne, popular college coaches, as individuals who were "pointing their ideals in the wrong direction." "All-cost Winning Scored by Udall," *New York Times*, 13 Jan. 1973, p. 25.

12. AAHPER, *Update*, Apr. 1973, p. 1.

13. The wording in the response sheets sent to the AIAW Executive Board and AIAW member institutions was slightly different from the wording sent to the DGWS Executive Council because of the procedural requirement and the position of the respondents. The response of the first group was obtained before the information was sent to the second; and in turn, the second before sending to the third. Rekstad and Hoyt, "*Kellmeyer, et al. v. NEA, et al.*, Summary of Action," p. 3; and "Response Sheet" (AAHPER, AIAW), ca. Feb. and Mar. 1973, AIAW Papers, box 67.

14. AIAW, "Policies on Women Athletes Change," AIAW news release, ca. end of March to beginning of April 1973, AIAW Papers, box 67, p. 1.

15. Ibid., pp. 1–2.

16. Carole Oglesby, personal interview by Virginia Hunt, 15 Nov. 1975, as quoted in Virginia Hunt, "Governance of Women's Intercollegiate Athletics: An Historical Perspective," pp. 139–40.

17. Carole Oglesby, e-mail correspondence to the writer, 16 Mar. 2000.

18. Ibid.

19. In a survey conducted by the Philosophy and Standards Section of the DGWS, over 18 percent of the colleges and universities responding to the survey indicated that athletic scholarships of one form or another were given to women student-athletes. Betty McCue, "Athletic Scholarships for Women?" *Journal of Health, Physical Education, and Recreation* 33 (Apr. 1962): 18.

20. Hunt, "Governance," p. 124.

21. Ibid, pp. 122–24.

22. Twenty men and women educators and administrators of interscholastic and intercollegiate athletics attended the meeting. The main outcome of the meeting was a set of guidelines for the conduct of interscholastic and intercollegiate competitive opportunities for girls and women. "Summary of the Study Conference on Competition for Girls and Women," 10–12 Feb. 1965, Katherine Ley Papers, box 6; Phebe Scott and Celeste Ulrich, "Commission on Intercollegiate Sports for Women," *Journal of Health, Physical Education, and Recreation* 37 (Oct. 1966): 10, 76; and Hunt, "Governance," pp. 124–25.

23. Even though Bill Reed was Big Ten Commissioner of a major big-time conference, he was likely opposed to full athletic scholarships based solely on athletic ability. In the 1950s, the Big Ten tried to prevent scholarships based only on athletic ability, but lost their efforts when other conferences decided to base their scholarships only on athletic talent.

24. Carole Oglesby, personal interview by Virginia Hunt, in Hunt, "Governance," p. 147.

25. AIAW, memorandum to AIAW member institutions, AIAW Executive Board, DGWS Executive Council from Special Committee to Reword DGWS Scholarship Statement and Revise AIAW Rules and Regulations, 2 Apr. 1973, AIAW Papers, box 67.

26. Joan S. Hult, "The Philosophical Conflicts in Men's and Women's Collegiate Athletics," *Quest* 32, no. 1 (1980): 83.

27. Minutes of CIAW and AIAW Transition Meeting, 1–4 June 1972, AIAW Papers, box 418, p. 8.

28. The actual wording of the motion was "that a student enters a tournament which awards cash prizes." AIAW, Minutes of the Executive Board, 7–9 Jan. 1974, AIAW Papers, box 418, p. 6.

29. The motion was passed unanimously by the AIAW Executive Board. A similar motion was passed by the AIAW Delegate Assembly in January 1977. AIAW, Official Minutes of the 1977 Delegate Assembly, 2–6 Jan. 1977, AIAW Papers, box 382, p. 39.

30. AIAW, Official Minutes of the Spring Executive Board Meeting, 19–22 May 1975, AIAW Papers, box 418, p. 9.

31. AIAW, Official Minutes of the 1977 Delegate Assembly, 2–6 Jan. 1977, AIAW Papers, box 382, pp. 37–38.

32. For instance, the NCAA required a one-year waiting period of championship eligibility for transfer students, but the AIAW did not (although the student might not be eligible for financial aid); the NCAA prohibited student-athletes from employment to coach or instruct in his/her own sport, whereas the AIAW allowed accepting coaching or officiating fees; the NCAA allowed off-campus contact with a prospect if permitted by the high school's authority, the AIAW prohibited off-campus contact with a prospective student-athlete; the NCAA considered loans, grants, work-study, and employment as athletic aid, but the AIAW did not; the NCAA deducted "training table" (special meals provided for student-athletes) from allowance, the AIAW did not; and the NCAA could provide financial aid as long as the student-athlete was an undergraduate, even if eligibility were exhausted, whereas the AIAW limited financial aid to a maximum of four years and the student must have been eligible to participate in order to receive athletic aid. For details, see AIAW, "Review of Significant Rules Difference Between AIAW, NCAA, and NAIA," July 1980; and Judith Holland to Ruth Berkey, 26 Sept. 1980, box "AIAW," folder "AIAW-NCAA Differences Concerning Rules."

33. AIAW, Official Minutes of the Spring Executive Board Meeting, 19–22 May 1975, AIAW Papers, box 381, p. 20.

34. AIAW, Official Minutes of the Fall Executive Board Meeting, 30 Sept.–3 Oct. 1975, AIAW Papers, box 269, pp. 2, 24.

35. AIAW, Official Minutes of the Fall Executive Board Meeting, 24–28 Oct. 1976, AIAW Papers, box 418, p. 16.

36. Joan S. Hult, personal interview by the author, Greenbelt, Md., 27 June 1995.

37. Official Minutes of the Third AIAW Delegate Assembly, 11–15 Jan. 1976, AIAW Papers, box 269, p. 36.

38. Ibid.

39. Ibid.

40. Kay Hutchcraft, AIAW executive secretary, reported that "although the financial outcome of the tour was disappointing inasmuch as the tour ended with a deficit, the fact that AIAW received National publicity and the good will between China and the United States was of tremendous importance." AIAW, Official Minutes of the Spring Executive Board Meeting, 29 May–1 June 1976, AIAW Papers, box 269, p. 11.

41. The contract between the AIAW and Sugarman Productions was a guaranteed $25,000 for the first year. AIAW, Official Minutes of Executive Board Meeting (part III), 4 Jan. 1977, AIAW Papers, box 382, p. 4.

42. AIAW, Official Minutes of the Executive Board and Delegate Assembly Meeting, 11–15 Jan. 1976, AIAW Papers, box 269, pp. 37–40.

43. AIAW, Official Minutes of the Spring Executive Board Meeting, 10–13 May 1977, AIAW Papers, box 269, p. 6.

44. Ibid., p. 14.

45. AIAW, Official Minutes of the Fall Executive Board Meeting, 10–13 Oct. 1978, AIAW Papers, box 269, p. 19.

46. Ronald A. Smith, *Play by Play: Radio, Television, and Big-Time College Sport* (Baltimore, Md.: Johns Hopkins Univ. Press, 2001), pp. 117–22.

47. The AIAW had 906 active members in 1979 while the NCAA had 725. AIAW, Official Minutes of the 1979 Delegate Assembly, AIAW Papers, box 418; and *1978–79 Annual Report of the NCAA.*

48. Charlotte West, AIAW president, "Welcoming Remarks for the 6th Annual AIAW Delegate Assembly," AIAW, Official Minutes of the 1979 Delegate Assembly, AIAW Papers, box 418, appendix 1, p. 2.

49. The NAGWS emerged from the DGWS in 1974.

50. AIAW, Official Minutes of the 1979 Delegate Assembly, 7–9 Jan. 1979, AIAW Papers, box 418, appendix 1, pp. 52–56.

7. Equality over Power: The Impact of Title IX
on Intercollegiate Athletics for Women

1. "Title IX—Prohibition of Sex Discrimination," Education Amendments of 1972, Public Law 92–318, 92d Cong., S. 659, sec. 901.(a), 23 June 23 1972.

2. For details, see *Final Title IX Regulation Implementing Education Amendments of 1972: Prohibiting Sex Discrimination in Education* (Washington, D.C.: U.S. Department of Health, Education, and Welfare/Office of Civil Rights, June 1975).

3. *New York Times,* 13 Jan. 1973, p. 25.

4. Ronald A. Smith, "Women's and Men's Models of College Sport from the Nineteenth Century to Title IX: Maternalism and Paternalism," paper presented at Raymond Weiss Lecture of 1996 AAHPER National Convention, 15 Apr. 1996, Atlanta, Ga., p. 3.

5. Minutes of the First AIAW Delegate Assembly, 4–6 Nov. 1973, AIAW Papers, box 269, p. 5.

6. Joanna Davenport, personal interview by the author, 12 July 1995, Marblehead, Mass.

7. See "Resolution and Rationale for Separate Intercollegiate Athletic Teams for Women," Minutes of the First AIAW Delegate Assembly, appendix.

8. Marjorie Blaufarb, "Solomon's Judgement on Women's Sports," p. 3, Minutes of the First AIAW Delegate Assembly, appendix.

9. Jack Whitaker, speech on Title IX, the First AIAW Delegate Assembly, 4–6 Nov. 1973, AIAW Papers, box 294, pp. 8–11.

10. Linda Estes to Carole Oglesby, 11 Aug. 1973, AIAW Papers, box 309.

11. The coordinator of AIAW national championships in 1973 was Laurie Mabry from Illinois State University, who became the AIAW president in 1975–76. Minutes of the First AIAW Delegate Assembly, p. 1.

12. Estes to Oglesby, 11 Aug. 1973.

13. The constitution of the AIAW designated the past president, president, and president-elect as elected top officials of the organization.

14. Linda Estes, memo to Carol Gordon, Leotus Morrison, and Carole Oglesby, 9 Oct. 1973, AIAW Papers, box 418.

15. For a more detailed discussion on the subject, see, for instance, Susan K. Cahn, " 'Play It, Don't Say It:' Lesbian Identity and Community in Women's Sport," in *Coming on Strong: Gender and Sexuality in Twentieth-Century Women's Sport* (Cambridge, Mass.: Harvard Univ. Press, 1994), pp. 185–206.

16. Leotus Morrison to Linda Estes, 14 Nov. 1973, AIAW Papers, box 418.

17. Linda Estes to Leotus Morrison, 11 Dec. 1973, AIAW Papers, box 418.

18. Ibid.

19. Ibid.

20. "Speech by Linda Estes to Student Action Council," Anaheim, Calif., 29 Mar. 1974, personal files of Linda Estes, p. 1.

21. Linda Estes to Leotus Morrison, 11 Dec. 1973.

22. For the AIAW's effort on the subject, see Jack Whitaker, speech on Title IX, the First AIAW Delegate Assembly, AIAW Papers, box 294. For the NCAA's effort to get legal advice, see Philip B. Brown to Tom Hansen, re Sex Discrimination Provisions of Education Amendments of 1972, 21 Dec. 1973; and Ritchie T. Thomas to Tom Hansen, re Office of Civil Rights proposed regulations regarding sex discrimination, Walter Byers Papers, box "Title IX, 1970–80," folder "Correspondence to Parties External to the NCAA."

23. Robert C. James, memorandum to chief executive officers of NCAA Member Institutions, 21 Feb. 1974, Walter Byers Papers, box "Title IX, 1970–80," folder "Correspondence to Member Institutions."

24. Ibid.

25. John A. Howard to Kenneth Cole, 1 Mar. 1974, Walter Byers Papers, box "Title IX, 1970–80," folder "Correspondence to Parties External to the NCAA."

26. Ibid.

27. Ibid.

28. Walter Byers to John A. Howard, 11 Mar. 1974, Walter Byers Papers, box "Title IX, 1970–80," folder "Correspondence to Parties External to the NCAA."

29. John W. Winkin to President Richard Nixon, 5 Mar. 1974, Walter Byers Papers, box "Title IX, 1970–80," folder "Correspondence to Parties External to the NCAA."

30. Alan J. Chapman to President Richard Nixon, 20 Mar. 1974, Walter Byers Papers, box "Title IX, 1970–80," folder "Correspondence to Parties External to the NCAA."

31. Politically, the NAIA had been an ally of the AAU, the AAHPER, and the DGWS/AIAW. The NJCAA had been an ally of the NCAA. Minutes of the First AIAW Delegate Assembly, 4–6 Nov. 1973, p. 6.

32. Carol E. Gordon, memorandum to Lee Morrison, Carole Oglesby, Laurie Mabry, et al., 22 Feb. 1974, AIAW Papers, box 70, "Appendix to Affidavit of AIAW President Donna A. Lopiano," appendix 36.

33. Ibid. The NJCAA began to offer national championships for both men and women at the junior college level in 1975.

34. See Carol Gordon, Lee Morrison, and Carole Oglesby, memorandum to AIAW Board of Directors, 5 Mar. 1974, AIAW Papers, box 294.

35. Leotus Morrison, memorandum to voting representatives of AIAW member institutions, 27 June 1974, AIAW Papers, box 418.

36. Carol Gordon, memorandum to presidents of AIAW member institutions, Mar. 1974, "Appendix to Affidavit of AIAW President Lopiano," appendix 44.

37. See Alan J. Chapman and Richard P. Koenig, memorandum to chief executive officers, faculty athletic representatives, and athletic directors of NCAA member institutions, 14 June 1974, "Appendix to Affidavit of AIAW President Lopiano," appendix 40.

38. "Comments of the Association for Intercollegiate Athletics for Women" (submitted to Director, Office of Civil Rights of the Department of Health, Education & Welfare), 15 Oct. 1974, AIAW Papers, box 294, pp. 2–6.

39. "No Sporting Chance: The Girls in the Locker Room," *Washington Post,* 12 May 1974, p. A14.

40. Chapman and Koenig, memorandum to chief executive officers, faculty athletic representatives, and athletic directors of NCAA member institutions.

41. Walter Byers to John Tower, 6 June 1974, Walter Byers Papers, box "Title IX, 1970–1980," folder "Correspondence to Member Institutions."

42. District Six of the NCAA consisted of its member institutions located in the states of Texas, Arkansas, and New Mexico.

43. Walter Byers, memorandum to Directors of Athletics of NCAA Member institutions in District Six, 10 June 1974, Walter Byers Papers, box "Title IX, 1970–80," folder "Correspondence to Member Institutions."

44. Chapman and Koenig, memorandum to chief executive officers, faculty athletic representatives, and athletic directors of NCAA Member Institutions.

45. Ibid.

46. Alan J. Chapman and Richard P. Koenig, telegram to Joint Senate-House Conferees on H.R. 69, 13 June 1974, "Appendix to Affidavit of AIAW President Lopiano," appendix 40.

47. Ibid.

48. The proposed regulations of Title IX were published on 20 June 1974 with the content of the Javits Amendment intact in the document.

49. Walter Byers to Eugene F. Corrigan, Clifford B. Fagan, John A. Fuzak, Carol Gordon, George E. Killian, Stanley J. Marshall, Mary Jean Mulvaney, Robert J. Scannell, and David Swank, 26 Feb. 1974, Walter Byers Papers, box "Title IX, 1970–80," folder "Correspondence to Member Institutions."

50. Ibid.

51. Ibid.

52. George Gangwere to Walter Byers, 18 Mar. 1974, "Appendix to Affidavit of AIAW President Lopiano," appendix 38.

53. Ibid.

54. "Resolution" (adopted by the Council of the NCAA), 6 May 1974, Walter Byers Papers, box "Title IX, 1970–1980," folder "Correspondence to Member Institutions."

55. *1973–74 Annual Reports of the NCAA,* p. 114.

56. NCAA, "Summary of NCAA Meetings Concerning Women's Athletics Matters," p. 9.

57. *1973–74 Annual Reports of the NCAA,* p. 145.

58. "Minutes of the NCAA Committee on Women's Sports," 10 Oct. 1974, Chicago, Ill.,

Walter Byers Papers, box "Title IX, 1970–80," folder "Reports/Minutes/Official Comments (1974)."

59. Ibid.

60. Leotus Morrison, memorandum to AIAW Executive Board, 15 Oct. 1974, AIAW Papers, box 418.

61. "The NCAA and Women's Intercollegiate Athletics" [A staff report prepared for and at the direction of the NCAA Council], Walter Byers Papers, box "Title IX, 1970–80," folder "Correspondence to Member Institutions," p. 1.

62. Philip B. Brown to Walter Byers, 20 Nov. 1974, Walter Byers Papers, box "Title IX, 1970–80," folder "Correspondence to Member Institutions," p. 1.

63. Ibid.

64. "The NCAA and Women's Intercollegiate Athletics," Walter Byers Papers, box "Title IX, 1970–80," folder "Correspondence to Member Institutions," pp. 3, 7.

65. Walter Byers to Alan Chapman, 21 Dec. 1974, Walter Byers Papers, box "Title IX, 1970–80," folder "Correspondence to Member Institutions."

66. *1974–75 Annual Reports of the NCAA*, p. 63.

67. Ibid.

68. *Proceedings of the 69th Annual Convention of the NCAA* (1975), p. 145.

69. Ibid., p. 58.

70. Ibid., p. 61. Swank's statement was misinterpreted by Donna A. Lopiano in her affidavit on the *AIAW vs. NCAA* lawsuit six years later in 1981. Lopiano gave the impression that the "some opposition" would come from the NCAA instead of the AIAW (see "Affidavit of Donna A. Lopiano," AIAW vs. NCAA, NCAA Papers, box "Testimonies and Affidavits," p. 75).

71. AIAW, Official Minutes of the Executive Board and Delegate Assembly Meetings, 4–11 Jan. 1975, p. 10.

72. See *Proceedings of the 69th Annual Convention of the NCAA* (1975), p. 146; and Ann Uhlir, "Political Victim: The Dream That Was the A.I.A.W.," *New York Times*, 11 July 1982, newspaper clipping in AIAW Papers, box 276.

73. *Proceedings of the 69th Annual Convention of the NCAA* (1975), pp. A82–84.

8. The Challenge to AIAW's Solitary Control: 1975–1979

1. Epigraph is from Leotus Morrison, letter to presidents of AIAW member institutions, 23 Jan. 1975, AIAW Papers, box 37.

2. Ibid.

3. *On Campus with Women*, no. 11 (Washington, D.C.: Project on the Status and Education of Women, Association of American Colleges, May 1975), p. 12.

4. Kenneth M. Mason, general manager of Motion Picture and Audiovisual Markets Division, Eastman Kodak Company, to Leotus Morrison and Mildred Barnes (president of NAGWS), 26 Feb. 1975, AIAW Papers, box 309.

5. AIAW, "Possible Alternatives for Future Governing Structures for Intercollegiate Athletics," ca. late Mar. 1975, AIAW Papers, box 70, "Appendix to Affidavit of AIAW President Donna A. Lopiano," appendix 53, p. 3.

6. Ibid.

7. NCAA, "Report of the Council of the National Collegiate Athletic Association on the Several Issues Involved in the Administration of Women's Intercollegiate Athletics at the National Level," 25 Apr. 1975, NCAA Papers, box 1, "The NCAA and Women's Athletics," p. 6.

8. Ibid., pp. 4, 9.

9. Leotus Morrison, memo to AIAW Voting Representatives, 29 Apr. 1975, "Appendix to Affidavit of AIAW President Lopiano," appendix 55.

10. AAHPER, "Executive Committee Response to the Report of the Council of the NCAA on the Several Issues Involved in the Administration of Women's Intercollegiate Athletics at the National Level," 12 May 1975, AIAW Papers, box 37.

11. Ibid.

12. L. Leotus Morrison, memo to Voting Representatives of AIAW Member Institutions, Director of Women's Intercollegiate Athletics of AIAW Member Institutions, or Chairperson, Department of Physical Education of AIAW Member Institutions, 15 May 1975, AIAW Papers, box 37.

13. The official AIAW response to the NCAA Council's report, completed in May 1975, was distributed in June after Laurie Mabry assumed the presidency of the association. Laurie Mabry to AIAW Voting Representatives, 10 June 1975, AIAW Papers, box 37; and AIAW, "Response of the Association for Intercollegiate Athletics for Women to the NCAA Report on the Several Issues Involved in the Administration of Women's Intercollegiate Athletics," May 1975, AIAW Papers, box 37, p. 1.

14. In 1974–75, the AIAW ran a budget deficit of more than 13 percent, with a total expense of $119,348 over an income of $105,569. "AIAW Financial Statement, June 1, 1974-May 31, 1975," AIAW Papers, box 262.

15. Official Minutes of the Third AIAW Delegate Assembly, AIAW Papers, box 269, p. 12.

16. Ibid.

17. Margot Polivy, memo to Executive Boards NAGWS and AIAW, 7 Apr. 1975, AIAW Papers, box 309.

18. Walter Byers to Selected Representatives of NCAA, 17 May 1975, David Mathews Papers, folder "Athletic Office #2, 1974–75," University of Alabama Archives, Tuscaloosa, Ala.

19. Walter Byers to Selected Representatives of NCAA, 30 May 1975, David Mathews Papers, folder "Athletic Office #2, 1974–75," University of Alabama Archives.

20. "Terps' Kehoe Criticizes New Sex Bias Rules," *Washington Post*, 5 June 1975, newspaper clipping in AIAW Papers, box 276.

21. Ibid.

22. Ibid.

23. Margot Polivy, memo to Laurie Mabry, 6 June 1975, AIAW Papers, box 309.

24. Ibid.

25. Ibid., p. 3.

26. Margot Polivy, memo to Presidents AIAW, NAGWS, 17 June 1975, AIAW Papers, box 309.

27. On 14 July 1975 the House Equal Opportunities Subcommittee rejected an amendment sponsored by James O'Hara, a representative from Michigan, which proposed the ex-

emption of "revenue-producing" sports from the implementation of Title IX. "HEW Rules Said Not to Match Laws," *Washington Post*, 15 July 1975. Representatives of the American Football Coaches Association, Darrell Royal of the University of Texas, Barry Switzer of the University of Oklahoma, and Bo Schembechler and Don Canham of the University of Michigan, met with President Ford in the White House shortly before the regulations became effective. After the meeting, the big-time college football coaches agreed that the rejection of the regulations was "no longer a viable possibility." Walter Byers Papers, NCAA Television Committee Minutes, 16–17 July 1975; and *Newsday*, 20 July 1975.

28. "Statement by Casper W. Weinberger, Secretary of Health, Education, and Welfare," *Final Title IX Regulation Implementing Education Amendments of 1972—Prohibiting Sex Discrimination in Education* (Washington, D.C.: U.S. Department of Health, Education, and Welfare/Office for Civil Rights, 1975), pp. 2, 4–5.

29. The meeting was held on 24–25 September 1975 at the O'Hare Hilton in Chicago. Representing the AIAW were Carol Gordon, Laurie Mabry, Peg Burke, Kay Hutchcraft (non-voting), and Roger Wiley (non-voting); NCAA representatives included Bill Orwig (committee chair), Bob Strimer, John Eiler, Ed Betz, Stan Marshall, and Walter Byers (non-voting). The minutes of the meeting were "revised" by the AIAW. "NCAA-AIAW Joint Committee Meeting Minutes," 24–25 Sept. 1975, "Appendix to Affidavit of AIAW President Lopiano," appendix 59.

30. The NCAA received only seventy-five responses to the NCAA Council's report: twenty-six (34.7 percent) favorable/favorable with reservations; thirty-three (44 percent) unfavorable/unfavorable with reservations; and sixteen (14.3 percent) undetermined. The AIAW received seventy-seven responses: twenty-two (28.6 percent) unqualified support/qualified support, forty-five (58.4 percent) unqualified/qualified rejection, and ten (13 percent) undetermined. The total number of "87" AIAW responses reported in the minutes seems to be an error in tabulation. "NCAA-AIAW Joint Committee Meeting Minutes," 24–25 Sept. 1975, "Appendix to Affidavit of AIAW President Lopiano," appendix 59, p. 2.

31. Ibid., pp. 2–7.

32. Ibid., p. 7.

33. Ibid., pp. 7–8.

34. Cox, Langford and Brown, and Swanson, Midgley, Gangwere, Thurlo and Clarke, "A Legal Opinion requested by the NCAA Council for its guidance and for the information of the membership of the National Collegiate Athletic Association," 21 Nov. 1975, NCAA Papers, p. 2.

35. Ibid., pp. 21–22.

36. *1974–75 Annual Reports of the NCAA*, p. 162.

37. Several members indicated that the NCAA should continue its negotiation with the AIAW in good faith instead of jeopardizing a healthy process by a unilateral action. At the suggestion of Stanley McCaffrey of the University of the Pacific, the convention avoided a possible defeat of the motion that would have put the NCAA on record as an organization for men only. "That," stated McCaffrey, "would be very unwise legally." *Proceedings of the 3rd Special Convention and 70th Annual Convention of the NCAA* (1976), pp. 206–13, A128–30.

38. Walter Byers to Edward S. Steitz, John R. Eiler, William Exum, Robert M. Strimer, Mel R. Sheehan, Harry Fouke, Lavon McDonald, Edward S. Betz, Ruth M. Berkey, and J. William Orwig, 28 May 1976, AIAW Papers, box 37.

39. Ibid.

40. Walter Byers to Ruth Berkey, 29 June 1976, Walter Byers Papers, box 159, folder "Women's Athletics."

41. AIAW, Official Minutes of the Spring Executive Board Meeting, 10–13 May 1977, AIAW Papers, box 382, p. 3.

42. AIAW, Official Minutes of the Fall Executive Board Meeting, AIAW Papers, box 382, pp. 34–35; and NCAA, "Summary of NCAA Meetings Concerning Women's Athletics Matters," pp. 25–26.

43. *1976–77 Annual Reports of the NCAA*, p. 170.

44. The motion was sponsored by six northeastern institutions: Bentley College, University of Hartford, LeMoyne College, Quinnipiac College, St. Michael's College, and Springfield College. *Proceedings of the 72nd Annual Convention of the NCAA* (1978), p. A-86.

45. AIAW, Official Minutes of the Winter Executive Board Meeting, 12 Jan. 1978, AIAW Papers, box 418, p. 2.

46. AIAW, Official Minutes of the Winter Executive Board Meeting, 7 Jan. 1978, "Appendix to Affidavit of AIAW President Lopiano," appendix 87, p. 8.

47. *1977–78 Annual Reports of the NCAA*, pp. 71–72.

48. *Proceedings of the 72nd Annual Convention of the NCAA* (1978), pp. 179–82.

49. Edward S. Betz, memo to chief executive officers, faculty athletic representatives, and directors of athletics of NCAA member institutions, 14 Feb. 1978, "Appendix to Affidavit of AIAW President Lopiano," appendix 88.

50. It was noted that the Division II results were established "almost entirely by favorable responses from NCAA members which do not belong to AIAW." No explanation was given to the Division I and Division III responses. *1977–78 Annual Reports of the NCAA*, p. 125.

51. Ibid., p. 182.

52. *1977–78 Annual Reports of the NCAA*, p. 215; NCAA, "Summary of NCAA Meetings Concerning Women's Athletics," pp. 29–30; and AIAW, Minutes of the Fall Executive Board Meeting, 10–13 Oct. 1978, p. 22.

53. *1977–78 Annual Reports of the NCAA*, p. 198.

54. NCAA, "Summary of NCAA Meetings Concerning Women's Athletics," p. 31.

55. At its October 1979 meeting, the NCAA Council reiterated its position on the issue that "national governance was not an appropriate issue for negotiation by national organizations until direction emanated from the institutional and conference levels." *1978–79 Annual Reports of the NCAA*, p. 218.

56. Charlotte West, memo to Presidents and Executive Directors of the NAIA and the NCAA, 24 Oct. 1978, "Appendix to Affidavit of AIAW President Lopiano," appendix 94.

57. Walter Byers to Charlotte West, 7 Jan. 1979, "Appendix to Affidavit of AIAW President Lopiano," appendix 96.

58. The average annual inflation rate during the 1970s reached 7.08 percent, three times the rate during the 1960s (2.36 percent) and more than three and one-half times the rate during the 1950s (1.98 percent). See "Consumer Price Indexes (CPI-U), Annual Percent Change by Major Groups: 1940 to 1995," in *Statistical Abstract of the United States*, 116th ed. (Washington, D.C.: U.S. Bureau of Census, 1996), p. 484.

59. "NCAA General Round Table" [Discussion of Title IX Policy Interpretation], 8 Jan. 1979, Walter Byers Papers, box "Title IX 1970–1980," folder "Title IX pre-1980," pp. 8–9, 67–68

60. By 1979–80, only 19.5 percent of women's programs in all competitive divisions were separately administered by female athletic directors, with 80.5 percent under a single male athletic director. Vivian Acosta and Linda Carpenter, *Administrative Structure and Gender of Personnel in Intercollegiate Athletics for Women* (New York: Brooklyn College, June 1980), as cited in "Affidavit of Donna A. Lopiano," *AIAW vs. NCAA*, p. 119.

61. The NCAA Council noted in 1979 that "there appears to be a clear pattern of a single athletic structure at the institutional level and in many conferences." *1978–79 Annual Reports of the NCAA*, p. 218.

62. Harry Fritz, NAIA Executive Director, to Members of the AIAW Liaison Committee on Men's Athletics, 19 July 1978, "Appendix to Affidavit of AIAW President Lopiano," appendix 91.

63. "For the past 15 year[s], NAIA has given full support and cooperation to the development of the then DGWS, now the AIAW." A. O. Duer to Presidents of NAIA Member Institutions, 9 June 1975, "Appendix to Affidavit of AIAW President Lopiano," appendix 52.

64. Charlotte West, "Welcoming Remarks for the 6th Annual Delegate Assembly," 7 Jan. 1979, AIAW, Official Minutes of the Executive Board and Delegate Assembly Meetings, appendix, p. 5, AIAW Papers, box 418.

65. According to Charlotte West, the AIAW "had no savings" by the 1978–79 fiscal year. AIAW, Official Minutes of the Executive Board and Delegate Assembly Meetings, appendix, p. 5, AIAW Papers, box 418, p. 2.

66. From 1972 to 1978, the average AIAW annual income was approximately $181,000 (range from ca. $28,000 in 1972–73 to ca. $386,000 in 1977–78) versus an average expense of about $196,000. "AIAW Financial Statements, 1971–79," AIAW Papers, box 262.

67. AIAW, Official Minutes of the Spring Executive Board Meeting, 29 May–1 June 1976, p. 32.

68. AIAW, Official Minutes of the Spring Executive Board Meeting, 10–13 May 1977, p. 5.

9. Margot Polivy, Legal Costs, and the AIAW's Financial Disaster

1. Margot Polivy to Donna Lopiano, 2 Sept. 1975, AIAW Papers, box 309.

2. In spring 1973, shortly after the settlement of the *Kellmeyer* case, the AIAW Executive Board voted to set up a separate legal fund within the AAHPER. The board recognized that the "AIAW needs its own lawyer to provide legal assistance for problems which might arise in the future." Minutes of the Executive Board of the AIAW, 31 May–4 June 1973, AIAW Papers, box 418, p. 7.

3. Only two AIAW leaders were involved in the hiring process, Leotus Morrison, AIAW president, and Kay Hutchcraft, AIAW program coordinator. Kay Hutchcraft, "Report of Legal Assistance," 30 Sept. 1975, AIAW Papers, box 309, p. 1.

4. Joanna Davenport, personal interview by the author, 12 July 1995, Marblehead, Mass..

5. "Retainer Agreement Between AIAW and Renouf, McKenna and Polivy [1975–76]," AIAW Papers, box 309; and Hutchcraft, "Report of Legal Assistance," p. 1.

6. "Analysis—Legal Services Expenditure," Jan. 1976, AIAW Papers, box 309; and "AIAW Financial Statement, 1 June 1974–31 May 1975," AIAW Papers, box 262.

7. Hutchcraft, "Report of Legal Assistance," p. 3.

8. In a memo sent to Leotus Morrison, 8 Dec. 1974, Estes questioned the sanity of AIAW's spending on Margot Polivy. AIAW Papers, box 309.

9. Subcommittee for Input to Executive Committee, memo to executive committee—AIAW, 3 Oct. 1975, AIAW Papers, box 309.

10. Laurie Mabry, memo to AIAW Executive Committee members, 6 Oct. 1975, AIAW Papers, box 309.

11. Ibid.

12. "Retainer Agreement [1975–76]," AIAW Papers, box 309.

13. Mabry, memo to AIAW Executive Committee members, 6 Oct. 1975.

14. Charlotte West to Laurie Mabry, 10 Oct. 1975, AIAW Papers, box 309.

15. Ibid.

16. Leotus Morrison, memo to AIAW Executive Committee, 14 Oct. 1975, AIAW Papers, box 309.

17. Ibid.

18. Margot Polivy to Kay Hutchcraft, 30 Oct. 1975, AIAW Papers, box 309.

19. Ibid.

20. Region 8 of the AIAW included the following states: California, Hawaii, and Nevada. Nettie Morrison to Laurie Mabry, 20 Nov. 1975, AIAW Papers, box 309.

21. Region 9 of the AIAW included the following states: Alaska, Idaho, Montana, Oregon, and Washington. Catherine Green to Laurie Mabry, 26 Nov. 1975, AIAW Papers, box 309.

22. "Legal fees" were covered under the "general operation" of the 1975–76 AIAW budget. By October 1975, the legal expenses had exceeded $19,000, overrunning the $18,124 annual budget for AIAW's "general operation." "Financial Statement, 1 June 1975–31 May 1976"; "1975–76 Financial Justification," AIAW Papers, box 262; and "Analysis—Legal Services Expenditures" (Jan. 1976), AIAW Papers, box 309.

23. As one alternative, Polivy suggested that the retainer agreement be modified to include "all legal services under monthly retainer with the annual retainer amount renegotiated annually at a flat rate, to be $17,000 of the last five months of this fiscal year and $60,000 for fiscal 1976–77." Margot Polivy to Kay Hutchcraft, 30 Oct. 1975, AIAW Papers, box 309.

24. Laurie Mabry to Margot Polivy, 16 Dec. 1975, AIAW Papers, box 309.

25. The disagreements on the three occasions were related to (1) AIAW's official response to the release of the Title IX regulations; (2) AIAW's response to the NCAA report on the implication of Title IX in intercollegiate athletics, and (3) AIAW's testimony at the congressional hearing regarding Title IX. AIAW Papers, box 309.

26. Ibid.

27. Ibid.

28. Ibid.

29. The AIAW Executive Committee consisted of the president, the past president, the president-elect, and the executive secretary. Laurie Mabry, telephone interview by the author, 15 Apr. 1997.

30. Margot Polivy to Laurie Mabry, 19 Dec. 1975, AIAW Papers, box 309.

31. Ibid. Polivy insisted that the NCAA structure was more desirable with its policies and direction coming from the executive staff. She was only partially correct. While the NCAA often derived its directions from the executive staff, its policies were made by the NCAA Council and, ultimately, the membership.

32. Ibid.

33. Ibid.

34. Ibid.

35. See "Potential Agreements Regarding Function of the AIAW Legal Counsel and Operational Policies and Relationships Between the AIAW and Its Legal Counsel," Appendix B in AIAW Official Minutes of the Executive Board and Delegate Assembly Meetings, 6–11 Jan. 1979, AIAW Papers, box 418, pt. 3, p. 69.

36. The extremely high percentage of legal expenses in 1981–82 (41.7 percent) was the combined result of reduced income and the extra cost of the *AIAW v. NCAA* antitrust lawsuit. See AIAW, "Financial Statements" (1974 to 1982), AIAW Papers, box 262.

37. Ranging from 6.4 percent to 9.4 percent during the eight-year period, the average share for AIAW national championships was only 8.0 percent of AIAW annual income. See AIAW Papers, box 262; AIAW, "Legal Counsel Cost Analysis," "Cash Disbursements, 1981–82," AIAW Papers, box 419; AIAW, "Analysis—Legal Services Expenditures," January 1976, AIAW Papers, box 309; and Ann Uhlir, memo to Cindy Jackson, AIAW administrative accountant, 13 May 1981, AIAW Papers, box 309.

38. Kay Hutchcraft, AIAW executive secretary, "Report of Legal Assistance," 30 Sept. 1975, AIAW Papers, box 309, p. 4; and "Retainer Agreement [1975–76]," AIAW Papers, box 309.

39. "Financial Statement, June 1, 1975-May 31, 1976," "1975–76 Financial Justification," AIAW Papers, box 262; and "Analysis—Legal Services Expenditures" (January 1976), AIAW Papers, box 309.

40. "Retainer Agreement Between AIAW and Renouf, McKenna and Polivy [1976–77]," AIAW Papers, box 309.

41. AIAW's 1975—76 budget for legal service was $18,800; the actual expense was $43,647. AIAW, "Financial Statement, June 1, 1975-May 31, 1976."

42. Ibid.

43. The attempt to get rid of Polivy's service failed after lengthy discussions during the spring 1976 AIAW Executive Board meeting. The minutes of the meeting indicate a marginal victory for those who wanted to retain the service of Polivy (11 for, 9 opposed, 1 abstain). Interviews by this author with several members (anonymous) who were at the meeting show that the original vote was a tie. Then the AIAW president, N. Peg Burke, broke the tie with a favorable vote. AIAW, Official Minutes of the Spring Executive Board Meeting, 29 May–1 June 1976, AIAW Papers, box 269, pp. 32–41.

44. Except for the singular vote from Judith Holland, then president-elect, the executive board overwhelmingly defeated the motion "that a Management Audit of AIAW be undertaken in the fiscal year 1977–78." AIAW Papers, box 269, p. 35.

45. As quoted in Linda Estes to AIAW Voting Representatives, 6 Nov. 1978, AIAW Pa-

pers, box 309. Region 7 of the AIAW consisted of the states of Arizona, Colorado, New Mexico, Utah, and Wyoming.

46. Linda Estes, memo to Judy Holland, Charlotte West, Carole Mushier, 24 Oct. 1978, AIAW Papers, box 309.

47. AIAW, Official Minutes of the Fall Executive Board Meeting, 10–13 Oct. 1978, AIAW Papers, box 269.

48. In order to put Region 7's resolution on the agenda of the delegate assembly, Estes had collected the required number of signatures through a petition and was requesting a response from the three AIAW presidents (president, past president, and president-elect). The actual AIAW budget for its legal counsel in 1978–79 was $75,000, 14.6 percent of the association's budget of $513,666. Estes, memo to Holland et al., 24 Oct. 1978; and "Financial Statement, June 1, 1978-May 31, 1979," AIAW Papers, box 262.

49. Charlotte West, Judie Holland, Carole Mushier, memo to Linda Estes, 10 Nov. 1978, AIAW Papers, box 309.

50. Ibid. There seemed to be no evidence to support the statement. In 1977–78, the total of NCAA's legal fees and expenses was $645,720. *1977–78 Annual Reports of the NCAA*, p. 252.

51. West et al., memo to Estes, 10 Nov. 1978.

52. Margot Polivy, telephone interview by the author, 11 Sept. 1997.

53. Linda Estes to AIAW Voting Representative, 6 Nov. 1978, AIAW Papers, box 309. According to Estes, the letter was mailed on 14 Nov. 1978, ten days after it was written and fifteen days before the 29 Nov. 1978 deadline for Delegate Assembly agenda items. Linda Estes, memo to Carole Mushier and Charlotte West, 29 Nov. 1978, AIAW Papers, box 309.

54. Judith R. Holland to Linda Estes, 21 Nov. 1978, AIAW Papers, box 309.

55. Bonnie Slatton to Linda Estes, 21 Nov. 1978, AIAW Papers, box 309.

56. Estes was referring to President Nixon and the Watergate scandal that led to his resignation. Linda Estes to Bonnie Slatton, 29 Nov. 1978, AIAW Papers, box 309.

57. Estes, memo to Mushier and West, 29 Nov. 1978.

58. Margot Polivy to Bonnie Slatton, 22 Nov. 1978, AIAW Papers, box 309.

59. Ibid.

60. Ibid.

61. Ibid. Apparently it was believed that the future would bring hope for the AIAW's financial situation. That was why Polivy's firm "rejected the proffered increase of $5,000 [for the retainer year 1978–79] because while it imposed an additional burden on AIAW's budget," Polivy stated, "it did not, to any significant extent, alleviate our financial suffering."

62. Ibid.

63. Ibid. Contrary to Polivy's statement, the NCAA's total legal fees and expenses in 1978–79 were $560,833, only 3.7 percent of the organization's income of $14,965,033. *1978–79 Annual Reports of the NCAA*, pp. 268–72.

64. Margot Polivy to Bonnie Slatton, 22 Nov. 1978, p. 5.

65. Carole L. Mushier, AIAW president, to Arlene E. Gorton, 20 Feb. 1979, AIAW Papers, box 309.

66. Linda Estes, telephone interview by the author, 17 May 1997.

67. Arlene E. Gorton to Charlotte West, 2 Feb. 1979, AIAW Papers, box 309.

68. The total payment, according to the contract, should not exceed $130,000. "Retainer Agreement Between AIAW and Renouf and Polivy [1979–80]," AIAW Papers, box 309. The law firm changed its name from Renouf, McKenna and Polivy to Renouf and Polivy after Francis G. McKenna left the firm.

69. AIAW, "Financial Statement, July 1, 1980-June 30, 1981," AIAW Papers, box 262.

70. Information on the subject was incomplete in the AIAW Papers. The AIAW paid the law firm at least $285,114, which was 41.7 percent of AIAW's total income of $684,245. It is worth noting that out of the $285,000 plus legal costs, only $132,000 was paid for the retainer fee; the $153,000 plus was spent on the *AIAW v. NCAA* litigation. AIAW, "Legal Counsel Cost Analysis," "Cash Disbursements, 1981–82," ca. July 1982, AIAW Papers, box 419; and "Financial Statement, July 1, 1981-June 30, 1982," AIAW Papers, box 262.

71. The 4,746 hours included 3,917 hours of work on the litigation and another 829 hours of work for the AIAW as covered by the retainer fee. AIAW, "Legal Counsel Cost Analysis," AIAW Papers, box 419.

72. According to the recollection of Polivy, there were, on an average, two full-time (Polivy and an associate) and two part-time lawyers working for the AIAW during the *AIAW v. NCAA* litigation. Another Washington, D.C., law firm—Dickstein, Shapiro and Morin (known for its expertise in antitrust laws, according to Polivy)—provided pro bono services to the AIAW. Margot Polivy, telephone interview by the author, 24 Sept. 1997.

73. AIAW, "Legal Counsel Cost Analysis."

74. Ibid.

10. From NCAA "Governance Plan" to the End of AIAW Operation

1. The chapter epigraph is from Christine H. B. Grant, "AIAW/NCAA Press Statement," Apr. 1980, AIAW Papers, box 404.

2. *Proceedings of the 73rd Annual Convention of the NCAA* (1979), pp. 136–40, A83-A84.

3. On 9 March 1979 Edward Betz, NCAA committee chair on women's athletics, phoned Mary Roby, AIAW committee chair on men's athletics, to arrange a joint committee meeting. Roby discouraged the meeting because of "questionable agenda" and schedule conflict. On 14 March 1979, Roby informed the AIAW committee that the proposed meeting was "inappropriate" at the time. AIAW, "CIAW-AIAW-NCAA Organizational Relationships Chronology, 1959–1980," Walter Byers Papers, box 1, "NCAA and Women's Athletics," folder "NCAA's Early Involvement with Women's Athletics, 1975."

4. McFadden was responding to West's letter of 31 Oct. 1978, when she was the president of the AIAW. Hugh B. McFadden to Charlotte West, 23 Apr. 1979, Walter Byers Papers, box 159, "Women's Athletics."

5. WAC stands for the Western Athletic Conference to which the University of Wyoming belonged. Walter Byers Papers, box 159, "Women's Athletics."

6. Ibid.

7. Ibid.

8. See Walter Byers to William J. Flynn and James Frank, 23 July 1979, Walter Byers Papers, box 159, "Women's Athletics."

9. Norman C. Crawford Jr., memo to Dr. William Gerbering, Dr. Hollis A. Moore, Dr. William J. Tietz, and Dr. Henry I. Willett Sr., 6 July 1979, Walter Byers Papers, box 159, "Women's Athletics."

10. "There is a reluctance (I believe an inability) on the part of AIAW to compromise any of its rules with those of either the NCAA or the NAIA," wrote Crawford. "There appears to me to be a division among the AIAW leadership in this regard which precludes any such compromise being harmoniously achieved." Walter Byers Papers, box 159, "Women's Athletics." Crawford's speculation on the situation seemed to be rather credible. Seventeen years later, Suzanne C. Willey pointed out in her doctoral dissertation that "there was major resistance, on the part of the AIAW leaders, to sincerely work towards a mutually beneficial governing organization." Suzanne C. Willey, "The Governance of Women's Intercollegiate Athletics: Association for Intercollegiate Athletics for Women (AIAW) 1976–1982" (P.E.D. diss., Indiana Univ., 1996), p. 239.

11. Crawford, memo to Gerbering et al., 6 July 1979.

12. Ibid. It would be hard to determine exactly how much Crawford's correspondence affected the evolution of NCAA's policies on women's athletics. The significance of the correspondence, however, apparently did not escape the attention of Walter Byers. The NCAA executive director, presumably as soon as he acquired a copy, made duplicates and sent them to William Flynn and James Frank, the president and secretary-treasurer of the NCAA. The importance of Byers' letter became self-explanatory. Byers pointed out in his correspondence that the five presidents involved served on the five-member AIAW chief executive officers advisory council, and that Crawford's memo "probably should be treated as confidential." Walter Byers to William J. Flynn and James Frank, 23 July 1979, Walter Byers Papers, box 159, "Women's Athletics."

13. Minutes of the NCAA Committee on Women's Intercollegiate Athletics, 16–17 June 1979, Walter Byers Papers, box 159, "Women's Athletics."

14. *1978–79 Annual Reports of the NCAA*, p. 181.

15. The five alternative governance structures were: (1) union of AIAW/NCAA, (2) federation-type linkage between AIAW/NCAA, (3) maintaining the two current separate associations, (4) federation of four-year athletic governing groups, and (5) a federation of coeducational associations that were established on the basis of divisional status. Minutes of the Meeting of the AIAW Committee on Men's Intercollegiate Athletics and the NCAA Committee on Women's Intercollegiate Athletics, 1–2 Oct. 1979, Walter Byers Papers, box 159, "Women's Athletics," attachment no. 1.

16. Ibid., p. 3.

17. NCAA Council Minutes, Resolution, 16–19 Oct. 1979, AIAW Papers, box 70, "Appendix to Affidavit of AIAW President Donna A. Lopiano," appendix 102; and Thomas Hansen to Mary Roby, 16 Nov. 1979, AIAW Papers, box 64.

18. AIAW, Official Minutes of the Fall Executive Board Meeting, 9–12 Oct. 1979, AIAW Papers, box 418, p. 26; and "Affidavit of Donna A. Lopiano," *AIAW v. NCAA*, 9 Oct. 1981, Walter Byers Papers, box "Testimonies and Affidavits," p. 126.

19. Carole L. Mushier to William Flynn, 19 Nov. 1979, Walter Byers Papers, box 159, "Women's Athletics."

20. William Flynn to Carole L. Mushier, 11 Dec. 1979, Walter Byers Papers, box 159, "Women's Athletics."

21. U.S. Department of Health, Education, and Welfare, "Statement by Patricia Roberts Harris, Secretary of Health, Education, and Welfare," 4 Dec. 1979, "Appendix to Affidavit of AIAW President Lopiano," appendix 103, p. 6.

22. Carole Mushier, memo to AIAW Voting Representatives, 7 Dec. 1979, AIAW Papers, box 28.

23. Ibid.

24. "Significant Issues to Face AIAW Delegate Assembly," AIAW News Release, 18 Dec. 1979, AIAW Papers, box 280.

25. Later on, the AIAW often used the term "alternative model" instead of "educational model."

26. Ibid., pp. 1, 4.

27. As early as October 1979 during the NCAA Council meeting, representatives of smaller institutions on the NCAA Committee on Women's Athletics had indicated that "they could best provide opportunities for their women athletes through NCAA championships because of the Association's payment of expenses for participants in its championships." *1978–79 Annual Reports of the NCAA,* p. 217; and NCAA, "Agenda, Special Committee on NCAA Governance, Organization and Services," 11–12 Dec. 1979, "Appendix to Affidavit of AIAW President Lopiano," appendix 105, p. 4.

28. Carole Mushier to presidents (of institutions holding both AIAW and NCAA memberships), 26 Dec. 1979, AIAW Papers, box 280.

29. Special NCAA Committee on Governance, Organization and Services, "Preliminary Report," 28 Dec. 1979, "Appendix to Affidavit of AIAW President Lopiano," appendix 106, AIAW Papers, box 280.

30. AIAW, Official Minutes of the Winter Executive Board Meeting, 5 Jan. 1980, "Appendix to Affidavit of AIAW President Lopiano," appendix 107, p. 3.

31. AIAW, Official Minutes of the 1980 Delegate Assembly, 6–9 Jan. 1980, AIAW Papers, box 418, p. 25.

32. *1979–80 Annual Reports of the NCAA,* p. 75.

33. See, for details, *Proceedings of the 74th Annual Convention of the NCAA* (1980), pp. 33–34.

34. The five sports were basketball, field hockey, swimming, tennis, and volleyball. Ibid., pp. 114–22, A42-A44.

35. An "open" championship was one in which schools in all three divisions of the AIAW were eligible to compete.

36. The AIAW's first attempt at television marketing, with Sugarman Productions, was a failure. In May 1978, the AIAW authorized Margot Polivy to recover monies due the AIAW under the contract. But the "Sugarman Debt," according to Polivy, was never fully recovered because the company went bankrupt. AIAW, Official Minutes of the Spring Executive Board Meeting, 9–12 May 1978, AIAW Papers, box 269, p. 8; and Margot Polivy, telephone interview by the author, 11 Sept. 1997.

37. Interviews with several former AIAW officials indicated that the one-million-dollar

TV rights contract with NBC was spread out for four years. "Presidential Address," Official Minutes of the AIAW Delegate Assembly, 6–9 Jan. 1980, AIAW Papers, box 418, p. 32.

38. Ibid., p. 34.

39. Ibid., pp. 34–35.

40. Christine H. B. Grant, "Presidential Address," Official Minutes of the AIAW Delegate Assembly, 6–9 Jan. 1980, AIAW Papers, box 418, p. 37.

41. Ibid.

42. Fey mis-termed the CCWAA as composed of "a few people in the middle," for it was the very "opposition party" within the AIAW. Karen Fey, interview by Gail F. Maloney, 20 Sept. 1993, as cited in Gail F. Maloney, "The Impact of Title IX on Women's Intercollegiate Athletics" (Ph.D. diss., State Univ. of New York at Buffalo, 1994), pp. 100–102.

43. Initiated by Barbara Hedges of the University of Southern California, the co-founders of the CCWAA also included Phyllis Bailey (Ohio State University), Jean Cerra (University of Missouri), June Davis (University of Nebraska), Kay Don (Texas A&M University), Della Durant (Penn State University), Linda Estes (University of New Mexico), Sue Garrison (University of Houston), Mary Alice Hill (San Diego State University), Judith Holland (University of California at Los Angeles), Mary Roby (University of Arizona), and Pamela Strathairn (Stanford University). Barbara Hedges, telephone interview with the author, 11 Aug. 1997. Durant recalled that Ellen Perry of Penn State University represented her at the first CCWAA meeting at Stanford University. Della Durant, telephone interview by the author, 20 July 1997. In 1991, the CCWAA changed its name to the National Association of Collegiate Women Athletic Administrators.

44. Karen Fey, as quoted in Maloney, "The Impact of Title IX," p. 101.

45. Christine Grant, interview by Gail F. Maloney, 20 Sept. 1993, "The Impact of Title IX," p. 89.

46. "Affidavit of Judith R. Holland," Walter Byers Papers, box "Testimonies and Affidavits," p. 2.

47. "AIAW Presentation to ACE Presidents' Committee on Collegiate Athletics," 25 Feb. 1980, "Appendix to Affidavit of AIAW President Lopiano," appendix 118, p. 2.

48. Ibid, p. 5.

49. James Frank (chair of NCAA Governance Committee), memo to Chief Executive Officers of Active Member Institutions, 31 Jan. 1980, "Appendix to Affidavit of AIAW President Lopiano," appendix 109; and James Frank, memo to Chief Executive Officers of NCAA Member Institutions, 2 June 1980, "Appendix to Affidavit of AIAW President Lopiano," appendix 116.

50. "Decision and Order," *AIAW v. NCAA* (U.S. District Court for the District of Columbia, Civil Action 81–2473), 25 Feb. 1983, personal files of Joan S. Hult, p. 9.

51. William J. Flynn and James Frank, memo to chief executive officers, faculty athletic representatives, and directors of athletics of NCAA member institutions, 5 Nov. 1980, AIAW Papers, box 64.

52. "The AIAW urged the ACE (American Council on Education) to adopt a position of formal opposition to the NCAA proposals and advise college presidents that ACE looked with disfavor on NCAA entrance into women's intercollegiate athletics, ACE took no formal

action at that time." See "Affidavit of Donna A. Lopiano," p. 162. In late June 1980, the AIAW Executive Committee solicited the support of the AIAW members in its opposition to the NCAA proposals. AIAW Executive Committee, memo to AIAW Voting Representatives, 26 June 1980, "Appendix to Affidavit of AIAW President Lopiano," appendix 120.

53. Christine H. B. Grant to Sarah Harder, co-chairperson, National Women's Conference Committee, 29 Aug. 1980, AIAW Papers, box 64.

54. Ibid.

55. Christine H. B. Grant, "A 'State of the Union' Message," *National Championship Newsletter* (AIAW), ca. fall 1980, NCAA Papers, box "Reactions."

56. In comparison, the AIAW had established forty-two national championships in nineteen different sports by 1981–82. Joan S. Hult, "The Story of Women's Athletics: Manipulating a Dream, 1890–1985," in *Women and Sport: Interdisciplinary Perspectives*, ed. D. Margaret Costa and Sharon R. Guthrie (Champaign, Ill.: Human Kinetics, 1994), p. 97. The NCAA proposal for Division I women's championships was eventually approved by Division I membership with a vote of 137 to 117. It was initially defeated on a tie vote, 124 to 124, then defeated on recount, 127 to 128. A motion for roll-call vote was also defeated, 114 to 133. A subsequent motion to reconsider the proposal was approved, 141 to 105. A motion to recess was defeated. A motion to cease debate was approved. Finally, it was approved by a vote of 137 to 117. *Proceedings of the 75th Annual Convention of the NCAA* (1981), pp. 167–80, A61-A67.

57. "Decision and Order," p. 10.

58. Ibid., p. 11.

59. "Affidavit of Donna A. Lopiano," Walter Byers Papers, box "Testimonies and Affidavits," p. 265.

60. The AIAW's total income in 1980–81 was $824,112. "Decision and Order," p. 11; and AIAW, "Financial Statement" (1 July 1980–30 June 1981), AIAW Papers, box 262.

61. The AIAW received a total of $2,372,039 from its membership dues between 1974 and 1982. AIAW, "Financial Statement" (1 June 1974–30 June 1982), AIAW Papers, box 262.

62. "Decision and Order," pp. 11–12; "Affidavit of Donna A. Lopiano," p. 266; and Donna A. Lopiano, "Presidential Address," 6 Jan. 1982, AIAW, Official Minutes of 1982 Delegate Assembly, AIAW Papers, box 418, p. 57.

63. Responding to NBC's concern, Margot Polivy indicated that "AIAW was ready, willing and able to provide the Division I and Open Championships program covered by the NBC contract." AIAW's 1981–82 television income of $55,000 represented in its entirety deferred payments for 1980–81 events. Margot Polivy, memo for NBC/AIAW files, 25 Nov. 1981, AIAW Papers, box 309; An NBC Sports representative (signature undeciphered) to Mimi Murray, AIAW, 7 Dec. 1981, AIAW Papers, box 309; Margot Polivy, memo to AIAW Executive Committee, 10 Dec. 1981, AIAW Papers, box 309; and "Decision and Order," pp. 12–13.

64. From 1977 to 1982, over ten commercial enterprises contributed to the AIAW monetarily. Besides Kodak and Broderick, sponsors at various levels represented Hanes, Tea Council, Coca-Cola, Nike, Sports and Leisure International, Louisiana Sluggers, Nissan, and Mikasa. These sponsors contributed a total of approximately $92,000 to the AIAW. AIAW, "Financial Statement" (1 June 1974–30 June 1982); "Decision and Order," pp. 13–14; and "Affidavit of Donna A. Lopiano," p. 282.

65. "Decision and Order," p. 14; and "Affidavit of Donna A. Lopiano," p. 283.

66. "Decision and Order," pp. 14–15.

11. The Final Judgment: A Tale of Two Trials

1. [Ann Uhlir], "Executive Director's Report," Jan. 1982, AIAW, Official Minutes of the 1982 Delegate Assembly, AIAW Papers, box 44.

2. Donna A. Lopiano, "Presidential Address," 6 Jan. 1982, AIAW Papers, box 44.

3. [Uhlir], "Executive Director's Report," Jan. 1982.

4. Donna A. Lopiano, "Presidential Address," AIAW, Official Minutes of the 1981 Delegate Assembly, 6–9 Jan. 1981, AIAW Papers, box 382.

5. Donna Lopiano to Linda Estes, 20 Feb. 1981; and Margot Polivy, memo to AIAW Executive Committee, re Duties and Obligations of Corporate Directors, 19 Feb. 1981, personal files of Linda Estes.

6. Executive Committee (AIAW), memo to AIAW Voting Representatives and Women's Athletic Directors, 11 Feb. 1981, personal files of Linda Estes.

7. " 'Cause' shall include, but not be limited to, fraud, conflict of interest and misuse of corporate funds." Lopiano to Estes, 20 Feb. 1981.

8. Linda Estes was elected by AIAW Region 7 membership in September 1980 as its representative to a two-year term on the AIAW Executive Board. Linda Estes to Walter Byers, 27 Jan. 1981, personal files of Linda Estes.

9. William E. Davis to Presidents of Division I and Region 7 Member Institutions of AIAW, 25 Feb. 1981, AIAW Papers, box 70, "Appendix to Affidavit of AIAW President Donna A. Lopiano," appendix 149.

10. See "Affidavit of Donna A. Lopiano," p. 245.

11. Betty Werner Miles, telegram to President of the AIAW, 2 Mar. 1981, personal files of Linda Estes.

12. "Temporary Restraining Order," *Linda Estes v. AIAW*, 3 Mar. 1981, personal files of Linda Estes.

13. "Affidavit of Donna A. Lopiano," p. 246.

14. AIAW, Official Minutes of the Special Executive Board Meeting, 4 Mar. 1981, "Appendix to Affidavit of AIAW President Lopiano," appendix 147.

15. Ibid. Pamela Strathairn, AIAW Region 8 Representative, protested several AIAW Executive Board actions, including the motions adopted after the adjournment hour. Pamela Strathairn to Donna Lopiano, 17 Mar. 1981, personal files of Linda Estes.

16. See minutes of "AIAW/NCAA Joint Meeting," 30 Apr. 1981, AIAW Papers, box 48; "Transcript: Meeting of AIAW and NCAA Representatives," 30 Apr. 1981; and AIAW Press Release, 1 May 1981, Walter Byers Papers, box "AIAW."

17. "Verified Complaint," 9 Oct. 1981, *AIAW v. NCAA*, personal files of Joan S. Hult, pp. 1, 37–38; and Donna A. Lopiano, "Presidential Address," 6 Jan. 1982; AIAW, Official Minutes of 1982 Delegate Assembly, AIAW Papers, box 418, appendix A.

18. "*AIAW vs. NCAA* Legal Action Chronology," 8 June 1982, AIAW Papers, box 70.

19. The meeting was held on 3 June 1982. The AIAW delegation was composed of presi-

dent Merrily Baker, past president Donna Lopiano, and legal counsel Margot Polivy. The NCAA delegation was composed of president James Frank, secretary-treasurer John Toner, and legal counsel William Kramer. Margot Polivy to William D. Kramer, 14 May 1982, Walter Byers Papers, box "AIAW"; William D. Kramer, memo to the AIAW Litigation/Settlement Proposals File, 8 June 1982, Walter Byers Papers, box "AIAW"; and AIAW, "*AIAW v. NCAA* Legal Action Chronology," 8 June 1982, pp. 3–4.

20. "Decision and Order," *AIAW v. NCAA* (U.S. District Court for the District of Columbia, Civil Action 81–2473), 25 Feb. 1983, p. 2.

21. "From the high school and junior college level to the United States Olympic Committee, governance organizations now typically serve both men and women." "Decision and Order," p. 7.

22. Ibid., p. 20.

23. Ibid., pp. 29–30.

24. Ibid., p. 44.

25. Ibid., p. 45.

26. Ibid., pp. 45–46.

27. Ibid., p. 46.

28. "Appeals Court Rejects Charges That NCAA Forced Women's Group Out of Business," *The Chronicle of Higher Education*, 30 May 1984, pp. 27–28; and "The Byers Era: How the NCAA Assumed Dominance in College Sports," *The Chronicle of Higher Education*, 3 Sept. 1986, p. 113. The three presidents of the AIAW Executive Committee decided not to pursue the case further because of lack of money as well as any legal indications that the AIAW would prevail, while legal counsel Margot Polivy wanted to take the case to the Supreme Court (Lopiano stated that money alone prevented the pursuit). Merrily Dean Baker, telephone interview by the author, 8 Aug. 1997; Virginia Hunt, telephone interview by the author, 18 Aug. 1997; Donna A. Lopiano, telephone interview by the author, 19 Aug. 1997.

29. Virginia Hunt, former AIAW president-elect and secretary-treasurer, telephone interview by the author, 18 Aug. 1997. G. Ann Uhlir, former AIAW executive director, believed the cost of the lawsuit was "on the upper end of one million dollars." Uhlir, telephone interview by the author, 7 Aug. 1997. Based on the records in the AIAW Papers housed in the University of Maryland's McKeldin Library archives, this writer could identify only a total amount of $661,200 in cashed checks payable to Polivy's firm, but was unable to determine the actual amount paid to the firm between July 1982 and May 1984 because of incomplete records after June 1982 in the AIAW Papers.

30. The total amount of retainer fee is based on the fact that the AIAW paid $132,000 for the twelve months in 1981–82 (July 1981 to June 1982) and $10,833 for the month of June 1981. "Legal Counsel Cost Analysis," AIAW Papers, box 419.

31. In addition to the $132,000 retainer fees, the AIAW also paid Polivy's law firm $153,116 for the *AIAW v. NCAA* litigation fees. The AIAW's total income that year was $684,246. AIAW, "Financial Statement, July 1, 1981-June 30, 1982," AIAW Papers, box 262; "Legal Counsel Cost Analysis," AIAW Papers, box 419.

32. Christine Grant, as quoted in Gail F. Maloney, "The Impact of Title IX on Women's Intercollegiate Athletics" (Ph.D. diss., State Univ. of New York at Buffalo, 1994), p. 89.

33. From 1974 to 1982, the average cost of legal service for the AIAW was 21.7 percent of the association's total income; the average cost of national championships was 7.8 percent. See AIAW "Financial Statement" from 1974–75 to 1981–82 in AIAW Papers, box 262.

34. Margot Polivy to Charlotte West, 6 Apr. 1978; and Margot Polivy to Bonnie Slatton, 22 Nov. 1978, AIAW Papers, box 309. In April 1979, Polivy indicated that her law firm was paid approximately 44 percent of "a normal client rate" for its service to the AIAW. Margot Polivy to Bonnie Slatton, 30 Apr. 1979, AIAW Papers, box 309.

35. The AIAW closed its bank account by paying its last $5,635.47 to Polivy's law firm in late May 1984. See canceled check #104, AIAW, Montana State Univ., and "Checking Account Summary," 25 June 1984, American Security Bank, AIAW Papers, box 419. The exact amount the AIAW owed Polivy's firm was $445,304.61. Renouf and Polivy, memo to Virginia Hunt, AIAW president-elect, 4 June 1984, AIAW Papers, box 419.

36. The Appeals Court was told that the "AIAW has been out of business since 1 September 1982 and is wholly without funds." Katrina Renouf to George A. Fisher, Clerk of U.S. Court of Appeals for the District of Columbia Circuit, 1 June 1984, AIAW Papers, box 419.

37. Hunt, telephone interview by the author, 18 Aug. 1997; G. Ann Uhlir to Merrily Dean Baker, 22 Apr. 1988, Ann Uhlir Papers, Texas Women's University Archives, Denton.

38. A representative of NBC Sports (signature undeciphered) to Mimi Murray, 7 Dec. 1981, AIAW Papers, box 309.

39. Ann Uhlir, memo to (AIAW) National Office Staff, 31 Mar. 1982, Ann Uhlir Papers.

40. Joan S. Hult, memo to AIAW Executive Committee (Merrily Baker, Virginia Hunt, Donna Lopiano, and Ann Uhlir), 29 June 1987, Ann Uhlir Papers.

41. Merrily Dean Baker, former AIAW President, to Joan S. Hult, 3 Aug. 1987, Ann Uhlir Papers.

42. G. Ann Uhlir, telephone interview by the author, 7 Aug. 1997.

43. G. Ann Uhlir to Merrily Dean Baker, 22 Apr. 1988, Ann Uhlir Papers.

44. Merrily Dean Baker to G. Ann Uhlir, 13 June 1988, Ann Uhlir Papers.

45. [Uhlir], "Executive Director's Report," Jan. 1982.

Epilogue: Reducing the Gap: Gender Equity in Intercollegiate Athletics at the Dawn of the Twenty-First Century

1. Christine H. B. Grant, "Presidential Address," 6 Jan. 1981, AIAW, Official Minutes of the 1981 Delegate Assembly, AIAW Papers, box 382, p. 66.

2. Hugh B. McFadden to Charlotte West, 23 Apr. 1979, Walter Byers Papers, box 159, "Women's Athletics."

3. Ronald A. Smith, *Sports and Freedom: The Rise of Big Time College Athletics* (New York: Oxford Univ. Press, 1988), pp. 216–17.

4. Ibid., pp. 213–18.

5. "Testimony of Nora Lynn Finch," *AIAW v. NCAA*, May 1982, NCAA Papers, box "Testimonies and Affidavits," p. 10.

6. Ronald A. Smith had suggested the idea of women's power and control through a separatist, maternalistic approach to women's athletics. See Ronald A. Smith, "Women's and

Men's Models of College Sport from the Nineteenth Century to Title IX: Maternalism and Paternalism," paper presented at the Raymond Weiss Lecture, AAHPER 1996 National Convention, 17 Apr. 1996; and Ronald A. Smith, "There's More Than One Story of Women's Competition: The NCAA, AIAW, and Title IX," paper presented at the Evalyn Clark Symposium on Athletics, Vassar College, 10 Nov. 1995.

7. Christine Grant, as cited in Gail F. Maloney, "The Impact of Title IX on Women's Intercollegiate Athletics" (Ph.D. diss., State Univ. of New York at Buffalo, 1994), p. 89.

8. Joan S. Hult, "The Philosophical Conflicts in Men's and Women's Collegiate Athletics," *Quest* 32, no. 1 (1980): 83.

9. At the junior/community college level, the National Junior Collegiate Athletic Association began to provide national championships for both men and women in 1975. The NAIA and NCAA followed suit in 1980 and 1981, respectively.

10. The only features left in the AIAW that differed significantly from the NCAA were recruitment rules and student representation. The AIAW rules were much more restrictive than those of the NCAA. Beginning in 1976, there was one student representative (with voting power) in the twenty-four-member executive board of the AIAW. That representation doubled in 1982. There was no student representation in the NCAA counterpart.

11. Joan M. Chandler, "The Association for Intercollegiate Athletics for Women: The End of Amateurism in U.S. Intercollegiate Sport," *West Georgia College Studies in the Social Sciences* 24 (1985): 15.

12. "Sports at Smith: Noted Women's College Going Athletic in Major Way," *Springfield (Mass.) Sunday Republican*, 6 Sept. 1981.

13. Chandler, "The Association for Intercollegiate Athletics for Women," p. 15.

Bibliography

Primary Sources

Manuscript Collections

AIAW Papers. Special Collections, Univ. of Maryland Libraries, College Park. By summer 1999, the massive collection—about five hundred boxes—was only marginally organized. One could find duplicates in various boxes, and many documents were not filed in folders.

Walter Byers Papers. NCAA Library, NCAA Headquarters, Indianapolis, Ind. (previously located in Overland Park, Kans.).

David Mathews Papers, Univ. of Alabama Archives, Tuscaloosa, Ala.

NCAA Papers. NCAA Library, NCAA Headquarters, Indianapolis, Ind.

NSWA Papers. Archives of the AAHPERD, Reston, Va.

Personal Files of Linda Estes. Univ. of New Mexico, Albuquerque.

Personal Files of Joan S. Hult. Univ. of Maryland, College Park, Md.

Personal Files of Ronald A. Smith. Lemont, Pa.

Special Collection of Katherine Ley. Archives of the American Alliance for Health, Physical Education, Recreation, and Dance (AAHPERD), Reston, Va.

Ann Uhlir Papers. Texas Women's University Archives, Denton, Tex.

Unprocessed Women's Athletic Papers, Ohio State University Archives, Columbus, Ohio.

Government Documents

Amateur Sports Act, Public Law 95–606, 95th Cong., 2d sess. (21, 22 June 1978).

Association for Intercollegiate Athletics for Women v. National Collegiate Athletic Association. U.S. District Court for the District of Columbia (civil no. 81–2473), 25 Feb. 1983.

Association for Intercollegiate Athletics for Women v. National Collegiate Athletic Associ-

ation. U.S. Court of Appeals for the District of Columbia Circuit (civil no. 83–1342), 18 May 1984.

Fern Kellmeyer, et al. vs. National Education Association, et al. U.S. District Court, Southern District of Florida (no. 73, 21 Civ NCR), 17 Jan. 1973.

Final Report of the President's Commission of Olympic Sports. Washington, D.C.: U.S. Government Printing Office, Jan. 1977.

Final Title IX Regulation Implementing Education Amendments of 1972: Prohibiting Sex Discrimination in Education. Washington, D.C.: U.S. Department of Health, Education, and Welfare/Office for Civil Rights, effective date 21 July 1975.

Memorandum to Chief State School Offices, Superintendents of Local Educational Agencies and College and University Presidents, Subject: Elimination of Sex Discrimination in Athletic Programs. Washington, D.C.: U.S. Department of Health, Education, and Welfare/Office for Civil Rights, Sept. 1975.

NCAA-AAU Dispute, Hearings Before the Committee on Commerce, United States Senate, Eighty-ninth Congress, First Session, on the Controversy in Administration of Track and Field Events in the United States. Washington, D.C.: Government Printing Office, 1965.

Nondiscrimination on the Basis of Sex in Education Programs and Activities Receiving or Benefitting from Federal Financial Assistance. Washington, D.C.: U.S. Department of Health, Education, and Welfare, Office of the Secretary, 6 Dec. 1978.

"Proposed Procedural Regulation for Civil Rights Enforcement." *HEW Fact Sheet.* Washington, D.C.: U.S. Department of Health, Education, and Welfare, June 1975.

"Statement by Joseph A. Califano Jr., Secretary of Health, Education, and Welfare." *HEW News.* Washington, D.C.: U.S. Department of Health, Education, and Welfare, 6 Dec. 1978.

"Title IX and Intercollegiate Athletics; Nondiscrimination on the Basis of Sex in Education Programs and Activities Receiving or Benefitting from Federal Financial Assistance." *Federal Register*, part 6, 11 Dec. 1978.

"Title IX—Civil Rights." *HEW Fact Sheet.* Washington, D.C.: U.S. Department of Health, Education, and Welfare, June 1975.

Title IX of the Education Amendments of 1972: A Proposed Policy Interpretation. Washington, D.C.: U.S. Department of Health, Education, and Welfare/Office for Civil Rights, Office of the Secretary, 6 Dec. 1978.

Title IX Questions and Answers. Washington, D.C.: U.S. Department of Health, Education, and Welfare, Office for Civil Rights, June 1975.

Title IX—Prohibition of Sex Discrimination, Education Amendments of 1972. Public Law 92–318, 92d Cong., S. 659, 23 June 1972.

U.S. Commission on Civil Rights. *More Hurdles to Clear: Women and Girls in Compet-*

itive Athletics. Clearinghouse Publication no. 63. Washington, D.C.: U.S. Commission on Civil Rights, 1980.

Organizational Publications

American Association for Health, Physical Education, and Recreation. *National Conference on Social Changes and Implications for Physical Education and Sport Programs.* Washington, D.C.: AAHPER, June 1958.

———. *Proceedings on the National Institute on Girl's Sports.* Washington, D.C.: AAHPER, 1963–69.

Center for the Study of Athletics. *Women in Intercollegiate Athletics at NCAA Division I Institutions.* Palo Alto, Calif.: American Institutes for Research, 1989.

Division of Girls and Women's Sport. *National Conference: Sports Programs for College Women.* Washington, D.C.: AAHPER, June 1969.

———. *Standards in Sports for Girls and Women.* Washington, D.C.: AAHPER, 1953–71.

Gender Equity—Men's and Women's Participation in Higher Education. Washington, D.C.: U.S. General Accounting Office, 2000.

Knight Foundation. *Reports of the Knight Foundation Commission on Intercollegiate Athletics, March 1991-March 1993.* Charlotte, N.C., 1993.

National Association for Girls and Women in Sports. *The Story of the National Leadership Conference on Girls and Women's Sports.* Washington, D.C.: AAHPER, 1956.

National Association for Physical Education of College Women and National College Physical Education Association for Men. *Title IX: Moving Toward Implementation, Briefings 1.* N.p.: n.p., 1975.

NCAA. *Annual Reports of the National Collegiate Athletic Association.* Overland Park, Kans.: NCAA, 1965–99.

———. *Gender-Equity Study.* Indianapolis, Ind.: NCAA: 1992, 1997, 1997–98.

———. *1999–2000 Gender-Equity Report.* Indianapolis, Ind.: NCAA, 2002.

———. *Proceedings of the Annual Convention of the National Collegiate Athletic Association.* Overland Park, Kans.: NCAA, 1960–83.

———. Revenues and Expenses of Divisions I and II Intercollegiate Athletics Programs: Financial Trends and Relationships, 1999. By Daniel L. Fulks. Indianapolis, Ind.: NCAA, 2000.

———. *Yearbook of the National Collegiate Athletic Association.* Overland Park, Kans.: NCAA, 1963–65.

Interviews by Author

Baker, Merrily Dean. Telephone. 8 Aug. 1997; 17 Sept. 1997.
Davenport, Joanna. Long Beach, Calif. 29 May 1995; Marblehead, Mass., 12 July 1995.
Durant, Della. Telephone. 20 July 1997; 23 Sept. 1997.
Estes, Linda. Telephone. 28 June 1997; 23 Sept. 1997.
Gangwere, George H. Telephone. 28 Apr. 1997.
Grant, Christine H. B. Telephone. 18 Aug. 1997.
Hedges, Barbara A. Telephone. 11 Aug. 1997.
Holland, Judith. Telephone. 8 July 1997.
Hult, Joan S. 29 May 1995, Long Beach, Calif.; 27 June 1995, Greenbelt, Md..
Hunt, Virginia. Telephone. 18 Aug. 1997.
Lopiano, Donna A. Telephone. 19 Aug. 1997.
Mabry, Laurie. Telephone. 22 Mar. 1997; 22 July 1997.
Magnusson, Lucille. Telephone. 19 Aug. 1997.
McKenna, Francis G. Telephone. 8 June 1997.
Mushier, Carole. Telephone. 22 July 1997.
Polivy, Margot. Telephone. 11 Sept. 1997; 24 Sept. 1997.
Uhlir, Ann. Telephone. 7 Aug. 1997.
West, Charlotte. Telephone. 6 Apr. 1997.

Secondary Sources

Acosta, R. Vivian, and Linda J. Carpenter. "Women in Athletics: A Status Report." *Journal of Physical Education, Recreation and Dance* 56 (Aug. 1985): 30–34.
Ainsworth, Dorothy S. *The History of Physical Education in Colleges for Women.* New York: A. S. Barnes, 1930.
Anderson, Margo Lynn. "A Legal History and Analysis of Sex Discrimination in Athletics: Mixed Gender Competition, 1970–1987." Ph.D. diss., Univ. of Minnesota, 1989.
Bandy, Susan J., and Anne S. Darden, eds. *Crossing Boundaries: An International Anthology of Women's Experiences in Sport.* Champaign, Ill.: Human Kinetics, 1999.
Berenson, Senda. "The Significance of Basketball for Women." In *Basket Ball for Women.* New York: American Sports Publishing, 1900.
Beveridge, C. P. "Title IX and Intercollegiate Athletics: When Schools Cut Men's Athletic Teams." *University of Illinois Law Review,* summer 1996, 809–42.
Birke, L., and G. Vines. "A Sporting Chance: The Anatomy of Destiny." *Women's Studies International Forum* 10 (1987): 337–47.

Birrell, Susan. "Women Athlete's College Experience: Knowns and Unknowns." *Journal of Sport and Social Issues* 11 (Dec. 1987): 82–96.

———. "Separatism as an Issue in Women's Sport." *Arena Review* 8 (July 1984): 21–29.

Birrell, Susan, and Cheryl L. Cole, eds. *Women, Sport and Culture*. Champaign, Ill.: Human Kinetics, 1994.

Birrell, Susan, and D. M. Richter. "Is a Diamond Forever? Feminist Transformations of Sport." *Women's Studies International Forum* 10 (1987): 395–409.

Blair, D. A. "Title IX Participation Opportunity, Compliance Strategies, and Encountered Obstacles of NCAA Division I Universities." Ph.D. diss., Univ. of Kansas, 1997.

Blinde, Elaine M. "Contrasting Orientation Toward Sport: Pre- and Post-Title IX Athletes." *Journal of Sport and Social Issues* 10 (winter/spring 1986): 6–14.

———. "Participation in a Male Sport Model and the Value Alienation of Female Intercollegiate Athletes." *Sociology of Sport Journal* 6 (Mar. 1989): 36–49.

Blumberg, J. H. "Constitutional Law—Brown University Violated Title IX in Not Providing Women Equal Opportunity in Intercollegiate Athletics." *Suffolk University Law Review* 31 (Mar.-Apr. 1998): 987–97.

Borries, Eline. *History and Functions of the National Section on Women's Athletics*. Washington, D.C.: AAHPER, 1941.

Bryson, Lois. "Sport and the Maintenance of Masculine Hegemony." *Women's Studies International Forum* 10 (1987): 349–60.

Byers, Walter, and Charles Hammer. *Unsportsmanlike Conduct: Exploiting College Athletes*. Ann Arbor: Univ. of Michigan Press, 1995.

Cahn, Susan Kathleen. "Coming on Strong: Gender and Sexuality in Women's Sport, 1900–1960." Ph.D. diss., Univ. of Minnesota, 1990.

———. *Coming on Strong: Gender and Sexuality in Twentieth-Century Women's Sport*. Cambridge, Mass.: Harvard Univ. Press, 1994.

Carnegie Foundation for the Advancement of Teaching. *Twenty-Fourth Annual Report of the President and of the Treasurer*. Boston: Merrymount Press, 1929.

Carpenter, Linda J. "The Impact of Title IX on Women's Intercollegiate Sports." In *Government and Sport: The Public Policy Issues*, ed. Arthur Johnson and James Frey, 62–78. Totowa, N.J.: Rowman and Allanheld, 1985.

Carpenter, Linda J., and Vivian R. Acosta. "Back to the Future: Reform with a Woman's Voice." *Academe* 77 (Jan.-Feb. 1991): 23–27.

Certo, M. J. "Reaching Gender Equity in Intercollegiate Athletics: Coaches' and Student-Athletes' Beliefs about Institutional Support for Men's and Women's Athletics." Ed.D. diss., Columbia Univ. Teachers College, 1997.

Chafe, William H. *Women and Equality: Changing Patterns in American Culture*. New York: Oxford Univ. Press, 1977.

Chandler, Joan M. "The Association for Intercollegiate Athletics for Women: The End of Amateurism in U.S. Intercollegiate Sport." *West Georgia College Studies in the Social Sciences* 24 (1985): 5–17.

Chepko, Steveda Frances. "The Impact of Mabel Lee, Ethel Perrin, and Agnes Wayman on Women's Intercollegiate Athletics." Ph.D. diss., Temple Univ., 1987.

Cheska, Alyce. *Historical Development and Present Practices of Women's Athletic/Recreation Association.* Washington, D.C.: AAHPER, 1966.

Choi, Precilla Y. L. *Femininity and the Physically Active Woman.* New York: Routledge, 2000.

Chu, Donald, Jeffrey O. Segrave, and Beverly J. Becker, eds. *Sport and Higher Education.* Champaign, Ill.: Human Kinetics, 1985.

Claussen, C. L. "Measuring Women's Interest in Participation in Intercollegiate Athletics: A Critique." *Journal of Legal Aspects of Sport* 7 (winter 1997): 5–11.

Cohen, Greta, ed. *Women in Sport: Issues and Controversies.* Newberry Park, Calif.: Sage Publications, 1993.

Davenport, Joanna. "Historical Development of AIAW." *Proceedings of North American Society for Sport History,* 1979, 35–36.

Dubley, E. C. Jr., and G. Rutherglen. "Ironies, Inconsistencies, and Intercollegiate Athletics: Title IX, Title VII, and Statistical Evidence of Discrimination." *Virginia Journal of Sports and the Law,* fall 1999, 177–235.

Duderstadt, James J. *Intercollegiate Athletics and the American University: A University President's Perspective.* Ann Arbor: Univ. of Michigan Press, 2000.

Dudley, Gertrude, and Frances A. Kellor. *Athletic Games in the Education of Women.* New York: Henry Holt, 1909.

Duncan, Margaret M., and Velda P. Cundiff. *Play Days for Girls and Women.* New York: A. S. Barnes and Co., 1929.

Emery, Lynn. "Women's Participation in the Olympic Games: An Historical Perspective." *Journal of Physical Education, Recreation, and Dance* 55 (1984): 62–63, 72.

Epstein, K. V. "Sameness or Difference? Class, Gender, Sport, the WDNAAF, and the NCAA/NAAF." *International Journal of the History of Sport* 9 (Aug. 1992): 280–87.

Espy, I. P. "A History and Analysis of Sports-Related Title IX Legislation and Litigation from 1972 to 1997." Ed.D. diss., Univ. of Alabama, 1998.

Evans, Sara M. *Born for Liberty: A History of Women in America.* New York: Free Press, 1989.

Evans, T. S. "Title IX and Intercollegiate Athletics: A Primer on Current Legal Issues." *Kansas Journal of Law and Public Policy* 5 (spring 1996): 55–64.

Falla, Jack. *NCAA: The Voice of College Sports. A Diamond Anniversary History, 1906–1981.* Mission, Kans.: NCAA, 1981.

Festle, Mary Jo. *Playing Nice: Politics and Apologies in Women's Sports.* New York: Columbia Univ. Press, 1996.

Fishwick, Lesley. "A Sporting Chance? Resegregation of Coaching Jobs in Women's Intercollegiate Athletics." Ph.D. diss., Univ. of Illinois-Urbana-Champaign, 1990.

Flath, Arnold William. *A History of Relations Between the National Collegiate Athletic Association and the Amateur Athletic Union of the United States (1905–1963).* Champaign, Ill.: Stipes Publishing Co., 1964.

———. "A History of Relations Between the NCAA and the AAU, 1905–1968." In *A History of Physical Education and Sport in the United States and Canada,* ed. Earle F. Zeigler, pp. 212–14. Champaign, Ill.: Stipes Publishing Co., 1975.

Fleisher, Arthur A., Brian L. Goff, and Robert D. Tollison. *The National Collegiate Athletic Association: A Study in Cartel Behavior.* Chicago: Univ. of Chicago Press, 1992.

Francis, L. P. "Title IX: Equity for Women's Sports?" In *Philosophic Inquiry in Sport,* ed. W. J. Morgan and K. V. Meier, 2d ed., pp. 305–15. Champaign, Ill.: Human Kinetics, 1995.

Frankfort, Roberta. *Collegiate Women: Domesticity and Career in Turn-of-the-Century America.* New York: New York Univ. Press, 1977.

Frey, James H., ed. *The Governance of Intercollegiate Athletics.* West Point, N.Y.: Leisure Press, 1982.

Gavora, Jessica. *Tilting the Playing Field: Schools, Sports, Sex, and Title IX.* San Francisco, Calif.: Encounter Books, 2002.

Gerber, Ellen W. *Innovators and Institutions in Physical Education.* Philadelphia, Pa.: Lea and Febiger, 1971.

———. "The Controlled Development of Collegiate Sport for Women, 1923–1936." *Journal of Sport History* 2 (spring 1975): 1–28.

Gerber, Ellen W., Jan Felshin, Pearl Berlin, and Waneen Wyrick. *The American Woman in Sport.* Reading, Mass.: Addison-Wesley, 1974.

Gissendanner, Cindy Himes. "African-American Women and Competitive Sport, 1920–1960." In *Women, Sport, and Culture,* ed. Susan Birrell and Cheryl L. Cole, pp. 81–92. Champaign, Ill.: Human Kinetics, 1994.

Gittings, Ina E. "Why Cramp Competition?" *Journal of Health and Physical Education* 2 (Jan. 1931): 10–12, 54.

Grant, Christine H. B. "Institutional Autonomy and Women's Athletics." *Educational Record* 60 (1979): 409–19

———. ."The Gender Gap in Sport: From Olympic to Intercollegiate Level." *Arena Review* 8 (July 1984): 31–47.

Greenberg, Randi J. "AIAW vs. NCAA: The Takeover and Implications." *Journal of the National Association of Women Deans, Administrators, and Counselors* 47 (1984): 29–36.

Guttmann, Allen. *Women's Sports: A History.* New York: Columbia Univ. Press, 1991.

Hargreaves, John. *Sport, Power and Culture.* Cambridge, UK: Polity Press, 1986.

Harris, Dorothy V., ed. *DGWS Research Reports: Women in Sports.* American Association for Health, Physical Education, and Recreation, 1971.

Hill, Phyllis. *The Way We Were, A History of the Purposes of NAPECW, 1924–1974.* Washington, D.C.: AAHPER, 1975.

Himes, Cindy L. "The Female Athlete in American Society, 1860–1940." Ph.D. diss., Univ. of Pennsylvania, 1986.

Hoepner, Barbara J., ed. *Women's Athletics: Coping with Controversy.* Washington, D.C.: AAHPER, 1974.

Hogan, Candace L. "What's in the Future for Women's Sports." *Women's Sports and Fitness,* June 1987, 43–48.

Holland, Judith R., and Carole Oglesby. "Women in Sport: The Synthesis Begins." *The Annals of the American Academy of Political and Social Science* 445 (Sept. 1979): 86.

Howell, Reet, ed. *Her Story in Sport: A Historical Anthology of Women in Sports.* West Point, N.Y.: Leisure Press, 1982.

Huckle, Patricia. "Back to the Starting Line: Title IX and Women's Intercollegiate Athletics." *American Behavioral Scientist* 21 (Jan.-Feb. 1978): 379–92.

Hult, Joan S. "The Philosophical Conflicts in Men's and Women's Collegiate Athletics." *Quest* 32, no. 1 (1980): 77–94.

———. "Have the Reports of the Death of Competitive Women's Athletics Been Greatly Exaggerated?" Unpublished paper presented at National Mid-West Convention of the AAHPER, Detroit, Mich., Apr. 1980.

———. "The Governance of Intercollegiate Athletics." *Proceedings, National Association of Physical Education in Higher Education Conference,* June 1980, 19–26.

———. "Women's Athletics: Power and Politics." Unpublished paper presented at the North American Society for Sport History Conference, Louisville, Ky., May 1984.

———. "The Governance of Athletics for Girls and Women: Leadership by Women Physical Educators, 1899–1949." *Research Quarterly in Exercise and Sport,* Centennial Issue, 1985, pp. 64–77.

———. "Lou Henry Hoover: Champion of Women's Sport." Unpublished paper presented at the NASSH Conference, Tempe, Ariz., May 1988.

———. "Women's Struggle for Governance in U.S. Amateur Athletics." *International Review for the Sociology of Sport* 24, no. 3 (1989): 249–63.

———. "The Governance of Athletics for Girls and Women: Leadership by Women Physical Educators, 1899–1949." In *A Century of Women's Basketball: From*

Frailty to Final Four, ed. Joan S. Hult and Marianna Trekell. Reston, Va.: AAH-PER, 1991.

———. "The Legacy of AIAW." In *A Century of Women's Basketball: From Frailty to Final Four,* ed. Joan S. Hult and Marianna Trekell. Reston, Va.: AAHPER, 1991.

———. "The Story of Women's Athletics: Manipulating a Dream, 1890–1985." In *Women and Sport,* ed. D. M. Costa and S. R. Guthrie, pp. 83–106. Champaign, Ill.: Human Kinetics, 1994.

Hult, Joan S., and Marianna Trekell, eds. *A Century of Women's Basketball: From Frailty to Final Four.* Reston, Va.: AAHPER, 1991.

Hultstrand, Bonnie J. "The Growth of Collegiate Women's Sports: The 1960s." *Journal of Physical Education, Recreation, and Dance* 64 (Mar. 1993): 41–43.

Hunt, R. R. "Implementation and Expansion of the Mandate: A History and Critical Legal Analysis of Twenty-Five Years of Title IX Athletic Policy Development." Ph.D. diss., Univ. of Utah, 1997.

Hunt, Virginia. "Governance of Women's Intercollegiate Athletics: An Historical Perspective." Ed.D. diss., Univ. of North Carolina at Greensboro, 1976.

Ireland, Valerie Kay. "Women's Collegiate Athletics: An Institution Within the Female Sphere, 1900–1930." M.S. thesis, Arizona State Univ., 1982.

Jensen, Judy. "Women's Collegiate Athletics: Incidents in the Struggle for Influence and Control." In *Fractured Focus,* ed. R. Lapchick, pp. 151–61. Lexington, Mass,: Lexington Books, 1986.

Johnson, Arthur T., and James H. Frey, eds. *Government and Sport: The Public Policy Issues.* Totowa, N.J.: Rowman and Allanheld, 1985.

Jurewitz, R. A. "Playing at Even Strength: Reforming Title IX Enforcement in Intercollegiate Athletics." *American University Journal of Gender, Social Polity, and the Law* 8 (spring 2000): 283–351.

Kerber, Linda K. "Separate Spheres, Female Worlds, Woman's Place: The Rhetoric of Women's History." *Journal of American History* 75 (June 1988): 9–39.

Kinavey, W. H. "Women in Collegiate Sports: The Struggle for Equity Since the 1972 Title IX Educational Amendment." Ed.D. diss., Univ. of Pittsburgh, 1998.

Lannin, Joanne. *A History of Basketball for Girls and Women from Bloomers to Big Leagues.* Minneapolis, Minn.: Lerner Publishing, 2000.

Leahy, C. D. "The Title Bout: A Critical Review of the Regulation and Enforcement of Title IX in Intercollegiate Athletics." *Journal of College and University Law* 24 (winter 1998): 489–543.

Lee, Mabel. "The Case For and Against Intercollegiate Athletics for Women and the Situation as It Stands Today." *American Physical Education Review* 29 (Jan. 1924): 13–19.

———. "The Case For and Against Intercollegiate Athletics for Women and the Situation Since 1923." *Research Quarterly* 2 (May 1931): 93–127.

————. *A History of Physical Education and Sports in the U.S.A.* New York: John Wiley and Sons, 1983.

Lenskyj, Helen. *Out of Bounds: Women, Sport and Sexuality.* Toronto: The Women's Press, 1986.

————. "Common Sense and Physiology: North American Medical Views on Women and Sport, 1890–1930." *Canadian Journal of History of Sport* 21 (May 1990): 49–64.

Ley, Katherine, and Sara Staff Jernigan. "The Roots and the Tree." *Journal of Health, Physical Education, and Recreation* (Sept. 1962): 34–36, 57.

Lichtenstein, Grace. "Competition: A Feminist Taboo?" In *Competition in Women's Athletics,* ed. Valerie Miner and Helen E. Longino, pp. 48–55. New York: Feminist Press, 1987.

Linhart, Cynthia A. *Common Rules in the Governance of Intercollegiate Athletics.* Washington, D.C.: American Council on Education, President's Commission on College Athletics, Apr. 1981.

Lopiano, Donna A. "I Am Woman: The NCAA and AIAW Draw the Lines." *Coach & Athlete* 44 (Oct. 1981): 28–30.

————. "A Political Analysis of the Possibility of Impact Alternatives for the Accomplishment of Feminist Objectives Within American Intercollegiate Sport." In *Fractured Focus,* ed. R. Lapchick, pp. 163–76. Lexington, Mass.: Lexington Books, 1986.

————. "Growing up with Gender Discrimination in Sports." In *Sport in Society: Equal Opportunity or Business as Usual,* ed. R. E. Lapchick, pp. 83–95. Thousand Oaks, Calif.: Sage Publications, 1996.

Lopiano, Donna A., and C. Zotos. "Equity Issues and Policy Problems in Women's Intercollegiate Athletics." In *The Rules of the Game: Ethics in College Sport,* ed. R. E. Lapchick and J. B. Slaughter, pp. 31–54. New York: Macmillan, 1989.

Lovett, D. J., and C. Lowry. "Gender Representations in the NCAA and NAIA." *Journal of Applied Research in Coaching and Athletics* 4 (1989): 1–16.

Lucas, John A. *The Modern Olympic Games.* New York: A. S. Barnes, 1980.

Lucas, John A., and Ronald A. Smith. *Saga of American Sport.* Philadelphia, Pa.: Lea and Febiger, 1978.

Maloney, Gail F. "The Impact of Title IX on Women's Intercollegiate Athletics." Ph.D. diss., State Univ. of New York at Buffalo, 1994.

Mangan, J. A., and Roberta J. Park, eds. *From "Fair Sex" to Feminism: Sport and the Socialization of Women in the Industrial and Post-Industrial Eras.* London: Frank Cass, 1987.

Marien, Jennifer. "An Analysis of the History of Women's Intercollegiate Athletics." Unpublished paper, Branford College, Yale University, 1994.

McCrone, Kathleen. *Playing the Game: Sport and the Physical Emancipation of English Women, 1870–1914.* Lexington: Univ. Press of Kentucky, 1988.

McCue, Betty. "Athletic Scholarships for Women?" *Journal of Health, Physical Education, and Recreation* 33 (Apr. 1962): 18.

McKenzie, R. Tait. *Exercise in Education and Medicine.* Philadelphia, Pa.: W. B. Saunders, 1910.

Messner, Michael. *Power at Play: Sports and the Problem of Masculinity.* Boston: Beacon Press, 1992.

Messner, Michael, and Donald F. Sabo, eds. *Sport, Men and the Gender Order: Critical Feminist Perspectives.* Champaign, Ill.: Human Kinetics, 1990.

Miner, M. Jane. "Women in Sport—A Reflection of the Greater Society." *Journal of Physical Education, Recreation, and Dance* 64 (Mar. 1993): 44–48.

Nelson, Mariah Burton. *Are We Winning Yet? How Women Are Changing Sports and Sports Are Changing Women.* New York: Random House, 1991.

Oglesby, Carole A. *Women and Sport: From Myth to Reality.* Philadelphia, Pa.: Lea and Febiger, 1978.

———. "Changed Times or Different Times: What's Happening with 'Women's Ways' of Sport?" *Journal of Physical Education, Recreation, and Dance* 64 (Mar. 1993): 60–62.

Oglesby, C., and K. Hart. "Time Has Not Yet Come: The Women's Feelings Toward John Toner's Proposed AIAW-NCAA Merger." *Athletic Purchasing and Facilities* 3 (Mar. 1979): 12–14, 16.

Oliphant, J. L. "Title IX's Promise of Equality of Opportunity in Athletics: Does It Cover the Bases?" *Kentucky Law Journal* 64 (1975/76): 432–65.

Park, Roberta J. "Sport, Gender, and Society in a Transatlantic Victorian Perspective." *British Journal of Sports History* 2 (1985): 5–28.

———. "Physiology and Anatomy Are Destiny!?: Brains, Bodies, and Exercise in Nineteenth Century American Thought." *Journal of Sport History* 18 (spring 1991): 31–63.

Park, Roberta J., and Joan S. Hult. "Women as Leaders in Physical Education and School-Based Sports, 1865 to the 1930s." *Journal of Physical Education, Recreation, and Dance* 64 (Mar. 1993): 35–40.

Plyley, Dale E. "The AIAW vs. the NCAA: A Struggle for Power to Govern Women's Athletics in American Institutions of Higher Education, 1972–1982." M.A. thesis, Univ. of Western Ontario, Canada, 1997.

Rader, Benjamin G. *American Sports, from the Age of Folk Games to the Age of Televised Sports.* 2d ed. Englewood Cliffs, N.J.: Prentice Hall, 1990.

Riess, Steven A., ed. *The American Sporting Experience: A Historical Anthology of Sport in America.* New York: Leisure Press, 1984.

Rosenberg, Carroll Smith, and Charles Rosenberg. "The Female Animal: Medical and Biological Views of Women and Their Role in Nineteenth-Century America." In *From "Fair Sex" to Feminism: Sport and the Socialization of Women in the Industrial and Post-Industrial Eras*, ed. J. A. Mangan and Roberta J. Park, pp. 13–37. London: Frank Cass, 1987.

Sandoz, Joli, and Joby Winans. *Whatever It Takes: Women on Women's Sport*. New York: Farrar, Straus, and Giroux, 2000.

Scott, M. Gladys. "Competition for Women in American Colleges and Universities." *Research Quarterly* 16 (Mar. 1945): 49–71.

Scott, M. Gladys, and Mary J. Hoferek, eds. *Women as Leaders in Physical Education and Sport*. Iowa City: Univ. of Iowa Press, 1979.

Scott, Phebe M., and Celeste Ulrich. "Commission on Intercollegiate Athletics for Women." *Journal of Health, Physical Education, and Recreation*, Oct. 1966.

Sefton, Alice Allene. *The Women's Division National Amateur Athletic Federation, Sixteen Years of Progress in Athletics for Girls and Women*. Stanford, Calif.: Stanford Univ. Press, 1941.

Shook, S. M. "The Title IX Tug-of-War and Intercollegiate Athletics in the 1990's: Nonrevenue Men's Teams Join Women Athletes in the Scramble for Survival." *Indiana Law Journal* 71 (summer 1996): 773–814.

Slatton, Bonnie. "AIAW: The Greening of American Athletics." In *Governance of Intercollegiate Athletics*, ed. J. H. Frey, pp. 144–54. West Point, N.Y.: Leisure Press, 1982.

Smith, Lissa, ed. *Nike Is a Goddess: The History of Women in Sports*. New York: Atlantic Monthly Press: 1998.

Smith, Ronald A. "Amateur Athletic Union." In *Encyclopedia: USA*, pp. 157–59. Gulf Breeze, Fla.: Academic International Press, 1983.

———. "The Rise of Basketball for Women in Colleges." In *The American Sporting Experience: A Historical Anthology of Sport in America*, ed. Steven. A. Riess, pp. 239–54. New York: Leisure Press, 1984.

———. *Sports and Freedom: The Rise of Big-Time College Athletics*. New York: Oxford Univ. Press, 1988.

———. "There's More Than One Story of Women's Competition: The NCAA, AIAW, and Title IX." Unpublished paper presented at the Evalyn Clark Symposium on Athletics, Vassar College, Nov. 1995.

———. "Women's and Men's Models of College Sport from the Nineteenth Century to Title IX: Maternalism and Paternalism." Unpublished paper presented at Raymond Weiss Lecture, AAHPER 1996 National Convention, Apr. 1996.

———. *Play by Play: Radio, Television, and Big-Time College Sport*. Baltimore, Md.: Johns Hopkins Univ. Press, 2001.

Smith, Ronald A., and James G. Thompson. *History of Sport and Physical Activity.* University Park, Pa.: privately printed, 1991.

Smith-Rosenberg, Carroll. *Disorderly Conduct: Visions of Gender in Victorian America.* New York: Alfred A. Knopf, 1985.

Solomon, Barbara Miller. *In the Company of Educated Women: A History of Women and Higher Education in America.* New Haven, Conn.: Yale Univ. Press, 1985.

Spears, Betty. *Leading the Way: Amy Morris Homans and the Beginnings of Professional Education for Women.* New York: Greenwood Press, 1986.

———. "Senda Berenson Abbott, New Woman: New Sport." In *A Century of Women's Basketball: From Frailty to Final Four,* ed. Joan S. Hult and Marianna Trekel. Reston, Va.: AAHPER, 1991.

Spitz, C. "Gender Equity in Intercollegiate Athletics as Mandated by Title IX of the Education Amendments Act of 1972: Fair or Foul?" *Seton Hall Legislative Journal* 21 (Dec. 1997): 621–56.

Staurowsky, E. J. "Blaming the Victim: Resistance in the Battle over Gender Equity in Intercollegiate Athletics." *Journal of Sport and Social Issues* 20 (May 1996): 194–210.

Struna, Nancy L. "Beyond Mapping Experience: The Need for Understanding in the History of American Sporting Women." *Journal of Sport History* 11 (spring 1984): 120–33.

Suggs, Welch. "Scholarships for Women Exceed Federal Guidelines." *The Chronicle of Higher Education,* 18 May 2001.

———. "College Presidents Urged to Take Control of College Sports." *The Chronicle of Higher Education,* 6 July 2001.

Sumption, Dorothy. *Sports for Women.* New York: Prentice Hall, 1940.

Swanson, Richard A., and Betty Spears. *History of Sport and Physical Activity in the United States.* 4th ed. Madison, Wisc.: Brown and Benchmark, 1995.

Theberge, Nancy. "Toward a Feminist Alternative to Sport as a Male Preserve." *Quest* 37 (1985): 193–202.

———. "Sport and Women's Empowerment." *Women's Studies International Forum* 10 (1987): 387–93.

Thomas, A., and J. Sheldon-Wildgen. "Women in Athletics: Winning the Game but Losing the Support." *Journal of College and University Law* 8 (1981–82): 295–330.

Thompson, James G. "Athletics vs. Gymnastics in Classical Antiquity." In *History of Sport and Physical Activity,* ed. Ronald A. Smith and James G. Thompson, pp. 67–72. University Park, Pa.: privately printed, 1991.

Tressel, R. E. "An Analysis of Strategies and Barriers Concerning Title IX Compliance of Intercollegiate Athletic Programs in NCAA Division III Institutions." Ph.D. diss., Univ. of Minnesota, 1996.

Twin, Stephanie L., ed. *Out of the Bleachers.* Old Westbury, N.Y.: Feminist Press, 1979.

Uhlir, G. Ann. "Political Victim: The Dream That Was the AIAW." *New York Times,* 11 July 1982.

———. "Athletics and the University: The Post—Woman's Era." *Academe* 4 (July-Aug. 1987): 25–29.

Verbrugge, Martha H. *Able-Bodied Womanhood: Personal Health and Social Change in Nineteenth-Century Boston.* New York: Oxford Univ. Press, 1988.

Vertinsky, Patricia. *The Eternally Wounded Women: Women, Doctors, and Exercise in the Late Nineteenth Century.* Manchester, England: Manchester Univ. Press, 1990.

———. "Women, Sport, and Exercise in the Nineteenth Century." In *Women and Sport: Interdisciplinary Perspectives,* ed. D. Margaret Costa and Sharon R. Guthrie, pp. 64–66. Champaign, Ill.: Human Kinetics, 1994.

Wade, Paul. *Winning Women: The Changing Image of Women in Sports.* New York: Harvey House, 1987.

Wade-Gravett, N. L. "Perceptions of California College Presidents, Athletic Directors, and Head Coaches Regarding Compliance with Title IX of the Education Amendments Act of 1972." Ed.D. diss., Univ. of San Francisco, 1996.

Wallechinsky, David. *The Complete Book of the Olympics.* New York: Penguin Books, 1984.

Weiland, Walter E. "The Changing Scene in Women's Intercollegiate Athletics: Point with Pride, View with Alarm, 1971–1981." *The Physical Educator* 45 (spring 1988): 74–79.

Welch, Paula D. "The Relationship of the Women's Rights Movement to Women's Sport and Physical Education in the United States." *Proteus* 3 (1986): 34–40.

———. "Tuskegee Institute, Pioneer in Women's Olympic Track and Field." *The Foil* 7 (spring 1988): 10–13.

———. *Silver Era, Golden Moments: A Celebration of Ivy League Women's Athletics.* Lanham, Md.: Madison Books, 1999.

Welch, Paula D., and D. M. Costa. "A Century of Olympic Competition." In *Women and Sport: Interdisciplinary Perspectives,* ed. D. Margaret Costa and Sharon R. Guthrie, pp. 123–38. Champaign, Ill.: Human Kinetics, 1994.

West, Charlotte. "The Environmental Effect on the Women in Athletics." In *Women's Athletics: Coping with Controversy,* ed. Barb J. Hoepner, pp. 93–97. Washington, D.C.: AAHPER, 1974.

Wheeler, E. "NCAA vs. AIAW: The Battle for the Control of Women's Collegiate Athletics Heats Up." *Women's Sports* 2 (June 1980): 20–23, 59.

———. "War of the Words. A Report from the Lines of the AIAW/NCAA Controversy." *Women's Sports* 3 (June 1981): 14–17.

Willey, Suzanne C. "The Governance of Women's Intercollegiate Athletics: Association for Intercollegiate Athletics for Women (AIAW), 1976–1982." P.E.D. diss., Indiana Univ., 1996.

Williamson, Claire Louise, Geoffrey Lawrence, and David Rows. "Women and Sport: A Lost Ideal." *Women's Studies International Forum* 8 (1985): 639–45.

Wong, Glenn M., and Richard J. Ensor. "Sex Discrimination in Athletics: A Review of Two Decades of Accomplishments and Defeats." *Gonzaga Law Review* 21 (1985/86): 345–93.

Wood, Nan Elizabeth. "An Analysis of the Leadership of the Association for Intercollegiate Athletics for Women, 1971–1980." Ph.D. diss., Univ. of Utah, 1980.

Wu, Ying. "The Demise of the AIAW and Women's Control of Intercollegiate Athletics for Women: The Sex-Separate Policy in the Reality of the NCAA, Cold War, and Title IX." Ph.D. diss., The Pennsylvania State Univ., 1997.

———. "Margot Polivy, Legal Costs, and the Demise of the Association for Intercollegiate Athletics for Women." *Sport History Review* 30 (Nov. 1999): 119–39.

———. "Early NCAA Attempts at the Governance of Women's Intercollegiate Athletics, 1968–1973." *Journal of Sport History* 26 (fall 1999): 585–601.

———. "Intercollegiate Athletics." In *International Encyclopedia of Women and Sport,* ed. Karen Christensen, Allen Guttmann, and Gertrud Pfister, pp. 567–75. New York: Macmillan Reference USA, 2001.

———. "Association for Intercollegiate Athletics for Women." In *International Encyclopedia of Women and Sport,* ed. Karen Christensen, Allen Guttmann, and Gertrud Pfister, pp. 69–70. New York: Macmillan Reference USA, 2001.

———. "Intramural Sports." In *International Encyclopedia of Women and Sport,* ed. Karen Christensen, Allen Guttmann, and Gertrud Pfister, pp. 582–85. New York: Macmillan Reference USA, 2001.

Wushanley, Ying. "The Olympics, Cold War, and the Reconstruction of U.S. Women's Athletics." In *Bridging Three Centuries: Intellectual Crossroads and the Modern Olympic Movement,* ed. Kevin B. Wamsley, Scott G. Martyn, Gordon H. MacDonald, and Robert K. Barney, pp. 119–26. London, Ontario: Univ. of Western Ontario, 2000.

Zimbalist, Andrew. *Unpaid Professionals: Commercialism and Conflict in Big-Time College Sports.* Princeton, N.J.: Princeton Univ. Press, 1999.

Index